The Ebb of the Pink Tide

The Ebb of the Pink Tide

The Decline of the Left in Latin America

Mike Gonzalez

First published 2019 by Pluto Press
345 Archway Road, London N6 5AA

www.plutobooks.com

British Library Cataloguing in Publication Data
A catalogue record for this book is available from the British Library

ISBN 978 0 7453 9997 3 Hardback
ISBN 978 0 7453 9996 6 Paperback
ISBN 978 1 7868 0339 9 PDF eBook
ISBN 978 1 7868 0341 2 Kindle eBook
ISBN 978 1 7868 0340 5 EPUB eBook

Typeset by Riverside Publishing Solutions, Salisbury, United Kingdom

Simultaneously printed in the United Kingdom and United States of America

Contents

For Nella, who lived it all

Introduction
Neo-liberalism on the attack

Nautical metaphors can be risky; comparing social processes to the movement of the tides might suggest that the rise of Latin America's left governments, and their subsequent crises, belong to a natural cycle. It would be an absurdly inaccurate explanation for the complex and profound political developments with which this book is concerned. Indeed, it seems to me that the term 'pink tide' has an ironic, critical implication. It was first coined in 2006 by the New York Times correspondent in Montevideo, Frank Lehrer, in reference to the government of Tabaré Vázquez in Uruguay, with more than a hint of mockery as if the election of left governments in several Latin American countries was all sound and fury, signifying nothing. Diane Raby subsequently attributed the phrase to Hugo Chávez, which is an error, but one intended to invest it with a more positive meaning. But the reality is that it has now been generally adopted as an analytical tool in the discussion and interpretation of the experience of left governments in Latin America, which may prove to be unhelpful.

The process begins, by common consent, with the election of Hugo Chávez to the Venezuelan presidency in 1998. Reflecting back on that moment from the perspective of 2018 is a demoralising experience. Hugo Chávez died in bizarre circumstances in 2013, to be succeeded by Nicolás Maduro who has overseen what is undeniably the catastrophic collapse of the Venezuelan economy, and whose government represents, to me at least, a grotesque parody of the society promised by the Bolivarian revolution. Rafael Correa, a relatively late recruit to the Bolivarian project, has left the presidency of Ecuador to which he was elected in 2007, denouncing many of the social movements that carried him to power. Bolivia continues under a government led by Evo Morales, a figure as representative of the Bolivarian project as Chávez himself; but the grassroots rebellion that carried him triumphantly to the Casa Quemada in La Paz has fragmented, with many of its components distancing themselves from

Morales. In Argentina, the administrations of Néstor and later Cristina Kirchner, inheritors of the Peronist mantle, promised – beginning in 2003 – a progressive project in the wake of the mass protests embraced by the Argentinazo of December 2001. It ended with an election in 2015 which brought to power Mauricio Macri, a trenchant advocate of neoliberal strategies which he is imposing on the country with relentless determination. And in Nicaragua, as the 40th anniversary of the 1979 Sandinista revolution approaches, Sandinista police and military are firing live bullets at demonstrators protesting at austerity policies imposed by Daniel Ortega, the leader of the Sandinista revolution now reborn as an authoritarian ruler. He has delivered the country into the hands of Chinese multinationals intending to build the transoceanic canal which has regularly re-emerged as a dream project for multinational capital.[1]

There was nothing predestined or inevitable about these developments; no simple movement of the tides. The corruption and centralisation of power that have accompanied them are not attributable to human nature or the character of certain leaders. There are features common to each national experience – above all the turn back towards extractivism. There are also elements which have to do with the specific history of each nation and its state formation. And in every case the particular characteristics of its bourgeoisie, the history of the class struggle and its many and different manifestations, interspersed with issues of race and tradition, and with the internal contradictions within the left, combined in different ways. It is important to identify these particularities, as well as the impact and influence of external forces, in particular the U.S. government and multinational capital, a category which today must include China and Russia as material actors in Latin America. The concept of a 'pink tide', therefore, can identify the common framing conditions, but the specificity of each experience alone can allow us to discuss how to overcome the present circumstances, and continue the process of social transformation whose first steps were marked by the early flow of the pink tide.

It is instructive to cast our mind back to the moment of Chávez's election to the presidency, or perhaps more significantly to the Cochabamba Water War that inaugurated the twenty-first century. Both marked an ending and a beginning, or at the very least a turning point in global politics, though that would only become clear after the event.

It was the ending of a decade which had begun with the collapse of the Soviet bloc and the final demise and exposure of what was left of the

Stalinist project, whose implications and effects would resonate through the post-1989 decade. It was not, as Francis Fukuyama[2] alleged, the end of history but the uncertain and tentative beginning of a new and different history whose polarities were multiple and which could no longer be defined, however falsely, in cold war terms. The 1990s were a decade in which a newly confident and ruthless capitalism continued to extend its reach across the planet – leaving devastation it as it went. Neo-liberalism did set out to impose its model on Latin America, through its financial agencies – the International Monetary Fund (IMF) in particular – subverting national states and setting out to integrate the individual economies into a regional and ultimately global project.

This neo-liberal assault was variously concealed behind notions of 'austerity', 'structural adjustment' and 'the anti-poverty programme'. For the region, the net result of the 1990s, the decade of globalisation, was a dramatic rise in levels of poverty, the displacement of millions and the weakening of the national state, as public resources were privatised. The signposts along this new route included the Venezuelan urban rising known as the *Caracazo*, the bargain sale of Argentina's public assets by Peronist president Carlos Menem in 1990, the dollarisation of the Ecuadorean economy and the declaration of the North American Free Trade Area (NAFTA) in 1994, whose triumphalist inauguration was overshadowed by an insurrection in the southern Mexican state of Chiapas led by the Zapatista National Liberation Army (EZLN).

It is important to emphasise that the 1990s were a decade in which the destructive progress of neo-liberalism across the region was met by resistance and protest. The left governments did not emerge out of the blue. They were not forged in the mind of some prominent individuals, nor by the corporate manipulators of global electoral campaigns. The first imposition of structural adjustment policies was marked by an urban uprising across Venezuela beginning on 23 February 1989; the *Caracazo* cost hundreds of lives at the hands of the state. It is widely regarded as the starting point for the process that brought Chávez to power in 1998. A year later, in Ecuador, the indigenous organisations, having forged a new combined instrument of resistance, the Confederation of Indigenous Nations of Ecuador (CONAIE), launched a nationwide rising. The Zapatista insurrection and its occupation of San Cristóbal de las Casas, state capital of Chiapas, in 1994 were a defiant and explicit answer to the formation of NAFTA. The journalists gathered for the press conference of the three NAFTA presidents – Bill Clinton, Carlos Salinas de Gortari of

Mexico and Brian Mulroney of Canada – were caught unawares by the events in Chiapas, and apparently ignorant of the long history of conflict between the indigenous communities of the Lacandon Forest and the powerful cattle-raising interests that had systematically encroached on their land during the previous decade. The balaclava-masked barefoot troops waving what were mostly wooden rifles seemed to emerge from the mists of a very different world. But however different they may have seemed, however remote from the modern metropolis of Mexico City, they were the direct and immediate victims of neo-liberal global expansion, just as the occupants of Caracas slums had been. They represented the extremes of a global reality.

The peasant communities of Chiapas grew maize, their principal food staple, on their small plots. The rules of the World Trade Organization (WTO), the regulator and overseer of the global market, made it a condition of external investment that state subsidies should be eliminated, characterising them as restraints on trade and unfair protective measures. The agricultural economy of Chiapas was dependent on government subsidies; the small local maize growers could not compete on price with the maize imported from the United States, the world's largest maize producer. The direct cause of the impoverishment of the small maize growers of Chiapas was neo-liberal capitalism. The victims of the global system, however, were rarely seen, still less heard – at least until Chiapas.[3]

By a wonderful irony, this isolated corner of Mexico was able to communicate directly and immediately with the world through the recently created world wide web. That was certainly not the purpose for which it had been set up shortly before by the U.S. military! And this despite the fact that half the households in the communities had no access to electricity or running water.[4] Their leadership included the mysterious Subcomandante Marcos, who it would much later emerge was an ex-philosophy lecturer from Mexico's Metropolitan University and a Maoist. He was also a brilliant communicator with a comprehensive grasp of the realities of the global capitalist system as well as being simultaneously embedded in the popular culture of the indigenous communities to which he had relocated with a small Maoist group in the early 1980s. His several personas[5] spoke as directly to the indigenous people of Mexico as they did to the urban youth movements like the Metropolitan Indians in Italy. Marcos' 'Dispatches from the Lacandon Forest'[6] are lengthy and well informed indictments of neo-liberalism which were read across the world, escaping the physical encirclement to which the Zapatistas had been subjected within weeks of their rebellion by the Mexican army.

Beginnings

The Caracazo and the Chiapas uprising were symptoms of the aggressive new phase of global capitalism that neo-liberalism represented. They were the voice of the millions of poor and working class people who would be driven from the countryside into the swelling urban *barrios*; the unemployed workers who would lose their jobs as a result of a world-wide 'rationalisation' of production in the cold neutral tones of late twentieth century capitalism, replaced by new technology on the one hand and by the mobility of capital on the other; the state workers dismissed from employment in public institutions drained of public investment by the rules of the WTO, and many others.

The paradox is that in Latin America, the 1980s had coincided not only with the final demise of Stalinism but also with a 'return to democracy' – the end of the military regimes which had prevailed through most of the previous decade. The Pinochet regime in Chile, which overthrew Salvador Allende's Popular Unity government on 11 September 1973, opened the door wide to the first generation of neo-liberals, the so-called 'Chicago Boys' who had sat at the feet of Milton Friedman. The referendum which rejected Pinochet's plan for continuity in 1989 did not usher in a radical new direction, nor even a return to the development agenda that Salvador Allende had presented to the country with his Popular Unity coalition in 1971, and which the military regime had destroyed and replaced. The 'democracy' to which Latin America was now returning was not in any sense the social democratic model drowned in blood in Chile on 11 September 1973.[7] In Argentina, the military regime of Videla had been formally removed from power in 1983 – but any expectation that justice would be done, their crimes and violence denounced, and their subordin-ation to the interests of global capital replaced by some variant of social democracy, was soon disappointed. The government of Raul Alfonsín's Radical Party surrendered to military pressure and passed a 'Punto Final' law in 1986, drawing a line under the responsibilities of the military regime. It effectively gave immunity to those directly responsible for the Dirty War of 1976– 83, and the murder of 30,000 people in its seven years. Alfonsín followed it up with a Due Obedience statute which exonerated the torturers. By 1990, a Peronist president, Carlos Menem, delivered the national economy to multinational capital, selling off all the state's assets and enterprises in a giant bargain sale. So much for the return to democracy! In Chile, Pinochet's privatised economy continued under the Christian Democrat Patricio Aylwin; Pinochet and his circle were given immunity from prosecution and his economic holdings assured. It seemed that very few people remembered that Aylwin had publicly discussed a coup against Allende in 1972–3, though he had favoured what was called 'the soft coup' – that is, using economic rather than military instruments to bring down the Popular Unity government.

In 1989 after a referendum that year had rejected his continuation in power,[8] Pinochet left the presidential palace in Santiago, though he remained a senator for life with parliamentary immunity. It was in the same year that Carlos Andrés Pérez, standing in the presidential election in Venezuela, dismissed the austerity measures demanded by the IMF, and then imposed them within a few weeks of his election. The result was the Caracazo, the insurrection of Venezuela's poor against the programme – a key moment in the evolution of the pink tide, to which we shall return.

In Chile, Aylwin and the Christian Democrats were able to bury their earlier advocacy of Allende's overthrow among the forgotten chapters of recent history. The political formation that returned them to power, the Concertación, was a coalition between conservative, liberal and socialist parties that had severed their links with any radical legacy and represented a conservative neo-liberal alternative. The democracy into which they had entered referred only to the return to bourgeois democratic institutions and to the state as providing infrastructural support and disciplinary control on behalf of a multinational capital preparing its new interventions in the far more amenable circumstances of post-dictatorship Latin America.

Pinochet's was perhaps the last authoritarian regime to fall. But the democracy it ushered in was limited to formal electoral processes. In economic terms, neo-liberalism had opened frontiers and re-imposed the dominion of capital across the continent as Menem's privatisation made clear. The early 1990s extended the process of privatisation with the accompanying liberalisation of the economies. Friedman's free movement of capital ensured that privatisation would, in the main, signify what might be called the 'transnationalisation' of the Latin American economies. In political terms it marked the definitive failure of dependency theory[9] to launch a strategy of national development through import substitution industrialisation. The Popular Unity strategy would never return, whether or not Pinochet remained in power.

The political implications were profound. If much of the left, decimated during the authoritarian period, continued to hold to some variant of dependency theory, with its consequential role for a national bourgeoisie, the neo-liberal period exposed the fallacy of a developmentalism that rested on alliances with the bourgeoisie, 'national' or otherwise. The state of the 1990s was an agent of multinational capital, its role limited to social control and sustaining infrastructure. Its other role – the provision of social services and public sector investment – would now be redefined in the neo-liberal framework as restraint of trade, and those functions and services privatised. The WTO was set up in 1994 – though its baptism was a quiet affair and made little impact on the political debate at the time. That would change at Seattle in 1999 when it was unmasked before the world by what, in hindsight, seems a small demonstration of 70,000. Its numbers, however, were less important than its composition, 'teamsters and turtles'; the siege of the WTO brought together trade unionists, human rights groups, environmental organisations, anti-sweatshop coalitions, anti-militarists, and supporters of the Zapatistas. It was one of the first formal outings of the anti-capitalist movement.

The WTO was setting the rules and conditions for the conduct of a new unipolar world, using patent law and intellectual property aggressively to restrict and control conditions in the world beyond the United States and Europe. Its first intervention was to impose severe restrictions on state intervention in the economy, which was characterised as interference with the free movement of capital.

This moment of capitalist overconfidence – characterised with familiar modesty as 'the end of history' – coincided with the collapse of Eastern Europe. Yet it would become clear very quickly to what extent Stalinist strategy still dominated across the Latin American left. The conception of a development process conducted in coalition with 'patriotic' sectors of the bourgeoisie still persisted. Developmentalism, after all, was a strategy for achieving capitalist growth and industrialisation shaped by the internal and external market – its rhetoric notwithstanding. Its attendant assumption was that growth would yield a surplus sufficient to fund a welfare state and a limited redistribution. The realities of the 1980s had put paid to that expectation. If Chile told us anything, it was that the bourgeoisie, whatever its internal differentiation, was united around its commitment to capitalist globalisation and its resolute resistance to redistribution or any authentic involvement of the popular classes in the shaping of political life. Neo-liberalism marked the return of multinational capital in a commodities boom, in which manufacturing industry, such as it existed, was geared towards external markets, and in which the dynamic sector of the economy would in some senses return to the pre-import substitution era. It was once again the oilfields, the mines, and the vast estates of export agriculture that would be the main source of income for the state in Latin America. The local bourgeoisie would enter into partnership with multinational capital (and it was now truly multinational) in the new media conglomerates and in the marketing of consumer goods, the new technology and the luxury items that this newly prosperous capitalist class would demand for its own consumption.

The neo-liberalism of the 1990s and globalisation, however, also represented a profound political crisis. Endogenous growth slowed dramatically, and the export and extractive sectors were the only growth areas.[10] The defeat in Chile in 1973, the devastating repression in Argentina during the Dirty War (1976–83) and the silence that settled on Uruguay after 1973 condemned a revolutionary generation to the depths of the ocean, the concentration camps and torture centres, or to exile. The armed struggle strategy linked to the name of Guevara entered into decline after his death in Bolivia in 1967. It was ostensibly still in place and hegemonic, in Colombia on the one hand and in Central America until the victory of the Sandinistas in Nicaragua. Yet the continuing domination of Stalinism ensured that the strategic project remained the conquest of the state, and the dominant politics electoral, despite the Chilean experience. The focus on taking power in the state remained central. The exceptions were Central America, where armed popular resistance was shaping the struggle in Guatemala and El Salvador, and Colombia, where the FARC in particular controlled large areas of the country. But its strategy was not the Guevarist foquismo, the creation of small and flexible units of armed revolutionaries based in the more inaccessible areas. Its origins in the peasant defence committees formed in the wake of the insurrection of 1948 gave its war with the Colombian state a mass character and direct military and political control of significant areas of the country – its war, therefore, was a war of position rather than a war of manoeuvre.

In Central America too the guerrilla strategy had a mass character. In Guatemala by the early 1970s, it was the armed resistance of the indigenous communities. In El Salvador it was built upon peasant resistance but with significant roots in the urban centres, particularly the capital, San Salvador. In Nicaragua, the Sandinista Front was committed to the military overthrow of the Somoza dictatorship from its foundation in 1963. Its political leadership at its foundation – Carlos Fonseca, Tomas Borge and Silvio Mayorga – were all members of the communist party and their successful demolition of the Somoza dictatorship was not in a real sense a military victory but a political one. The political and symbolic impact of the FSLN's presence, and its spectacular actions like the occupation of the national parliament building which they held hostage until they won passage to Cuba, exposed the weaknesses of the dictatorship. But in strategic terms, the end of Somocismo was achieved by a Sandinismo dominated by a popular front conception, the forging of an alliance with the bourgeois opposition to Somoza engineered principally by Daniel Ortega.[11] Though political memories are sometimes surprisingly short, the Sandinista victory was not expected. The process of resistance was more advanced in El Salvador, the mass struggle in the countryside and the city more clearly coordinated there – though there were internal conflicts within and between the guerrilla organisations.[12] The expectation in 1979 was that the struggle in El Salvador would produce a major leap forward. In fact, a quarter of a million marched through the capital in January 1980, carrying arms and chanting the slogans of both the armed groups and the political and trade union organisations.

But the course of events, and the hegemonic strategy on the Central American left, was dramatically changed by the Sandinista victory of 19 July 1979. The Sandinista project had changed in the year preceding that victory when an internal political battle within the FSLN was definitively won by Daniel Ortega and his Tercerista (Third position) faction. Its arguments for a coalition with middle class anti-Somocista forces had prevailed over Tomas Borge's Prolonged Popular War faction and Jaime Wheelock's Proletarian Tendency. While the final blow against Somoza was probably the rising in the *barrios* of the town of Masaya, the Sandinistas were in fact not present at its beginnings – the three factions had stopped communicating with one another at the time. The youngest of the Ortegas, Camilo, was sent to establish connections with the insurgents; unfortunately he was killed there.

As a consequence of the overthrow of Somoza, however, it was Sandinismo – and its dominant faction, Ortega's Terceristas – who enjoyed the authoritative position in political debates about the future direction of the struggle in Central America. Thus it was the pursuit of a unilateral peace process at the expense of regional revolutionary politics built around solidarity that prevailed.

My purpose in revisiting the politics of the 1980s is not simply to locate the pink tide chronologically, but rather to seek out its political consequences for the left in the wake of the collapse of Stalinism and the era of neo-liberal globalisation. There was no avoiding the reality of defeat, with the exception of Nicaragua, or at least the sense of the failure of a socialist project that had focussed on the conquest of state power in order to pursue a programme of independent development built from the state. But the organisational expressions of that strategy had failed across the continent, and its representatives would return in the early 1990s to a role in a state with limited and conditioned powers subordinated to the control of the global agencies of capital and the multinationals. Only Cuba survived, but in conditions of near collapse after its abandonment by the Soviets. In 1991, Cuba was living through a 'special period in time of peace' in which the population was barely surviving and living standards fell catastrophically.

The reality, as John Beverley puts it, was that this was not a new stage so much as a restoration of the domination of the global market.[13] But the additional factor, as we shall see, was that neo-liberalism was committed not just to economic domination but also to cultural and political hegemony – that was one implication of Fukuyama's emblematic book. The electoral defeat of the Sandinistas in 1990 was the direct result of the support for the counter-revolution given by the United States and its economic siege of Sandinista Nicaragua. But it was also the expression of a political failure on the part of Ortega and the Sandinista leadership who had lost a significant proportion of their support as they were increasingly seen as remote from their mass base, and corrupt. The new government of Nicaragua, under Violeta Chamorro, was financed and supported by imperialism and included in the new administration a number of people who had led the *contras*, the anti-Sandinista coalition whose 15,000 armed men were financed and supplied by the United States both directly and indirectly.[14]

The international left had celebrated the Sandinista revolution just eleven years earlier as a turning point in a decade that began with the crushing of the Allende government. The real fragility of the Nicaraguan revolution was rarely addressed, the problem of a revolution conducted entirely from the state and by the state unacknowledged; analysis was set aside in favour of a political celebration. Any trace of its internal contradictions was buried within the public unity of the leadership, and any proposal for the democratisation of the process under way, condemned as collusion with imperialism.

After ten years of a vicious counter-revolutionary war, those internal contradictions were, of course, exacerbated. But no-one in the solidarity movement posed the question or identified the mounting tensions. When the electoral defeat of Sandinismo came in 1990, and they departed without protest from power, the experts and commentators were silent. And they kept their counsel when corruption on the part of the Sandinista leadership was exposed. Thus the revolution ended with the 'piñata', the appropriation – or to call it by its proper name, the theft – of state properties by leading Sandinistas. The electoral defeat was explained by the support of the United States for Chamorro's right-wing coalition – as if, after a decade of besieging the Nicaraguan revolution, this could not have been predicted with certainty. But there was no criticism of the Sandinista leaders, no attempt to critically analyse the sudden defeat of the people who had overthrown the universally hated Somoza just over a decade earlier. It was as if the overriding consideration was loyalty to the Sandinistas, rather than to the people of Nicaragua and their revolution.

We will have occasion to return to this phenomenon, this refusal to look defeat in the eye and seek out its causes, in the recent trajectory of the pink tide.

In Argentina, Menem – a Peronist – auctioned off state assets in 1990 at a huge profit for the private sector – and himself. In Venezuela the imposition of the harshest version of the IMF's austerity measures and the brutal repression of the popular protests in 1989 broke the consensus that had sustained the Venezuelan state for four decades, and left a political vacuum. It is hardly surprising that in such circumstances the mood that prevailed was what Beverley describes as 'the melancholia of defeat'.[15]

The Neo-liberal Strategy

Once again, as in 1973, Latin America became a laboratory for the strategies of global capital, in conditions that offered few obstacles to its triumphant march across the continent.

Freed of constraints, capital migrated en masse to the financial sector through the purchase of public debt and stock market movements.

Simultaneously there was a weakening of the regulatory capacity of states and a scaling back of social policies – as a result of growing debts and the letters of intent imposed by the IMF – alongside the privatisations of public assets and the opening up of the economies internationally.

A new power bloc was installed, led by finance capital, which was now allied to big groups of exporters and gave a new importance to agribusiness, especially soybean cultivation.[16]

In Mexico, the growth of the maquiladora manufacturing zone along the U.S. border was the evidence that it was the market to the north for which Mexican labour was producing electronics and consumer goods. The maquilas operated under advantageous financial conditions that provided minimal tax income to the Mexican state, as well being exempt from Mexican labour legislation. At the same time, by 1993, in anticipation of the declaration of NAFTA the following year, the Mexican financial sector was virtually in U.S. hands.[17] Further plans for the creation of regional economic formations had already been announced.

Neo-liberalism was not simply an economic strategy. The creation of a global system in which no obstacles or trammels were placed in the way of the movement of capital required both cultural hegemony and political control – and this touched directly on the role of the state. The redistributive role of the state in social democratic thinking implied both the allocation of resources and the provision of services and subsidies, as well as 'the domestication of the potential for a "politics of the people"' and 'the barring of other political possibilities'.[18] Ideologically, in Muñoz's terms, the state in neo-liberalism required 'the simplification and erasure of conflict from the idea of politics' in a technocratic state. The absence from the political arena of any authoritative counter-hegemonic proposal, for reasons addressed above, left a clear field for neo-liberalism. And the crisis was deepened as many individuals and groups associated in the past with more progressive projects entered the new states. Whatever their justifications, this appeared as surrender, and an abandonment of any version of socialist transformation.

The role of trade union leaders was also transformed. In the neo-liberal state there was no negotiating role for the trade unions, themselves regarded as restraints on the freedom of capital. The shift from production to speculation, which Sader notes as a central feature of neo-liberalism,[19] involved large scale job losses in the Latin American industrial sector, which severely weakened and limited the role of trade unions, and compromised the politics of engagement and negotiation with the state for which the left organisations stood. As social services were increasingly privatised – health, education, transport and housing in particular – the state withdrew from any arbitration or negotiating role in the relations between capital and labour. And the rising rates of unemployment marginalised the trade union organisations too. It was not just the material reality of workers that was affected; Marxist political ideas were themselves compromised. The centrality of the working class in the struggle for social change seemed challenged by the declining weight of the working class among the poor and exploited population.

Export agriculture and the extractive industries were the areas that attracted new external investment throughout the 1990s, from China in particular, at the expense of manufacturing and services.[20] Production was concentrated in the making of consumer items – electronics pre-dominantly; direct foreign investment in agriculture grew exponentially, but in areas of export agriculture only. Soybean cultivation and cattle-raising spread across the region at an accelerated pace, together with maize production – not for consumption but to produce ethanol as fuel. The devastation this expansion caused was and is most visible in Brazil, where vast swathes of the Amazon rain forest were cut down to permit the conversion of the land to arable and cattle-raising use. Soy, palm oil, maize and cattle occupied lands that had hitherto produced varied crops for domestic consumption. These were in many cases grown by peasant farmers with varying sized landholdings,[21] sometimes small family plots, sometimes quite large farms employing numbers of workers. Not only was the land lost to local consumption; their populations were driven off the land to add to the swelling populations of the marginal communities around the exploding cities of the region. The numbers involved are astonishing. It was often impossible to imagine where these people were in the overcrowded *barrios* of Latin America, with their various special names; the *callampas, pueblos jóvenes, barrios nuevos, poblaciones, villas miseria* and so on. It seemed inconceivable that so many human beings should be crammed into such restricted space and continue to function. Yet they did and they do, although it is the women who organise and maintain these impossibly densely populated hillsides (for they are usually hillsides, with makeshift homes clinging to unstable soil as they rise to the summits along carved out stairs that take the place of streets).

But they were also making a living in the city, in the booming street markets where the street sellers offered the products of the hidden factories of the east or the veiled Colombian or Haitian workshops which, between them all, produced mirror images of the luxury goods of the developed world, from handbags and clothing, to batteries and mobiles and everything between. They worked in these unsupervised, unorganised and low-paid sectors, or as domestics serving the middle class. And from time to time, as conditions became intolerable, they rose up in rage – as they did in 1989 in Venezuela. Those who work in precarious and temporary jobs were never represented by the trade unions, or by anyone else. And as the strategies of neo-liberalism narrowed down their options, their cost of living rose as an increasing proportion of their food was imported through the shrinking number of multinational companies – Cargill[22] chief among them – that profited both from the products of export agriculture and from the declining supply of basic foods for the majority population. The gulf between the poor and the comfortable middle classes who benefitted from a degree of redistribution in their favour as luxury goods replaced staples, grew wider. 'Never' as Sader put it 'has the North been further away from South',[23] even though they often live cheek by jowl in the vast cities of Latin America.

The extractive industries are located in the mountains, in the rain forests and the remoter regions, the areas occupied by indigenous populations who in many cases have eked out a living there over time from dry and unyielding land, and facing cold, heat or hunger. But neo-liberalism recognises no traditional occupancy or historic rights – these too would be unacceptable shackles on the free movement of capital. The rising in Chiapas, for example, involved indigenous communities and small farmers who depended on the cultivation of maize subsidised by the state. The Zapatista rising in 1994 coincided with the ending of those subsidies, and the Zapatistas reclaimed control over their *territorios*. For indigenous movements *territorio* is a category far wider and more all-embracing than 'property'. The division of land into individually owned properties, and the issuing of deeds to that effect, was perhaps the single defining act of imperialism. The indigenous cultures did not recognise individual ownership; the *territorio* was a cultural concept that embraced collective memory, tradition, patterns of shared production, and a relationship with the natural world which was one of mutual dependence and recognition rather than ownership and exploitation. The collectives were not separate, be they the *ejidos* of Mexico or the *ayllus* of the Incas, to name but two.[24]

By definition they could not be ceded, or alienated; nor could they be exploited, for exploitation meant wresting surplus value from working the land or the subterranean mineral veins, rather than accumulating their product to satisfy need.

As the state increasingly limited its functions to social control and/or repression, on the one hand, and to the administration of foreign investment on the other, its functions in the area of social provision and services were outsourced to NGOs, financed either by governments or by donations, or privatised. They were not the only organisations setting out to fill that vacuum. Religious groups, and specifically the largely U.S.-based Protestant evangelical groups with their vast wealth, became active on a huge scale in establishing links and networks with those sectors of the population who had been abandoned by the state.

The role of NGOs is ambiguous and often contradictory. Recent scandals have exposed the behaviour of many agents of the NGOs towards the people they were working for as patronising and imperious at best, exploitative and violent at worst. The scale of these revelations suggests a structural problem rather than a case of individual abuse. The presence of the NGOs from the outset was to compensate for the absence of the state or public agencies in the areas of welfare and services. Neo-liberalism privatised those services, placing them beyond the reach of the poorest. This was the political result of the transformation in the nature of the state as a consequence of capitalism's freedom of movement. The response should have been equally political, but the NGOs' role was to address this privation as an administrative or technical problem which could be solved by the provision of resources with external funding for specific and time-limited projects. They would often provide genuinely needed services, but they were always an emergency response that implied no long-term commitment or permanent provision, let alone structural change. This is not to deny that many of the individuals involved were genuinely concerned and committed to the cause of the poor and the oppressed. But they did not and could not address the issue of exploitation, the systemic extraction of value from the unpaid labour of workers. That was the dynamic of the system, whereas the non-governmental sector addressed its consequences – poverty, privation of resources, lack of minimal services like water, electricity, health and education – as if they were problems arising from technical failures or maladministration. The structural nature of that exploitation could not be addressed by organisations enjoined to avoid politics; the direct and deliberate consequences of neo-liberal strategies and programmes could only be addressed by them as conjunctural and accidental. But how could the consequences of the systematic dispossession of indigenous lands be addressed, without acknowledging that they had been taken in pursuit of a specific profit-making enterprise? How could urban unemployment be solved in discussion with the very agencies and enterprises who had created unemployment as a matter of policy? Sympathy and goodwill, and short-term grants could not even approach the problem.

The statistics told a very clear story as the decade wore on, and the distribution of income across the region revealed a deepening gulf and a growing inequality.[25] The most notable problem, however, was the absence of an alternative global strategy. In the early part of the decade, reviving the project for industrialisation and national economic growth seemed very remote. Memories of the failure of such a project were too recent, and the tradition from which such a proposal had come, the social democratic logic of it, the vision of an interventionist state, had little purchase in the realities of Latin America, where the state was withdrawing into a role of handmaiden to multinational capital.

As the impact of globalisation intensified, the resistance grew in step. The intervention of NGOs was largely conducted with the approval or complicity of the local state. Individual solutions were negotiated, but the structural responsibilities were not within the purview of the international organisations, except for the issue of human rights violations which were addressed in the context of international law, and which applied largely to the military dictatorships of the early 1980s. The battle against the impunity of those responsible for torture and murder on a massive scale was pursued through the cumbersome machinery of the international courts. But it was wholly compatible with neo-liberalism, insofar as it was pursued at all, since it did not address economic issues. The issue did serve, however, to establish a clear distinction between the earlier authoritarian regimes and the new regimes who offered legitimacy to neo-liberal programmes. The point that this demonstrated was that neo-liberalism did not require authoritarian regimes in power to carry through its programmes; on the contrary, the new governments, many of which included ex-opponents of the military regimes, were able to reconcile the defence of human rights and the advocacy of democracy to veil and soften neo-liberalism. In exchange for that collusion, the ex-reformists and social democrats were given access to the state. In 1994, Fernando Henrique Cardoso, once a Marxist and a theorist of dependency, implemented a comprehensive neo-liberal programme in Brazil from the presidency he had recently won. As we shall see, many of the components of his policy were continued by Luiz Inacio da Silva, known as Lula, the charismatic Workers Party leader who became Brazil's president in 2003.

The impact of those policies was felt at the local level and by sections of the community who responded with resistance, but from a perspective of difference. The Caracazo had not happened spontaneously, though it was widely presented that way. There was no leadership from any of the left *parties* but the insurrectionary impulse came from networks of pre-existing grassroots organisations, whether embedded in the urban *barrios*[26] or in the indigenous territories that would later provide the mass social base for the governments of the pink tide. In Ecuador, the formation in the mid-1980s of CONAIE provided a coordinating centre for the struggles of indigenous groups over a range of local and specific issues. It would confront the state,[27] in association with the trade unions, in the battle against Mahuad's dollarisation of the economy in 1999. In Bolivia, indigenous struggles proliferated from the Altiplano to the Cochabamba region through the 1990s. In Argentina, where the left organisations were the strongest in Latin America, but which were bitterly divided, it was the radical actions of the *piqueteros* movement that began to shape a new grassroots resistance. And in Chile, it was the students who in 1998 and 1999 would inspire a new mood of rebellion and protest with their brilliantly creative demonstrations of 2012.[28]

In Brazil the MST, the *Movimento dos Sem Terra* or Landless Workers Movement, was set up in 1984 under the leadership of Joao Stédile. Ideologically it had its roots in liberation theology and in popular movements mobilising the poorest and most marginal elements of society around a concept of self-activity. Although its leadership was closely linked to the PT, the *Partido dos Trabalhadores* founded in 1980, it maintained a rigorous independence, and has continued to do so throughout its history.

In Mexico, the Zapatistas had been surrounded and isolated by the state very quickly – but their dispatches from the Lacandón Forest continued to circulate across the world through an emerging anti-capitalist movement defined by its combativity but also by its lack of an overarching strategy. This was a movement of movements. And Subcomandante Marcos, in his dialogue with the new anti-capitalists, was offering a political direction defined by his characteristically paradoxical commitment to *mandar obedeciendo* – to lead by obeying. The perspectives of Zapatismo were set out by British academic John Holloway, working at Mexico's University of Puebla, in his influential book *How to change the world without taking power.*[29]

The title of Holloway's book resonated with a new post-Stalinist generation wrestling with the implications of a post Cold War world. The concept of socialism had, for a new generation confronting the naked reality of capitalism in its latest manifestation, lost credibility as the crimes and contradictions of Eastern Europe were exposed. In Latin America the first symptoms of neo-liberal austerity strategies were appearing and their victims beginning to travel on the freight trains through Honduras to the U.S. border. The reality of rural poverty may not have been visible, but the burgeoning slum cities arising in and around the major cities of the region were impossible to hide. The corruption of politicians from Argentina to Italy provoked protests that would prove to be the first expressions of an anti-capitalism that took many forms across the globe but which united around identifying as the villains of the piece the multinational corporations and the world financial agencies. The Zapatistas in a pre-world wide web world would have been easily consigned to a catalogue of minor local conflicts. But Marcos spoke to the world and he was heard. Neo-liberalism's victims now had their spokesperson.

Marcos was eloquent in describing what neo-liberalism, until then perhaps a slightly abstract concept, meant in reality – impoverishment, the removal of minimal state protection, leaving the indigenous communities at the mercy of people like the land-grabbing governor of Chiapas state, who was a major cattle rancher. Little was known about Marcos' political trajectory at that point, but he was identified with the disillusionment that the youthful protestors felt with a socialism that had lost its credibility and its authority. It was significant that an early expression of this new movement, the movement of young people in Italy, should have called itself the Metropolitan Indians.

Anti-capitalism was at that time a mood rather than a movement, as Chris Harman described it in a prescient early article.[30] He was responding to the extraordinary demonstration at the WTO meeting in Seattle in November 1999. It was an event organised in a new way, not from a single organising centre but from a multitude of small struggles, activities, protests that coincided in the second half of the 1990s, across the world. Harman quotes a Mexican journalist, Luis

Hernández Navarro, writing in the newspaper *La Jornada*, who described the Seattle gathering.

> Ecologists, farmers from the First World, unionists, gay rights activists, NGOs supporting development, feminists, punks, human rights activists, representatives of indigenous peoples, the young and not so young, people from the United States, Canada, Europe, Latin America and Asia. What united them, he says, was rejection of the slogan 'All power to the transnational corporations!' present on the free trade Agenda.

What united this vibrant and heterogeneous movement, which included trade unonists (teamsters) and ecologists (some in turtle outfits) was a hatred of capitalism, a scream of protest against oppression, a range of small struggles against the might of global capital. The movement had no shared strategic alternative. It was unclear what kind of future it was demanding, but it was united in what it did *not* want it to look like. A beautifully naive slogan suggested 'Abolish capitalism and replace it with something nicer.' Given the dramatic impact of the collapse of Stalinism on the left globally, it is hardly surprising that this largely spontaneous and unpredictable movement had no overarching narrative to offer. But it left no doubt that capitalism could not claim to have won its argument that it alone had the future in its hands, as Fukuyama had claimed. The anti-capitalist movement, varied, diverse, multiple and eclectic as it was, was agreed on that.

But if the lack of a strategy was a wholly understandable response to the history of Stalinism, and indeed of the experience of social democracy and reformism in Latin America, now in many places inescapably compromised with state regimes collaborating with neo-liberalism, the absence of an alternative political vision was a problem that the movement, as it grew, would have to address. Holloway, however, while he offered an authentic version of the dominant thinking within the movement as reflected in the words of Subcomandante Marcos and the actions of the Zapatista communities in Chiapas, presented the problem as a virtue, as evidence of their ideological purity and incorruptibility.

Ultimately the Zapatistas withdrew into their communities, their *caracoles*, the snail shells that both protected their communities and isolated them. It was a contradictory decision, emphasising the autonomy and independence of the movement on the one hand, but on the other isolating it from the emerging movement it had helped to inspire.

A Paler Shade of Pink

At various times during the first two decades of the twenty-first century, regimes of very different colours have presented themselves for inclusion in the pink tide. It is important to be clear that even the designation 'pink tide' lends itself to different interpretations at different times. A number of governments and states, for example, claimed an association for very limited material reasons, while their own political trajectories moved in a very different direction. Much seemed to depend on the relationship with Hugo Chávez – or perhaps, without wishing to be excessively cynical, with Venezuela's oil as generously dispensed by Chávez. I always felt it was a stroke of near genius to offer free energy to the South Bronx at the very moment when George Bush and his fellow advocates of the New American Century were preparing the destruction of Iraq and, as it proved, much of the Middle East as well. Some have made the case that Bush's preoccupation with Iraq distracted his attention from what was happening in Venezuela – but that belongs to myth. The reality is that his government's inattentiveness may have had more to do with the fact that Chávez at that point located himself within the 'third way' politics of Tony Blair and Anthony Giddens, neo-liberal to the core. Chávez's nationalism evolved into a more radical expression under the pressure of mass movements responding to an attack on his government by the national bourgeoisie. When hundreds of thousands took to the streets to defend his government, the Bolivarian revolution can be said to have begun. Perhaps against that background it would be important to address what we mean by a revolution in Latin America. We will return to the larger issue with the benefit of a narrative of the unfolding of these processes.

Some general issues arise at the outset, however. To take an extreme example, Daniel Ortega, self-appointed lifelong president of Nicaragua added his country's name to the list of 'left governments' supporting ALBA and the other regional expressions of Bolivarianism – and the description has been accepted by a number of commentators. It is true that Ortega was the leader of the 1979 Sandinista revolution that over-threw the odious Somoza dictatorship. It is important to add, however, that the FSLN (the Sandinista National Liberation Front) was deeply divided when the uprising of the impoverished *barrio* of Monimbó, in the city of Masaya, announced the imminent fall of the tyrant. Ortega led the so-called 'third faction' which argued for building a broad front with elements of the Nicaraguan bourgeoisie not directly complicit with Somoza. This was a politics from above, as all armed struggle is; the Sandinista guerrillas adopted the command structure that they had learned from Cuba as both a military and a political model, and retained it after the overthrow of the dictatorship. The internal discussions of the nine-man (they were all men) national directorate were closed, but the expectation that their decision would be obeyed without demur was enshrined in the slogan shouted on demonstrations – '*Dirección Nacional Ordene*': 'Give Us Your Orders, National Leadership' (the slogan loses its rhythm in translation). The guerrilla war tradition has no space for discussions of democracy – perhaps for understandable tactical reasons. As a result the Masaya rising, which had features recognisable in later social movements – the population of the district was mainly indigenous, and very poor, and the rising appeared to be a spontaneous action – was unexpected. The Sandinistas were certainly unaware of its potential, and were absent when it began. Once in government, the Sandinistas created a number of mass organisations, but they were characteristically created from above and acted as conduits from the leadership to the people. After the fall of the Sandinista government, Ortega retained his domination of the Sandinista group. His methods were often strong-arm, manipulative and unscrupulous. They included reaching agreements with the bourgeoisie and ultimately with the leader of the virulent anti-Sandinista opposition of the 1980s, Bishop Miguel Obando y Bravo, since elevated to Cardinal. The agreement involved accepting the most reactionary prohibition of abortion under any circumstances. That was the price of power. With the support of the church, Ortega fulfilled his ambition to be president, then acted swiftly to make himself indefinitely re-electable. His negotiation of a transoceanic canal through Lake Nicaragua, the principal source of fresh water for the nation, in a $40 billion contract was the acme of neo-liberal projects, and when the other face of public spending on infrastructure, austerity measures, was unveiled he sent police and military against the demonstrators, killing over three hundred. Speeches referring to socialism of the twenty-first century hardly compensate for this ruthless neo-liberal commitment! And there is nothing in the Sandinista tradition that Ortega represents about partici-patory democracy – except in the current of liberation theology, with its emphasis on community. Several of the exponents of that tradition have since been expelled from the FSLN and remorselessly persecuted by Ortega, among them the prominent poet and ex-Minister of Culture in the Sandinista government, Ernesto Cardenal. At the very least this calls into question the meaning of 'left leaning governments'.

James Petras wrote an important article[31] discussing the paradoxes of the pink tide – or more specifically the nature and horizons of anti-imperialist governments. He defines three groups and their relation not just to imperialism but to neo-liberalism as its expression in the age of globalisation. Though some of what he says is open to debate, it is a useful place to start an analysis of the pink tide. In twenty-first century Latin America, he argues, there is one group of countries which sits wholly within the ambit of imperialism/neo-liberalism. Colombia, Peru, Mexico in particular, and most of Central America, not only bend to the imperial will of their northern neighbour, but support the 'war on terror' and the 'war on drugs' as the current expressions of U.S. military expansionism. They are also countries who have assimilated the neo-liberal agenda – in Mexico's case entering and supporting NAFTA, holding down wages at their lowest level in the region, privatising the national oil company, Pemex, and providing cheap labour as well as access to primary materials for multinational companies, in the former case for the *maquiladora* assembly plants along the border.[32] Colombia has for many years through the Plan Colombia (1993) provided the platform for the American military presence in the region, in part on the pretext of the war against drugs. Peru, after brief progressive period under Ollanta Humala, turned back to the neo-liberal agenda and opened its economy to the most aggressive mining and extraction industries. There are nuances of difference between them, but Petras identifies them on the basis of an orthodox fiscal policy, the priority given to extractive industries, and thus a dependence on foreign multinationals. Yet Mexico may be on the brink, with the recent election to the presidency of Andrés Manuel López Obradors (or AMLO as he is known), of moving into the moderate group (see below), though the alarmists of the right are seeing his candidacy as an opening towards a new Venezuela, which seems to me to be a deliberate misreading of AMLO's campaign and intentions.[33] Santos of Colombia, by contrast, tried to differentiate himself from the openly reactionary perspectives of ex-president Uribe (whom he served as Minister of Defence) by moving from blanket reprisals against opponents to selective assassinations combined with lengthy negotiations with the guerrilla movement, the FARC, brokered by the Cuban and Venezuelan governments. What identified them all, despite their differences, was a continuing and unbroken commitment to neo-liberalism.

The recent election to the presidency of an avowed Uribista, Iván Duque Márquez would seem to confirm the analysis, and to place the reality of a new political space for demobilised guerrillas in question.

Petras's second group, which he describes as 'eclectic and pro-imperialist' embraces Brazil, Uruguay, Argentina and Chile. All four have been happy to expand trading relations with other Latin American countries through various associations – ALBA, Celac, Unasur and Mercosur. They differ in many ways, even in their relations with U.S. imperialism: each of them has pursued an independent foreign policy, which has meant taking an independent stance on the 'war on terror', for example, and adopting progressive positions on gay marriage (Argentina), marijuana (Uruguay) and human rights (Argentina and Chile). Each of them, Petras suggests, accept 'moderate foreign involvement' and assume soft neo-liberal positions on social issues while pursuing a hard economic agenda. In the case of Brazil, its sub-imperialist ambitions opened the possibility of Brazil's independent participation in global financial networks, which hardly places it in the anti-imperialist camp. But the reality is that each of the four, and indeed Peru as well, have diverted at least some of the revenues from the extractive industries into minimal social welfare programmes. And in the aftermath of the oil price fall in 2015, the countries in both this moderate, and the so-called militant anti-imperialist groups have welcomed a growing participation of multinational corporations in an increasing dependence on extractive industries.

Petras identifies as the 'militant quartet' those countries which have broken with imperialism and neo-liberalism. But as we shall show, this rupture is open to question, since all four have reverted to dependency in one form or another. Venezuela, Bolivia and Ecuador represented, in the early 2000s, the promise of a new direction, based on an explicit critique of neo-liberalism and imperialism. Claudio Katz, writing in 2007, expressed an excited optimism shared by many at the time: 'Latin America has broken that cumulative sequence of popular defeats on which neo-liberalism rests.'[34] Only Latin America, he argued, has developed a democratic, anti-imperialist project without religious elements (unlike the Middle East). Certainly Hugo Chávez's increasingly radical denunciations of the Iraq war, and of neo-liberalism in general, won the attention of radicals around the world. Venezuela's oil wealth gave it a weapon to use and a means of generating an income to finance its promised social welfare programmes. Bolivia too, having nationalised its oil company (at least in part) had the resources for an ambitious programme of social provision. Ecuador, the third member of the group, also had mineral wealth to use in carrying out such programmes. Cuba is a recipient rather than a producer of oil, and Venezuelan oil was certainly the Cuban economy's salvation through the late 1990s. Chávez's offer of oil in exchange for medical and educational services was a gesture of solidarity, but was also a commercial arrangement, though provision to small Caribbean island-states, and to New Orleans after Katrina, were acts of solidarity.

What united the proposals of the militant quartet, or perhaps it is more accurate to say that what was *assumed* to unite them, was a commitment to use oil as a spur to development. The pink tide *governments* restricted their opposition to neo-liberalism, at first, beyond more general and fairly abstract arguments, to the unjust and exploitative conditions of the relationship, and called, as Petras puts it, for 'a more equitable distribution of revenues from free trade'. Important though this was in releasing revenues that made it possible to redress some of the cutbacks and reductions in public spending that the IMF's austerity measures had imposed, it still did not constitute a proposal to transform that relationship. What marked the pink tide as a new era of class struggle, was the high level of popular mobilisation against the impacts of neo-liberalism, its diversity, and the demands around which they organised, all of which implied a resistance to neo-liberalism. The beginning of these new popular struggles was certainly the *Caracazo* of 1989, followed by the Zapatista rising. That is not to deny the continuity of resistance across the region throughout these years, but to identify how and at what point neo-liberalism became the explicit target of their opposition. In this sense, though *Zapatismo* very quickly limited itself in space, it was able to transmit its anti-neo-liberal analysis of the world without restriction, even as its communities were enclosed within an ever-tighter military embrace by the Mexican government.

A significant political feature of the movements was the absence from them all of the traditional slogans and positions of the organised, revolutionary left, expressed in what was often described as 'anti-politics', particularly by the autonomous currents that took their ideological lead from Chiapas. The term seems dubious to me, since every one of these mobilisations was directed against powerful interests in the state or in the economy. These were the enemies of the 'democracy' that came to be the central demand of these movements. The term, of course, had been appropriated by actors right across the political spectrum. Some saw it as the reconstitution of the institutions of formal bourgeois democracy which had disappeared under the heel of the military regimes of the 1970s and 1980s. The restoration of that system was a call issued by a range of social democratic parties, whose spokespeople in many cases had moved from much more radical positions held before the military regimes established their dominion. When the new social movements took on the demand for democracy, however, its content was both political and economic. The single word sheltered a multiplicity of resonances across a growing anti-capitalist movement in Europe and the United States which in some cases took its lead from Latin America. The absence of the left – compromised with the new centrist regimes in some cases, destroyed by repression in others, disillusioned in some cases, disoriented by the collapse of Stalinism in others – had its impact on the new movements too. Yet in many cases the social forces now in movement had been marginalised by a left focussed, above all, on the power of the organised working class. In very few cases was the left's understanding of the working class sufficiently flexible to embrace peasants, indigenous communities, the inhabitants of poor urban *barrios*, precarious or transient workers, the young, the victims of racism. And one effect of neo-liberalism's deindustrialising strategies, and its concentration on the extractive industries and export agriculture was the severe weakening of trade union organisation. Combined with the impact of the collapse of Eastern Europe and what looked very much like the surrender of layers of the social democratic left absorbed into the new, slimmed-down state or para-statal organisations, the discourse of socialism and workers revolution seemed to lose its impact. But politics did not disappear; it was reconfigured instead in the context of the new resistances. The struggle now was in defence of life, which translated into the fight to retain public control of water, to defend public health, to resist the contamination of the planet, to fight against the dispossession of indigenous communities by the multinational mining and oil companies. In urban settings, the focus was on unemployment against a background of austerity which cut back on benefits for the unemployed; the deterioration of living and housing conditions while huge infrastructural projects like the World Cup and the Olympics not only consumed public spending budgets but condemned them to indebtedness, sometimes for decades to come.

And in the course of those struggles new forms of organisation emerged that were, and could become, the seeds of a new kind of democratic power and the basis of new national communities. New ideas grew in such fertile ground, and new social imaginaries, contesting the failing neo-liberal hegemony in political life, the economy and culture. As the cracks widened, crisis followed and new political actors were carried into power.

Now the issue was the construction of alternatives – new societies based on something other than capitalist exploitation: programmes for the elimination of inequality; social imaginaries that could embrace and build on indigenous traditions and experience; cultures that fought machismo and discrimination; economies that produced for use not exchange. The new discourse described it in the indigenous languages as *sumac karsay*, 'the good life': forms of production that would not exhaust the land and the rivers.

The new 'militant' governments adopted many of these ideas in the abstract. But in economic terms their perspectives appeared to be 'developmentalist'. What did this and could this mean? In the 1940s and 1950s the dependency school had agued that Latin America's historical dependence on primary products had imprisoned its societies in a per-manent underdevelopment – importing its consumer goods and means of production in exchange for oil. Since all discussion about 'develop-ment' seemed to be based on reproducing the pattern of the growth of capitalism in Europe, there seemed to be no escape from the closed circle. The response of the Latin American economists was import substitution industrialisation (ISI), creating the capacity to produce the previously imported goods within the country. This involved protectionism and the diversification of the economy, aided by public investment. For complex reasons, but principally because the new industrial sectors were mainly financed through debt, later recalled by the international financial insti-tutions in the 1980s, the initiative failed in its purpose. In the decade that followed, global capitalism reclaimed the economies of Latin America in the brutal way we have described.

But the resistance across the region placed a different possible future on the agenda. The governments of the pink tide identified themselves with it and returned to a form of developmentalism. The dramatic rise in the price of oil certainly provided revenues on a scale that might have been able to finance diversification and break the cycle of dependency. And yet, despite the continuing demand that that be done, an overview of the experience and actions of these governments reveals something very different: that the relationship with neo-liberalism has continued and that its essential motor, the ironclad dependence on oil, gas and mineral production, has not only remained the same but has, in fact, grown stronger and deeper. As this volume is completed, the pink tide governments are drowning in a morass of corruption which is the expression of that failure. What was achieved by those governments in terms of welfare and the improvement of public services is now being eroded; poverty is returning and with it repression of the very resistance that carried these 'left leaning governments' to power.

There are many ways to explain this crisis, some of which we have tried to address here. In the end it is not about individuals, except to the extent that they were willing collaborators within the system that is the origin of the crisis. In the end, once again, faith in the power of the state to transform a global system has proved misguided. Taking your distance from U.S. capital while colluding with Chinese and Russian capitalism's global aspirations does not remove you from a system in which those capitals increasingly collaborate and collude. Socialism, I am convinced, remains the only international answer, but a socialism that has learned from this crisis. Of one thing I am certain; to veil or deny the damage that has been done in the name of revolution discredits the very concept for its victims. We are still obliged, if we are worthy of the name, to speak the truth to power from the grassroots – whatever disguise power may wear.

1

From the Caracazo to Chávez

The election of Hugo Chávez to the presidency of Venezuela in late 1998 was a critical event, though its implications would take a little time to filter through to the rest of Latin America. The opposing candidates were Irene Sáez, an ex-beauty queen and mayor of the bourgeois Chacao district of Caracas, who represented the white middle class that had been a key beneficiary of the consensual pact that had run the Venezuelan state for four decades. The other candidate was Henrique Salas-Romer, the governor of Carabobo state who was endorsed by the two puntofijo parties, COPEI and Acción Democrätica representing the bourgeoisie.

Chávez had famously made his mark on Venezuelan politics with a phrase he used on television during a speech conceding the failure of a short-lived attempted coup he led in February 1992. Our action has failed, he said, 'for the moment' (*por ahora*). These two words became legendary, appearing on walls and fences in various colours and smuggled into texts of every kind. Chávez spent the next three years in prison at Yare, where he was involved in a continuous conversation with the other political forces in the country. There were several currents vying for his attention. As Cicciarello-Maher describes in detail,[1] the previous decade had seen the rise and demise of the guerrilla movements led by the PRV,[2] the party formed by Douglas Bravo after an internal disagreement inside the Communist Party over strategy. Bravo had broken with Cuba over what he saw as Castro's abandonment of guerrilla warfare and of the still existing movements in Latin America. In the wake of Guevara's death in Bolivia, the Cuban regime changed direction, turning towards what might be described as realpolitik; it was symbolic that in 1970, Castro had spoken at the Algiers conference, supporting the role of the Soviet Union on the continent, and more generally Soviet geopolitics. It was the same conference where, just five years earlier Guevara had expressed frustration at the reluctance of the Soviets to support national liberation movements and the armed struggle, which had created a rift between him and Castro after the Soviets protested at Guevara's political misbehaviour. Guevara departed for the Congo shortly thereafter and only returned to Cuba once, in secret and heavily disguised, to form the group that would later go to Bolivia, where he was killed in October 1967.[3]

The Venezuelan guerrilla movement has been largely ignored by the left outside Venezuela, as has its brutal repression by President Rómulo Betancourt during the 1960s.[4] Betancourt was elected after the overthrow of the Pérez Jiménez regime in 1958, with the support of the communist party, many of whose members were now being tortured, 'disappeared' or killed. Several thousand guerrillas died in what were called the 'theatres of operations'. Others survived in a range of different organisations, but key figures, like Fabricio Ojeda,[5] did not survive the wave of repression launched by a politician (Betancourt) regarded abroad as a paragon of democracy. Chávez's brother, Adán Chávez, was a member of the PRV and close to Bravo; it was he who had earlier introduced Hugo to Bravo, who would become a key political influence. Bravo describes himself as a Bolivarian Marxist; his interpretation of Simon Bolivar's legacy shaped Chávez's concept of Bolivarianism[6] in these early days. But Bravo and Adán Chávez were not the only visitors. Alfredo Maneiro (1937–82), an extremely influential thinker and organiser had split from the communist party to form CausaR; he saw the working class as the centre of a revolutionary movement, and built a base in the steel complex of SIDOR in Guayana. CausaR also worked with students and in the Caracas *barrio* of Catia. Maneiro died in 1982, and CausaR's effective leader became Andrés Velazquez, ex-general secretary of the steel workers union. He was later elected governor of Bolivar province and was CausaR's presidential candidate in 1993, winning 22 per cent of the vote. Both SIDOR and the emblematic aluminium factory Alcasa are based in Bolivar state The other formation which played a key role in Chávez's political thinking was the group of military men who plotted the February coup with him.

The point here is that Chávez was subject to a range of influences from the left. His own basic position was, as he himself described it, more akin to the ideology of military nationalists like Velasco Alvarado in Peru or Omar Torrijos in Panama. By contrast his political reputation among the mass of Venezuelans, the consequence of the failed coup of 1992, was based on his brief television appearance, and the claim he made then and thereafter to be the voice of the Caracazo. Ciccariello-Maher shows how the decimation of the guerrillas led to the growth, or reinforcement of the grass roots groups and community organisers within the *barrios* who represented a network of resistance. Their presence, and their permanence calls into question the simple definition of the 1989 rising, the Caracazo, as we have argued, as a spontaneous outburst. It was certainly an immediate reaction to Carlos Andrés Pérez's betrayal of his election promises in imposing IMF austerity measures. It did not have any central coordinating organisation at its heart, but it did activate the networks across the city. It might be best described as a coincidence of resistances that rose up together in the face of a universal assault on the living standards and conditions of the poor, born out of the widespread repression under Betancourt and his successors. The nature of the identification between these social forces and Chávez is critical to an understanding of his future relationship with the mass movement, and its unique character.

The barrios identified more easily with Chávez than with any members of the traditional political class who were by and large white, male, educated and clearly middle class in their background. Chávez, by contrast, looked and sounded like them. He had not grown up in the urban *barrios* but in the state of Barinas in a household of poor teachers, and with a background that placed him clearly with the *pueblo*, that social layer that embraces workers, the unemployed, small local businesses, street traders, among others. In the racial hierarchy of Venezuela, significant despite its claim to be a racially blind society, Chávez's chiselled face announced his indigenous origins. In other Latin American, countries his membership of the armed forces might have aroused suspicion, but in Venezuela, in marked contrast to neighbouring Colombia, there was a career path in the military for people of humble origins. It is part of the Chávez myth that he was really only interested in baseball, and joined the army to be a pitcher in a military team. His rise was rapid, and he graduated quickly to the military academy as a tutor. There his immersion in Venezuelan history and his fascination with Simon Bolivar in particular, was his trademark. Bolivar has an enormous significance for Venezuelans, and particularly so for Chávez, but the content of his Bolivarianism varied over time. Bolivar himself came from the colonial elite and led the independence movement with a vision of the unity of Latin America, and the creation of a Gran Colombia independent of imperialist control and set on the road to national capitalist development. For Chávez, he represented a heroic struggle for national independence, but for Douglas Bravo Bolivarianism was revolutionary,[7] embracing nationalism and social revolution.

At this stage Chávez's links to a number of political and left-wing organisations served to develop his general political education, but he remained a radical nationalist in ideology, and a radical military reformist in his concept of organisation. His decision to stand for election, for example, did not meet with universal support on the left, and there was a clear reaction in left circles against a military man standing for the presidency – with the recollection of Pérez Jiménez and Gómez before him still fresh in the popular memory. Chávez's identification with the popular rebellion of 1989 and more generally with the traditions of grass roots mobilisation were not translated into strategy. The February coup was just that – an attempted military takeover of power.[8] Douglas Bravo is emphatic in his criticism of Chávez in that respect; according to Bravo there were popular forces ready to enter the fray with Chávez, to take up arms on the streets in support of his bid for power, but Chávez chose not to mobilise them. For Bravo it was a replay of the overthrow of Perez Jimenez in 1958, when the social forces on the ground were marginalised in a political action.[9] In 1958, the decision not to mobilise the popular forces, fundamentally by the communist party, was the price paid for an alliance with Acción Democrática, and Rómulo Betancourt, in exchange for a share in power. Shortly after entering the presidential palace, and having publicly expressed support for the Cuban revolution, Betancourt launched the repression that introduced the concept of the 'disappeared' into the political vocabulary of Venezuela.

Chávez's commitment to an electoral strategy involved a number of compromises, and a distancing from the left groups he had been dealing with until then. The implications were not immediately obvious, and the more optimistic – or romantic – commentators at the time and afterwards insisted that Chávez's long term objectives were more revolutionary than his manifesto or his political practice suggested. For Bravo, however, Chávez's compromise, particularly with a figure as emblematic of the old political arrangements as Luis Miquilena[10] reflected a political shift away from revolutionary Bolivarianism. For Bravo this was all too closely reminiscent of what had happened after the overthrow of Pérez Jiménez. And there was, for him, a second problematic element in the equation, whose consequences would emerge as fundamental in the future direction of Chavismo – the role and influence of Cuba, and of Fidel Castro in particular. Bravo had broken with Castro in a very public way at the end of the 1960s over the abandonment of guerrilla strategy.

Chávez's electoral base was the Movement of the Fifth Republic, the MVR, which reflected an alliance between his group within the military and politicians seeking a return to the state after the virtual collapse of the 40-year puntofijista agreement, which locked the main bourgeois parties into a long term, consensual, power-sharing agreement. But the reality was that the brutal economic realities of the 1990s had undermined their earlier influence – the crumbs from the table were growing scarce, and the levels of poverty in the population were rising at an alarming rate. Yet there was no organisation at a national level capable of channelling and shaping the popular discontent, and none of the traditional political forces could do so either. Among those who had entered the state and taken responsibility for the imposition of the IMF rules for survival were those who had not long before been members of guerrilla organisations, among them the extremely influential ex-guerrilla and tireless political commentator, Teodoro Petkoff, who had directly imposed austerity measures through the so-called Venezuela Agenda during a brief period as minister of planning in the mid-1990s.

The 1998 election was a manifestation of the decline, if not collapse, of the political compromise that had controlled the Venezuelan state for 40 years. It was exactly the condition which exposed what Laclau had called 'the empty signifier'. Without accepting the totality of Laclau's theory, this concept is useful. The emptiness, to which Laclau and Mouffe refer, is best seen as the absence of a dominant discourse, where no political force has, for any number of reasons, the capacity to establish political hegemony. This political or ideological crisis was obvious in Venezuela in 1998. The right-wing candidates were unable to deploy again the dominant populist language which had prevailed throughout the puntofijista period; it had functioned because its maintenance of social equilibrium could be financed from oil profits. In the conditions of the 1990s this was not possible; the state could only offer austerity, poverty and subordination to the menaces of the global market. The political terrain was therefore unoccupied in any real sense, and the language of nationalism, the symbolism of Bolivar, a broad anti-imperialism, a rejection of the old politics, and a populist imaginary, combined convincingly in the person of Chávez who could represent all of these things, occupied the political space. It could fill the empty space precisely because of its imprecision, of its generality. But the signifier had to be able to carry the responsibility for winning ideological dominance in this confused and contradictory moment. At such times, individuals count. Laclau had developed his theory in his exploration of the phenomenon of Peronism; he found similar characteristics in Chávez.

Even some very serious political analysts in the Marxist tradition have found themselves seduced by a notion of the special and unique nature of Chávez as an individual, his very ambiguities transformed into special personal qualities. Much the same, of course, was done with Castro, whose undoubted political skills metamorphosed into almost super-human characteristics over time.

Chávez's programme was radical and liberal. Despite his already intimate relationship with Cuba, it did not in any sense present a revolutionary or a socialist character. It was liberal in its emphasis on human rights, nationalist in its central assertion of national sovereignty, and reformist in its insistence on the renegotiation of the contribution that the oil industry should make to the national exchequer. Immediately after his election Chávez announced the calling of a Constituent Assembly to rewrite the Venezuelan Constitution for the new Bolivarian Republic.

Constituent and Constituted

The concept of the Constituent Assembly or *Constituyente* is central to the political discourse of the pink tide, but it is not always clear when it is translated. For the key intellectuals of the revolutionary process in Latin America it is fundamental – for Roland Denis, for example, it defines a different concept of power – and yet it is ambiguous. Cicciarello-Maher describes the grassroots response to the attempted coup against Chávez in 2002 in this way:

> This was a central moment for grappling with the peculiar relationship that exists in contemporary Venezuela between movement and state, constituent and constituted. Again, however, an apparent paradox disintegrates once we recognize that it was not a constituted order but a process – itself comprising the dynamic interplay between constituent and constituted that the most revolutionary elements of the Venezuelan people were defending in those fateful days.[11]

The issue re-emerges at every stage of the flowing of the pink tide, so it is important to clear about its meaning.

The *constituyente* is not the elected assembly itself, but the new social forces it represents and that speak through it. In appearance the assembly and the parliament may look very similar, especially once the latter has been transformed into a plurinational institution. But it is not the form nor the appearance that distinguishes the constituent from the constituted, nor solely the content of its deliberations, but rather the relationship between the assembly and its social base. The constituted, by contrast, is that complex of institutions and structures through which bourgeois democracy functions, an expression of a relationship of representation, or to give it another name, substitution. The constituted reflects a marginalisation of the majority population who exist politically as voters only. It is the representatives who act on their behalf. The *constituyente*, by contrast, is not different simply because it elects delegates charged to present the views of those they speak for but because those delegates are accountable at every stage. They are answerable not simply because they see themselves differently but because they are in a direct relationship with an active and mobilised base through organs of direct democracy.

The argument thus returns to the core debates on the left, to the distinction between reform and revolution. What has changed, of course, from earlier debates is the concept of revolution itself. The state is a class formation, the executive committee of the bourgeoisie, as Marx admittedly crudely put it. In the modern world, that executive is surrounded and bolstered by networks of institutions which administer the apparatuses of power and the structures which sustain the relationship between the state and the population at large. Their role is essentially mediation, or to put it another way the smoothing of the rocky road between the social base and the leadership. The relationship is, in its essence, confrontational – the ground between a ruling class and the producing classes is a terrain of negotiation and mediation between unequal powers. It is a terrain where that fundamental conflict, the class struggle, is hidden behind modes of arbitration, negotiation and the creation of cultural diversion – the fostering of the illusion that beyond class lies some shared territory, some level ground where we are 'all human'. The illusion of choice, of election, is created in the political arena. Electoral politics are essentially ritualistic, an enactment of an illusory equality which, as Paul Foot used to say,[12] provides around 5 minutes 20 seconds of equality in every lifetime. Under neo-liberalism, that terrain of choice has shifted to consumption, to the market place, where the proliferation of things enacts the multiplicity of choices. The ideological shift has closed the circle; the decline of politics, or anti-politics, may appear to be a rejection of bourgeois politics – that is how the left would like to think of it, finding reassurance there. But for the majority, outside the anti-capitalist circuits and immune to its mood, it *is* a rejection of politics understood as the shaping of priorities, relations and values. These now arrive on the shelf, ready made and double-wrapped. Fascism presents itself as anti-politics too, as a renunciation of that right to shape and construct the future, a utopia. Fascism as Mariategui describes it[13] is a reactionary myth, a collective conservative utopia imposed by authority. The absence of politics is common to all fascisms – replaced by ritual, performance, the refuge of the individual.

The problem is that social democracy functioned in the interstices of the constituted state, in the mediating terrains. They have now gone, and social democrats are either functionaries of the state, with no possibility of critical distance, or they exist in a kind of wilderness of nostalgia, a melancholia of regret or yearning. Where there is no negotiation to be conducted they have no place, no space in which to exist; when politics shifts to the market all that can be discussed is price, and that is beyond the reach of any ordinary mortal in the global marketplace.

The constituent, however, is more than and different from 'civil society', essentially because it includes those elements of society which have no civil society representation either – the poor, the marginalised, the unregistered and undocumented, the propertyless. It is a force far wider than the working class, as diverse and inchoate as the concept of *el pueblo*.

Nevertheless the question that Cicciarello-Maher poses is central to an understanding of the pink tide. When he describes the constituent-constituted relationship as a process, he is identifying a dynamic. As Beverley puts it:

> What should be the relation of formal or informal social movements to the new governments of the marea rosada they have helped bring to power? Do the social movements capture the state, or are they instead captured by it, limiting the radical force and possibility they carried initially...[14]

Beverley's question could be the epigram to this book as a whole, but with one critical addendum. Cicciarello-Maher's 'process' is by definition time-limited; for the two parties to the encounter can fulfill their objectives only by the eventual disappearance of the other. There is no timetable to the process, but there is a development, though how it unfolds, and at what point it prevails is a question of a shifting balance of forces.

Yet it is the central question. The constituted (the state as it exists) may set out to co-opt and absorb the social movements into the task of governing within the framework and according to the priorities of the capitalist system which it was designed to oversee, or it may be replaced by a new form of power. These are the options to be fought for on this terrain of competition and contradiction. In the rest of what follows it will be the implicit question in all the processes of the pink tide. There will be debates on the left, of course, about how this changes the politics of the conquest of the state, and above all about agency in that process; there will be disagreements about when the critical conjunctures come and how they may be recognised. There may even be attempts to merge the two ideologically and organisationally in a new discourse, which may be called populist among many other epithets. Or it may result in the victory not of the people's power implicit in the notion of the *constituyente* but of the constituted, wearing new clothes and speaking a new language, but whose conduct will be remarkably familiar.

Perhaps the constituted/constituent binary is simply a reworking of the representative versus delegate controversy. The representatives are chosen from a pre-existing list drawn up from above; the delegate is also elected, from a wider sample perhaps, but the critical difference is accountability. The delegate is not the substitute for the electors, but their direct voice, answerable to them. The constituent, then, is not a formal question of the manner of election – a cleaner electoral process, invulnerable to distortion or misuse, be it by secret ballot (the finest method of social fragmentation) or show of hands in open assembly. Of course in the latter case the delegate is identifiable, known, accessible as well as recallable. But that in itself is not what makes a constituent process. It is the permanent nature of the assembly. That doesn't necessarily mean that it continues uninterrupted forever, but only that it can be reconvened at any time by the will of is members. But it is also more than that. What makes it constituent is its control over the agenda, the priorities of the administration of society. So popular power is *constitutive* of the constituent power, rather than mere effect.

There is an argument that Ciccariello-Maher offers that the two can, for a time, exist side-by-side, taking some part of social territory each:

Rather than the revolution under way in Venezuela… some see merely the continuity of the state, of corrupt institutions, of charismatic lead-ers. It is in contrast to this view – the blind insistence that all power must be immediately dispersed in the here and now, that Ali Primera describes his people as… precious hope, precious wood… In other words we must first strategically accumulate, consolidate and develop our own power...[15]

That may be true insofar as there will be a struggle for domination. He seems to suggest some functions adapt to one form of control, others to the other. But they will still be in conflict. This will characterise any process of transition which must by necessity be brief, or at the very least a period of authentic and visible change.

Once elected, Chávez immediately announced the calling of a Constituent Assembly. In 1999, the enormous enthusiasm of the majority of Venezuelans was manifest in the participation in the public debates that preceded their election. Delegates were elected and the Assembly met and debated, but the referendum vote to approve the new constitution had to take place amid a devastating national tragedy – the *vaguada* or mudslide that engulfed whole areas of the state of Vargas and killed tens of thousands.[16] The devastation involved enormous costs and extraordinary efforts in the relocation of people. It seemed emblematic that one major casualty should have been the main motorway between the airport at Maiquetia and the capital – it would take ten years to repair. Nonetheless participation in the vote was extraordinarily high.

The vote reflected a promise to raise the levels of tax and royalties paid by the oil companies, the commitment to the eventual nationalisation of the national oil corporation PDVSA and the redistributive undertaking at its heart. Yet Douglas Bravo considers it to have been neo-liberal in its economic proposals, since it did not challenge globalisation or its impact on Venezuela directly, did not include labour rights at its centre and confirmed that it would observe its international financial obligations. At the time, Chávez rejected the nationalisation project in the immediate on the grounds that 40 per cent of PDVSA's earnings came from the United States. What Chávez did launch immediately, however, was a process carried by Ali Rodríguez Araque to strengthen and revive OPEC, which had lain virtually dormant for a decade in the face of Saudi indifference to the pursuit of an agreement among oil-producing countries. It was undoubtedly Venezuela's intervention[17] that reinforced OPEC and achieved agreement on limiting production in order to raise prices on the world market. But the constitution's key provision in terms of political change was the affirmation of the *participatory and protagonist* character of the new democracy and the clause that permitted the recall of any public official by a referendum.

Chávez's supporters, then and since, enthusiastically evoked the Paris Commune, which had adopted the principle of recall; but the echoes of the Commune stopped there. There was no *replacement* of the army by a citizens' militia and no suggestion that the salaries of public officials should be restricted to the average wage. The concept of participatory democracy would be further developed in Chávez's pronouncement of '21st century socialism' in 2005. For Bravo, from whom the concept of the Constituent Assembly derived – though he was not by any means the only political intellectual discussing it – it represented the highest expression of mass participation, replacing representatives with delegates and private negotiation with publicly accountable decision-making. But Bravo makes a fundamental point when he insists that it could only function in conjunction with an 'act of force' – a physical rising of the masses which would give its participatory character a meaningful content. This is not necessarily armed struggle, or insurrection – though it may be. It may take other forms, as it would do through the pink tide era. But without the act of mass involvement, the material presence of the masses in the political process, he argues, decisions would not be democratic but taken by a political leadership, in this case by Chávez.[18] The issue would become central.

In this sense I would argue that the Bolivarian revolution, in the sense that the masses became the direct leading participants in the political process and determined the outcome of events, began on 11 April 2002, defeating by mass action the attempted coup against Chávez by the Venezuelan right. Until then, the Bolivarian process was essentially a process of reform, a renegotiation of the *terms* of the relationship between Venezuela and the global market in the context of its total dependence on oil exports, but not a challenge to that relationship in itself. There was an early assumption, recalling the CEPAL theory of dependency, that the increased oil revenues would permit a policy of economic reorganisation and a diversification of the economy, investing in the expansion of other and new areas of the economy – industrialisation predominantly, but also the capitalisation of national agriculture, since at this stage something like 60 per cent of the country's food requirements were imported, mainly from the United States. A much higher proportion of consumer goods, technology, machinery, and knowhow were imported – a phenomenon common to all oil-producing countries, all the more so in the country with the second highest reserves in the world, Venezuela. Despite later claims, Chávez's programme was not anti-imperialist nor did it challenge the local bourgeoisie at that point. This would change after 2002, as we shall see.

Tension increased through 2001, with the first attempt at a bosses' strike. On 11 April 2002, the president of Fedecámaras, the employers' organisation, Pedro Carmona, appeared on television to announce the removal of Chávez. The ground had been well prepared previously with increasing street violence by the right. The bourgeoisie's key ally was the Venezuelan Workers Confederation, CTV, whose general secretary, Carlos Ortega, joined with the employers in opposing the nationalisation of the oil industry. The coincidence was not accidental. The traffic in jobs in the oil industry was part of the puntofijista arrangements, and although the royalties for oil production brought only 1 per cent of returns to the Venezuelan state, a slice of the rest was distributed across the state machine and oiled the wheels of corruption for that section of the population benefitting directly or indirectly from the industry. By the time of Chávez's election, however, the days when part of those profits did trickle down through society had long since passed, reclaimed by the IMF and the multinational companies after the boom times of the 1970s. By 1998 some 65 per cent of the population were living in poverty according to UN figures. This was the inequality that the coup-makers undertook to protect and maintain in their arrogance. In a rare conjunction of circumstances, an Irish television team from RTE was filming a documentary[19] in Venezuela, and were inside the Miraflores presidential palace when the coup began. They filmed the short-lived elation of the Venezuelan bourgeoisie as Carmona anointed himself president with a conveniently available orange sash, applauded by members of the military command, the representative of the Catholic church, and other leading capitalists. The camera captured their frozen smiles as they turned towards the windows of the palace through which the massive gathering crowd demanding the return of Chávez could be seen. Their baseball caps and t-shirts were sufficient evidence of where they had come from. The poor of Venezuela had 'come down from the hills' to surround the palace and reverse the coup. Though it had only lasted 48 hours, the threats and naming of names on television, and the revenge killings that left over 100 dead, were an unmistakable sign of what could have been expected had the coup succeeded. In fact, the interests of the capitalist class in Venezuela had, at that stage, remained untouched. Chávez's radical discourse won him the affection of Venezuela's majority and the optimistic support of an international left. Yet there was as yet no evidence of any strategic intention to restructure the society, reshape the economy or address its class structure.

The coup-makers fled to their havens in Miami and Colombia. What was significant, in the light of what happened subsequently, was the immediate response of Chávez. It was conciliatory, and the first meeting after his return to the presidential residence of Miraflores included the most powerful Venezuelan capitalist, Gustavo Cisneros.[20] Those who were present noted Chávez's deferential attitude to Cisneros, and the latter's contemptuous attitude to Chávez, who despite his role had not made public identification with the coup, although it was his private helicopter that had taken Carlos Andrés Pérez to his refuge in Curaçao during the Caracazo. Indeed he appears also to have enjoyed a privileged relationship with Chávez and his successors ever since. It would be empty speculation to suggest any kind of deal between them. What that encounter does reveal is a degree of insecurity in Chávez. There were those in his inner circle who argued fiercely that this was a moment to take the revolution forward, to carry through the nationalisation of PDVSA aggressively, to expropriate the property and interests of those who had organised the coup, and to pursue and detain the leading public figures in the reaction. His hesitation may explain the events that followed. In December 2002, the right launched a strike, focussed on PDVSA. The corporation's white collar employees, technicians and managers did not simply walk out: they sabotaged the enterprise, directly by damaging equipment, cutting cables and so on, and indirectly by concealing passwords for the multiple processes on which a highly automated enterprise like oil production and distribution rests. The information systems and IT sectors of PDVSA had been outsourced to SAIC, an IT company based in the United States and linked to the CIA.

The object of the strike was to sabotage the entire operation. The technology gave access to every level of information – the location of tankers around the world, the financial activity of the corporation – but also governed the refineries, pipelines, the temperature in the oil containers – if the temperature was not maintained, the oil would solidify and the containers collapse. The importance of control of the huge tankers was dramatically illustrated by the incident of the 'Pilín León' on Lake Maracaibo, abandoned by its crew as it drifted towards the bridge across the lake. The consequences of a collision are not hard to imagine! It was the intervention of a retired tanker captain that enabled the ship to be turned in time to avoid a disaster.

The Venezuelan economy was very nearly brought to its knees. The major refineries and oil installations were picketed by armed right-wing thugs; the IT assault, which was organised from outside the country, with clear Israeli involvement, was beaten back by students and staff from the universities, who hacked into the system before a disastrous collapse. Production fell to 200,000 barrels. Internal petrol supplies were reduced to almost nothing, as the huge unmoving queues at every service station testified. The private commercial sector joined the bosses' strike. Yet three months later, production had resumed, and the lockout had failed. What made the difference were two linked factors; the self-sacrifice of millions of ordinary Venezuelans, who accepted the intolerable conditions in solidarity with the Chávez administration, and the active involvement of communities in protecting oil installations, beating back the armed threat, and ensuring the continuing, if badly bruised, functioning of society and economy.

The two logics set in motion after the election of Chávez pointed towards two different political strategies.

Two Logics, Two Directions

The defeat of the bosses' strike, and the dismissal of 19,000 recalcitrant management personnel was indisputably a political victory. The right-wing opposition was down, though not yet out. It would go on to exploit the progressive recall clause in the Constitution in an effort to bring down Chávez and recover its control of the golden goose of the Venezuelan economy. The response was to mobilise the grass roots support for Chávez through the Bolivarian Circles, small local groups organised by local activists to ensure that the referendum proposal of the right would be rejected. It was highly successful, both in electoral terms and politically, continuing the process of public discussion and debate, basically of political education, at the grass roots. Militants of the old parties and of the trade unions certainly took an active part in these debates – but as local activists or individuals rather than in any collective way. Nevertheless it was a critical moment in *el proceso bolivariano*. The opposition was on the defensive, the mass movement growing in confidence. After the referendum, in 2004, the process moved in a significantly more radical direction. In PDVSA, for example, for a year thereafter, there was a shift towards control by an assembly of all workers, expressed in the production of an internal newspaper which included contributions from every sector of workers and employees of the corporation. It has been argued that this was a move against the unions, but it should be remembered that the existing trade unions were complicit in the coup, through the CTV, and had long acted in concert with the corporation's management.

In this period there was active discussion of workers control of industry, led by the Marxist ex-guerrilla Carlos Lanz,[21] who was later nominated to be the first director of the emblematic aluminium processing Alcasa plant in Puerto Ordaz in Guayana. It reflected a profound discussion about the nature of Chavismo which was taking place not just among the higher echelons of the state but also at the grass roots among the social movements and organisations of local activists. But for others, the workers assembly looked more like incorporation than a move in the direction of people's power. The contradictions of the *proceso* were unfolding even then.

The internal debates ranged around the role of the military, the character of the MVR, the nature of a socialist economy. Jorge Giordani, Minister of Planning, came from a communist background and championed the concept of a centralised, state-owned economy. Roland Denis, a revolutionary thinker and writer, was vice-minister, a post he accepted in anticipation of a radical move on the economy along the lines advocated by Carlos Lanz. He resigned within a year, convinced that the Chávez government was under other influences which were arguing for a more limited and slower process. It was always difficult to know which influences were affecting Chávez at any given moment, but his uncontested domination of the process at that stage made these questions significant.

The *Misiones*, whose formation began in 2003 in the wake of the bosses' strike, were the object of much debate. These were effectively social programmes directed at the social base of Chavismo. The first were the result of an agreement with Cuba, whereby Venezuela provided some 100,000 barrels of oil per day in exchange for numbers of Cuban medical personnel to staff the new local medical primary care centres through the *Misión Barrio Adentro* (Into the Barrios). The education *Misiones* – Robinson (for literacy) Ribas (for secondary high school education) and Sucre (for access to higher education) – were directed at people who had no access to education until then; they also employed Cuban personnel. At the same time, Venezuelan students were sent to Cuba to train in Integral Medicine to replace, eventually, the large number of Venezuelan medical personnel who had deserted the state sector, and the Cubans who were filling the gap. The *Misiones*, in the first place, were social welfare programmes for those who had no access to state services, be it in health, education or housing. Other Missions involved support for indigenous communities; one was designed to encourage people to return to productive work on the land

(Vuelvan Caras), reversing the direction of internal migration towards the cities, and Caracas in particular, from the 1960s onwards.

The Missions also had a political function in carrying through programmes which were often opposed by the state, where the right still retained considerable power. In this sense they were represented as a devolution of power to the grass roots, actively engaging and integrating local communities in the administration of public services. The reality was significantly more complex. Despite the events of 2002–5, the Venezuelan state remained in the hands of the previous generation of functionaries. It was extraordinarily resistant to change or democratisation. The same was true of PDVSA, despite the attempt to transform its internal political culture; it was finally nationalised in 2005. Its role in the Bolivarian project was unclear in many ways. Oil revenues would not be passed to the state; given the obdurate resistance of the state and the deliberate interference with or direct blocking of government decisions, the resources for the Missions would be administered and distributed directly through PDVSA. This involved a number of contradictions. If the central objective of Chavismo was to take control of the state, the new role of PDVSA appeared to avoid confrontation with the state sector, diverting many of its functions to the nationalised PDVSA which was directly under Chávez's control, through his personal nominee for director of PDVSA and Minister of Energy, Rafael Ramírez. As soon as he assumed his new role, Ramírez dismantled the workers assemblies and installed a clear regime of one man management, pyramidal and hierarchical, as symbolised by the main Caracas headquarters, La Campiña, a tower block overlooking the Avenida Libertador where Ramírez occupied the top floor.

What then was the role of *Misiones*? At the grass roots they were seen as a first stage in the development of the participatory, protagonist democracy promised in the 1999 Constitution. The expectation was that they would become, over time, a parallel state, distributing state resources through direct community participation. In a word, they were organs of grass roots democracy, deepening the role the social movements and local organisations had played in the resistance to the 2002 coup, the reaction to the bosses' strike and the mobilisation of the Bolivarian Circles. Alternatively, they were organs of patronage, conduits for state investments and government decisions. In the following months, it was becoming clear that a new layer of state functionaries for Venezuela was being created, trained and prepared politically in Cuba.

The majority of this new bureaucratic layer were young and from poor backgrounds. This was to be a new segment of the political class, unconnected to the previous system of clientilism and patronage and unconditionally loyal to Chávez himself and his inner circle. The upper echelons of government were nominated, and dismissed by the personal fiat of Chávez; there were no other publicly accountable mechanisms for the nomination or replacement of public officials, despite the constitutional clauses. Democratic procedures were increasingly replaced by internal rivalries, plots and counter-plots, rumour and counter-rumour. Key figures would disappear from politics overnight or be sent to remote diplomatic posts or administrative responsibilities far from power. Chávez himself was increasingly surrounded by circles of power brokers and sycophants, flattering and isolating him from the grass roots. For the moment, his personal power was still undiminished, however; his incontestable charisma and his enormous popularity were reinforced by his intensive and skilful use of the mass media, symbolised by his long, Sunday morning televised encounters with the people – *Aló Presidente*. The 2006 re-election campaign won Chávez his largest popular vote – some 62 per cent of the total. Chávez's popularity was never in doubt; it was not entirely spontaneous but well organised and maintained by large-scale public sector investment on the one hand, and on the other by high levels of spending on political campaigns and propaganda.

There was, inescapably, a contradiction developing within the Chavista project. D.L. Raby, writing in 2006,[22] posed the issue as a tension between 'formal or substantive democracy', where the latter was the 'direct democracy of the Commune, the soviets, Spain in 1936'. She described Venezuela as 'the greatest hope for progressive movements throughout the world'[23] and its constitution of 1999 as embodying 'a revolutionary concept of direct popular sovereignty' in which 'the conventional army has been in large part transformed into a revolutionary army'.[24] It was, Raby asserted, 'the most profoundly democratic revolution the world has yet seen.'

These hyperbolic claims were repeated by many commentators. But the issue here is not simply that these interpretations have proved to be ill-founded; they were a complete misreading of what was happening at the time. It might be argued that the left needed an injection of optimism so some exaggeration was understandable. But the problem is that truth is the first guiding principle of any revolutionary theory. Most significantly, the fact is that these descriptions and paeans of praise distorted both the external and the internal debate. Far from creating a revolutionary army, Chávez created 2500 new generals and continued to rely heavily on his network of military allies. The civic-military alliance did not subordinate the military to popular control. It remained an entirely autonomous structure. Over time, as we shall see, it was society that would be absorbed into a dominant and expanding military structure, and not the reverse. On the question of democracy, the test of a protagonistic, participatory democracy is not its formal declaration but the reality of direct involvement, its transparency and the accountability of public officials as a first step. It certainly bore no relation, even then, to the soviets or the anti-fascist committees in Spain in 1936–7. In Raby's terms, then, this was not a substantive democracy, but a formal one in which national elections were, and increasingly became, the focus of political activity.

What was understood by revolution in the Venezuelan context? I have argued that if revolution is defined politically as the moment when the protagonist of revolution, its subject, becomes the mass of working people, then it can be described as the sign of a profound political change. What happened on 12–13 April, as the mass movement descended on the presidential palace demanding the return of Chávez, was such a sign. But that is all it was. The bosses' strike, and the attempt to sabotage the oil industry and bring down the Chávez government with it, deepened the class confrontation, and marked a second phase in the class struggle. The social movements were central to the mobilisation against the strikers, but it was the intervention of organised workers that ensured the continuity of production that was the key to victory.[25]

Raby discusses the 'Chávez-people dialectic', a concept that seems perilously close to mysticism; Chávez became the symbol of popular resistance, and its voice. But that resistance was the action of thousands, tens of thousands even, who had entered directly into the arena of struggle, recognising their own strength and their own initiative as the definitive factor in defeating the capitalist class. This was the leap taken between April and December. In April, the demand was the return of Chávez and, although under the pressure of the physical presence of the working people, the resolution was the result of the intervention of the military – in many cases, furthermore, only when the balance of forces was tipping against the coup-makers. Between December 2002 and March 2003, it was mass militant action, with organised labour at its heart, which won.

It would have seemed the ideal moment to begin to implement the radical democracy that Raby had seen in Venezuela, though it was not yet real. It was a moment to build upon the actual participation and protagonism of the movement, to begin a deeper process of transformation. In the event, Alí Rodriíguez Araque invited the 19,000 or so managers and technical personnel to return to their posts – a gesture of conciliation which could be interpreted as a sign of strength or weakness. The right certainly interpreted it as weakness, and felt confident enough to immediately organise a recall referendum to bring Chávez down, taking advantage of a constitution they had criticised and satirised.

The mass media still remained predominantly in private hands, and they would be used to build an anti-Chávez campaign. The state remained obdurately resistant to change. If there was a moment to challenge the conservatives in the state machine and to punish the capitalist class that had enthusiastically supported the coup, it was then. It was also a moment to show that the Constitution meant what it said, and that there was a revolution in the offing. There were signs of a deeper transformation to come, as Chávez announced the creation of the Social Property Enterprises (EPS) and a programme to stimulate the growth of cooperatives.[26] The ideas of Carlos Lanz on worker management of enterprises were acknowledged and applied at the aluminium plant Alcasa and announced for the steel complex at Sidor. In PDVSA the move to workers assemblies suggested an imminent radicalisation of the control of the oil industry. And most centrally, the Missions whose formation began in 2003 could be seen as the embryo of a parallel state, putting flesh on the promise of a social revolution – not to fight for control of the state but to replace it. This was the most optimistic interpretation of what was happening in what seemed to be a clear move to the left on Chávez's part.

Yet if the fundamental contradiction at this point is between strengthening the state, which remains a bourgeois state in its personnel as well as its functions, and reinforcing the emerging organs of popular power, in other words moving in the direction of social revolution, it is not necessarily the case that the emphasis was on the former. The Missions were programmes to improve the lives of the people and provide basic social services in health and education. The creation of cooperatives – some 84,000 involving a million people according to Martha Haernecker – was a positive move, but with an average of ten members they could not be seen as a step towards the expropriation of private property or of the means of production. Indeed by 2007, according to Steve Ellner, the numbers involved had fallen dramatically.[27] In Alcasa, for example, the enterprise passed into the hands of its workers under the management of Carlos Lanz. By 2008, production at Alcasa had been devolved to a number of internal cooperatives, carrying out specific jobs in the plant, but they were essentially small businesses, sharing profits but earning nothing when there was no work and with no involvement in the global process of production. The workers had been transformed into small businessmen, keen to raise their profits and resentful of those who earned a regular wage.

The EPSs for their part were mainly enterprises which had been abandoned or decapitalised by their owners which the state bought and paid for at the market rate, compensating their owners. These included the emblematic Invepal, Inveval and Alcasa among others. The Missions in their turn were certainly placed under the control of the community councils formed two years earlier. They were forms of local government at the micro level, but their role was the implementation of social programmes conceived and financed from the state or by PDVSA.

Most importantly, the funding of all these social programmes was to come from oil revenues, and would continue to do so. By 2005, with Missions well under way and Venezuela supplying a number of countries with oil in exchange for their services, there was no perspective of diversification of the economy or the development of other, industrial or manufacturing sectors of the economy.

Meanwhile... in Cochabamba

The election of Hugo Chávez to the presidency in Venezuela proved to be, at first, a slow-burning fuse – viewed from abroad with curiosity amid some anticipation in its first year. But even before the masses had descended from the hills to defend, and win, 'their' president back from his bourgeois kidnappers, the population of the city of Cochabamba had set a new marker in the anti-capitalist struggle. The independence of the movement of resistance, its diversity, its distance from politics and its open forms of organisation announced a new kind of struggle against neo-liberalism driven from below. Its roots and its unfolding will form part of the next chapter.

2
Bolivia Rises

A History of Rebellion

For an outside world largely ignorant of Latin America for much of the last century or two, the explosions of popular rage and resistance that ushered in the pink tide will often seem to be spontaneous reactions to momentary situations. In fact, the struggle against exploitation and colonial oppression has been relentless. Nowhere illustrates that long and courageous defence of life more clearly than the history of the Bolivian people against the series of exploiters, foreign and domestic, who have torn out the country's mineral heart over the centuries. In the mid-sixteenth century, the silver hill of Potosí spawned a city larger than London, famed for its decadence and hedonism; the ornate silverwork in its churches was paid for by the wealthy colonists to preserve them from the fires of hell. These were reserved for the indigenous people driven deep into the mines where they died in huge numbers, from mercury poisoning or suffocation or starvation. When the silver veins were finally exhausted, the tin mines of the high Andes enriched the 'tin barons' like Simon Patiño,[1] whose enormous wealth allowed him to reproduce the palaces of Europe in his home outside Cochabamba. It was, once again, the miners who paid for his suite at the Waldorf Astoria in New York and for his enormous mausoleum. Today, the dramatic Altiplano, the high plateau between Bolivia and Chile, is witnessing the arrival of new colonists – Japanese and Chinese multinationals preparing to wrench the coltan and lithium from the belly of the mountain. These were the 'open veins of Latin America' that Eduardo Galeano[2] described in his brilliant, iconic history of the exploitation of Latin America.

The uninterrupted exploitation of Bolivia sustained an economy shaped by the external market from the sixteenth to the twenty-first century. The vast profits and luxurious living of the mineowners were paralleled by the slave labour conditions in the mines and the extreme poverty of the indigenous rural population who fed their bodies to the malevolent gods of the mine. These were the two faces of an extractive economy. Rebellion was a permanent response to these inhuman conditions, and in the late eighteenth century it reached insurrectionary proportions with the rising of Túpac Amaru (1780–82) and the siege of La Paz by Túpac Katari in 1781. The conditions of life, the enduring poverty, the exploitation and the resistance remained embedded in the collective memory of the indigenous communities, and were passed on in song and ceremony.

The Federal War of 1898 was described as a 'race war' – but it was in fact a war over land. The seizure of indigenous territories and the repression that followed left its residue in the collective memory and fuelled the conflicts of the 1920s and 1930s. In 1927 an indigenous congress in the mining town of Oruro declared itself for community government, but the subsequent rising failed to spread to the capital, La Paz. In 1932 Bolivia declared war on Paraguay over the arid region of the Chaco. The objectives of the war remain a topic of dispute, but the consequences do not. Some 250,000 people fought in the Chaco War, and over 52,000 died – many of them of starvation. The socialists, anarchists and trade unionists who protested were sent to die on the front line. It goes without saying that the majority of the dead were the indigenous foot soldiers.

> …the Chaco war called into question the legitimacy of the old regime, the racist foundations of Bolivian society, and the exploitative bases of an economy organised around the interests of… the tin-barons and the landed elite.[3]

The post-Chaco war military government introduced some reforms and nationalised the Rockefeller-owned Standard Oil Company. Into the 1940s two currents emerged – fascist groupings defending the interests of the old oligarchy and the MNR (Revolutionary Nationalist Movement), which would dominate Bolivian political life through most of the second half of the century. Originally influenced by fascist ideas, the MNR built its base in the 1940s among the miners, as the Second World War produced a new demand for the tin of which Bolivia was the world's largest producer. At the same time Trotskyism won a major base of support among the miners.[4] A turning point in this radicalisation was the massacre of miners and their families by government troops in the mining town of Catavi in 1942. Two years later the miners union, FSTMB, was formed and for the next 40 years led the labour movement in Bolivia.

Although they were only 3 per cent of the workforce, the miners' labour produced 95 per cent of the country's exports and 45 per cent of government revenues. As the struggle between the ruling oligarchy and the mineworkers intensified, in 1948 Catavi was again the scene of a terrible massacre of miners and their families.

The most militant and revolutionary sectors of the miners union were also working with a growing resistance in the countryside; in 1945 an Indigenous Congress brought together representatives of over 1500 communities, and although the congress was originally conceived as an exercise in incorporation by the government, it was shaped by grassroots organisations gathered in the CIB (The Bolivian Indigenous Committee). In 1947 an insurrection embraced the majority of indigenous communities. In the event it failed to achieve its central aims – the return of their land. The oligarchy held out against them; in 1947 4.5 per cent of rural proprietors still owned 70 per cent of the land, but the seeds of the 1952 national revolution had been sown. In 1946, the miners union adopted the Pulucayo Theses, a definitive revolutionary programme.

The 1952 Revolution

The MNR was a revolutionary nationalist organisation with basically two internal currents. Its right-wing supported a programme of reform and the development of a Bolivian state capitalism; it was fundamentally anti-communist. The left emerged from the revolutionary trade unionism of the miners, informed and shaped by Trotskyism. In April 1952, the MNR leadership launched an insurrection, but as Webber points out it rapidly broke the boundaries set by its leadership. The miners drove the revolution.

> Popular militias of factory workers and miners and MNR rank and file militants and urban dwellers, overran most of the armed forces of the ancient regime... Chaco veterans were armed with their twenty year old weapons, miners were armed with the dynamite of their trade, and the mutinous troops who joined the insurrection brought with them arms of the state.[5]

Essentially, the old order caved in. In the following three years the revolution reached beyond its reformist intentions. Its key achievements – the nationalisation of the mines, a far-reaching agrarian reform and universal suffrage – were driven from below. Although the indigenous movements had played a limited part in the insurrection itself, they mobilised on a large scale behind the demand for redistribution of land and for political integration. The reform, however, was largely limited to the highland indigenous communities; it did not extend to the eastern lowlands, although it was a 1953 law allowing the occupation of unused lands that would drive the indigenous movements of the east 20 years later. There is no doubt that the 1952 revolution initially represented a major advance for working class and indigenous interests. The nationalism of the MNR, however, was expressed in a concept of a mestizo nation, in which the indigenous culture would be absorbed and ultimately perhaps disappear. It was a powerful ideology which only began to be challenged in the 1970s.

The 1952 revolution confirmed the role of the miners as the vanguard of the working class; they combined revolutionary Marxism and anarcho-syndicalism with 'ongoing allegiances and attachments to pre-conquest, precapitalist Quechua-Aymara indigenous traditions and rituals' including the traditions of resistance held in the collective memory. This was expressed in 'an emphasis on participatory democracy' and 'the primacy of independent syndicalism over party politics'.[6]

The subsequent move to the right of the MNR was reflected in the clashes between Hernán Siles Suazo, its leader, and Juan Lechín, the head of the miners union and the Minister of Labour in the first MNR government. It was symbolised by Siles's reconstitution of the state-led armed forces against the workers militias. The new regime remained dependent on the flow of U.S. aid, which continued in support of the anti-communist leadership. Foreign investment was renewed, and a new highway built to open the east of the country. The state capitalist project of the MNR succeeded in breaking the unity of peasant and worker struggles, and Siles's Stabilisation Plan, and the inflationary crisis that followed, led the revolutionary workers movement to break with the MNR. The contradictions had been there at the outset of course; the nationalisation of the tin mines was an advanced expression of the revolution – the payment of compensation to the tin barons, with over $300 million to Simon Patiño for what were in fact deposits in decline,[7] expressed the contradictions clearly.

Neo-liberalism's First Interventions

The military regime of René Barrientos (1964–9) continued the strategy adopted by the MNR after 1956, in close alliance with the United States,

the IMF and the international financial agencies. But two further elements were added; as a fluent Quechua speaker, Barrientos forged
alliances with the leadership of the indigenous movements in a Military-
Peasant Pact, while an intensifying repression was directed against the
working class movement, and the miners in particular.[8] The sustained
assault on the miners claimed a rising list of victims, but the turning point
came with Massacre of San Juan in 1967, a surprise attack on a mining
community in the early hours of the morning after a festival. The official
death toll was over 70 – the reality almost certainly higher. It was a clear
signal that the repression was a generalised form of state terror. When
Barrientos was killed in an air crash, his successor Ovando adopted a
more conciliatory line with the workers and announced the nationalisation of Gulf Oil, the U.S. corporation which owned 80 per cent of Bolivia's
oil. He was in turn replaced by the short-lived radical regime of Juan
José Torres, whose tenure was dependent on the support of the workers
movement. But his government lasted only some ten months (October
1970 to August 1971), before it was overthrown at the second attempt by
the neo-fascist General Hugo Banzer. The ferocity of the repression he
unleashed, especially against the indigenous peasantry, brought down
the Military-Peasant Pact, spurring a resurgence of militant indigenous
resistance under the aegis of the Movimiento Katarista, its name a com-
memoration of the eighteenth century rebellion of Túpac Katari. During
the brief Torres interregnum, new possibilities found expression in the
Asamblea Popular which convened on 22 June 1971. It brought together
the militant workers organisations and the peasant movements around
revolutionary proposals from the left, who had some 25 per cent of the
delegates. All the documents discussed by the delegates saw the Assembly
as a manifestation of dual power, with the government on one side and
the Asamblea on the other. By its very nature that situation was unstable,
and it was clear when Banzer's second coup came in August that the conservative sectors saw the situation in a similar way – as threatened by an
insurrectionary popular power. In reality the pact forged by Barrientos
was still not broken, as indigenous and left organisations regarded one
another with suspicion across the Assembly floor. But Banzer's sustained
assault on the indigenous movement ensured the Pact's demise, and a
new indigenous leadership emerged as the alliance between the peasant
organisations and the state fell apart.

The new Katarista leadership emphasised the cultural roots of indigenous struggles to replace the assimilation that had underpinned both

the MNR and Barrientos's development strategy. The Asamblea Popular would remain a point of reference for the movements of resistance that followed, a lived example of dual power and disengagement from the state which would certainly shape the new social movements from the mid-1980s onwards.

At the same time the centre of the national economy was shifting from the highlands towards the eastern, Media Luna provinces, with Santa Cruz as the most important city. In 1985, Bolivia was chosen to be the second experimental laboratory (after Chile) for neo-liberalism, as originally conceived and shaped by Milton Friedman and implemented in Bolivia by the Harvard economist, Jeffrey Sachs. Victor Paz Estenssoro, the MNR president who, in 1952, had led what was called the 'national revolution', was brought back to administer what was euphemistically described as 'structural adjustment'. Bolivia was Latin America's poorest nation, after Haiti. Its revolution had been led by the organised working class, and had won not just the nationalisation of the mines but also agrarian reform and universal suffrage. The shift in the economic centre of the country, combined with systematic repression weakened and undermined the power of the miners, but it was by no means easy for the Banzer regime, brutal though it was, to suppress the working class organised in the COB, the Bolivian Trade Union Federation. The murder of Torres in Buenos Aires, in what was clearly an operation linked to the Plan Condor,[9] produced a mass mobilisation followed by a miners strike.

In these threatening circumstances, the peasant and workers movement began to re-forge the unity of workers and peasants that had been built at the beginning of the 1952 revolution. A series of coups followed the Banzer government, each committed to continuing the repression against the working class and the indigenous organisations. They also shared the determination to continue to enjoy the profits from drug trafficking largely administered through the military regime under Banzer. In the 1980 elections, however, Siles Suazo, the historic leader of the MNR and now leader of a new coalition, the UDP (Popular Democratic Unity), was elected, but was only allowed to assume power in 1982. Suazo attempted, in the midst of an almost uncontrollable economic crisis, to reconcile the interests of the popular movement, the capitalist class, and foreign capital. The COB, with its revolutionary traditions, mounted a sustained resistance to the UDP's populist policies. In 1985, the miners occupied La Paz for a week, striking terror into the urban middle class.

But the COB had no alternative strategy to offer, and Siles Suazo mobilised the military to end the strike. It was, undeniably, a shattering defeat.

Against that background Paz Estenssoro was called back to implement a neo-liberal strategy. His presidency (1985–9) and that of his successor Paz Zamora (1989–93) set in motion a series of measures which would lead to the privatisation of much of the economy, including education, one result of which was a dramatic rise in the levels of illiteracy. The policy of privatisation was continued and intensified under the first presidency of Gonzalo Sánchez de Lozada – or Goni as he was contemptuously known. He initiated the so called Plan for All (*Plan de Todos*) that enabled him to sell off all Bolivia's publicly-owned utility companies – electricity, telephones, railways and, most significantly of all, the Bolivian national oil company YPFB. Little wonder the Jeffrey Sachs described him as one of the most creative politicians of the age.

The reality was that the programmes imposed by the IMF met little resistance. Coca cultivation guaranteed a higher income than any other cash crop to small farmers, including the 20,000 ex-miners relocated to the Chapare as the diminished mining industry was privatised. And the world trade in cocaine was booming, though it was a legal crop in Bolivia. The traditional organisations which stood in the leadership of every struggle in the decades since 1952, the miners' union and the national trade union federation (COB) which it dominated, were disarmed by the dismantling of the mining industry and the migration of its social base. The economic crisis of the 1980s had exhausted the Bolivian working class, and its national profile gave way in those years to more local and sectoral forms of resistance. The neo-liberal shock therapy cut taxes, dramatically reduced public sector employment, eliminated subsidies on basic foods, 'liberalised' both trade and the labour market and 'freed' prices. The March in Defence of Life from Oruro to La Paz in August 1986 numbered around 10,000, but it failed to mobilise any major support. According to Hylton and Thomson

> Left political parties, which had long followed in the wake rather than led, national-populist movements, declined precipitously after 1986.[10]

As Webber put it:

> The imposition of neo-liberal restructuring domestically required a coherent ruling-class political as well as economic project of dismantling the infrastructures of popular class-power.[11]

This consolidated the end of an economy based on mining, and marked a shift towards drugs and export agriculture, on the one hand, and on the other on the growth of small-scale industry, especially in and around the capital, La Paz. Privatisation drew in external loans, but it also reflected the increasing integration into the global market of a new Bolivian oligarchy partly based in the expanding economy of Santa Cruz in the eastern lowlands, where Bolivia's oil was to be found and where the burgeoning new industries of soya cultivation and cattle rearing were located, developed in conjunction with Brazilian and Argentine capital.

As elsewhere in Latin America, neo-liberalism brought windfall fortunes to those who represented its interests, and sold off the state's assets at preferential prices. The economy was sluggish. Bolivian exports at the beginning of the 1980s were worth $1300 million – in 2003 the figure was $1600 million, a minimal improvement. Meanwhile the average per capita income in 1980, $940, rose by only $20 in the same period.[12]

As Crabtree and Chaplin argue,[13] the nature of Bolivian politics changed. Teachers and workers in small factories became the new militants; the miners were dispersed to the Chapare coca fields in some cases, in others to the indigenous city of El Alto. The claim that the period would bring a fall in unemployment was a trick of the light; the real issue was *under* employment, and the falling value of wages.

The COB was no longer able to coordinate struggles, as it had for over three decades. The result was that the leadership of the resistance passed in the 1980s to the peasant federation CSTUCB whose emphasis moved from the commonality of class to a shared ethnic identity, expressed through the Katarista movement. The movement was divided, however, and was in crisis by the end of the decade, though a new expression of it – the organisation Condepa – emerged in El Alto and La Paz where Carlos Palenque was elected as mayor. One of the Katarista leaders, Victor Hugo Cárdenas, became vice-president to Lozada in his 1993–7 regime. It may seem paradoxical that Cárdenas should share power with a neo-liberal who had privatised the Bolivian economy and imposed aggressive policies against the mass of the population. But this was a neo-liberalism with a socially conscious face. Under Lozada the state was redefined as pluri-national in a strategy of incorporation and division of the indigenous communities. Ideologically, neo-liberalism was presented as a solution to the crisis of the state, bringing in private capital to finance development and to manage public services.

There were divisions within the indigenous movement, and between it and the *cocaleros*, the coca farmers of the Chapare, who brought the traditions of struggle and trade union organisation from the mining regions to the Cochabamba region. In 1992 the ASP (Assembly for the Sovereignty of the Peoples) acknowledged the need for a 'Political Instrument' to confront the attacks on the livelihood of the *cocaleros* – but agreement was very slow in coming. In the 1995 municipal elections the ASP won a number of key posts in the Cochabamba region. It defined itself as fighting for a 'communitarian, multinational, socialist Bolivia' – but it eventually fell apart in the face of internal disputes between its president, Alejo Vélez, Felipe Quispe, the leader of the CSUTB, and Evo Morales. Two new organisations then emerged – the Movimiento Indígena Pachakuti and what eventually become the MAS, or Movement towards Socialism, which would represent the grassroots movement of the cocaleros but which also had an explicit anti-neo-liberal position while merging it with indigenous issues.

Hugo Banzer succeeded Lozada in the presidency (1997–2001), this time as an elected president, continuing Lozada's neo-liberal strategies. It was widely known that in his earlier presidency, Banzer and his cabinet had been deeply embroiled in the growing drug trade of the times, and there was little attempt to conceal the fact that military aeroplanes regularly transported coca out of the country. So it was particularly ironic that Banzer's return to power, in 1997, should coincide with the U.S. government's much-vaunted 'war on drugs'; its first public manifestations were directed against the coca growers of the Chapare, whose militant trade union organisation would become central to the new phase of resistance led by the social movements.

The Water War

In 1999 President Banzer announced the sale of Cochabamba's public water enterprise to a new company, Aguas del Tunari, a subsidiary of the giant U.S. corporation Bechtel, whose name would be associated, for the anti-capitalist movement, with the destruction and rebuilding of Iraq.

The privatisation of water was a central plank of neo-liberal strategy, inaugurated by Margaret Thatcher with her sale of England's public water companies to the highest bidder. The transfer of water provision was emblematic of the dismantling of the state;[14] it was also a hugely profitable strategy, as the big players in the world water industry, like Vivendi and

Suez, watched their profits soar and enter the tens of billions of dollars annually. Water was not simply one more mineral resource; it would represent, and could eventually replace in terms of world trade, the oil industry – but with deeper implications. To deliver water into the hands of global capital was, not to put too fine a point on it, to surrender control over life itself. But it was, at the same time, a source of cheap and available energy that could replace, or at least combine with oil and gas, and 25 per cent of the world's water was in the Amazon Basin.

The World Bank's June 1999 country report for Bolivia was clear. There would be 'no public subsidies' to hold down water price increases. In a process with just one bidder, local press reports calculated that investors put up less than $20,000 of upfront capital for a forty-year exclusive contract granted by the Bolivian state. The World Bank also threatened to withdraw $600 million unless these provisions were implemented. Alternative forms of water distribution – specifically self-built community wells and even rainwater collection were specifically forbidden.[15]

Cochabamba's population had reached half a million by the end of 1999; just 60 per cent were reached by the notoriously inefficient local public company Semapa. The rest of the population were served by traditional water systems, which were now forbidden under the Water Law 2029 passed at the same time. Even the collection of rainwater was covered by the new law. It was the final straw.[16] The supply of water from Aguas de Tunari would cost a third of the minimum wage of $60.

The explosion of popular rage embraced both urban and rural populations. Local farmers marched towards the city; communities blocked highways. Local communities met to protest at the new costs which would wreck the fragile household economy of the poor. In December 1999 the Coordinadora del Agua was formed under the leadership of Oscar Olivera,[17] an anarchist machinist in his mid-forties, Olivera was a union leader in a new mould; the Fabriles (small factories) organised at the rank and file level, but in the framework of what Webber calls 'social movement unionism' which drew together precarious and temporary workers, community activists, women and young people. Indigenous activists in the region had been fighting over the issue of control of water supplies for many years – defending the *regantes* or locally constructed irrigation systems. The *cocaleros*, miners dispersed from the high Andes in the 1980s to grow coca in the Chapare, had brought with them the experience of decades of militant trade union organisation combined with the solidarity of their indigenous communities. They had fought a continuous battle throughout the decade over the coca leaf, and had gained both confidence and organisational experience in the course of it. Local residents' groups, especially from the marginal *barrios*, had organised in defence of their own survival in the preceding years. These were the forces that gathered under the banner of the Coordinadora for the demonstration in Cochabamba's central square on 4 February 2000, a month after Aguas de Tunari's formal takeover.

From the early hours, the repressive forces sent from La Paz and Oruro began to wield their clubs and fill the streets with tear gas. By the end of the day, after ferocious street battles, an uneasy truce was negotiated and the government agreed to review the Bechtel contract. The government dragged its feet, however, and the Coordinadora organised a 'consulta popular', which overwhelmingly called for ending the Tunari contract. By now, peasant and indigenous organisations were blocking highways around the city. On 4 April a general strike in the city and a province-wide blockade were launched. Two days later the Coordinadora representatives negotiating with government were arrested. Sixty thousand gathered in protest in the city of Cochabamba and Banzer responded by declaring a state of emergency. The battle in the streets intensified until, on the 10 April, the agreement with Aguas del Tunari was annulled.

As each new discovery of the market value of Bolivia's natural resources has provoked new forms of exploitation, there has always been resistance – from silver to tin and now to water. What was most impressive about the Cochabamba water movement was that it gathered into a single stream the whole range of currents of resistance that had grown up, mainly around local issues, in the preceding years. Here indigenous and community organisations marched with market traders, coca farmers (the *cocaleros*), organised workers, students and civil servants. On 4 February and subsequent days, they took on armed police, and returned the teargas hurled at them.

> Everyone took a role, (says Oscar Olivera). Youth were on the frontlines, the elderly made roadblocks. When protest leaders called on the radio for a citywide transportation stoppage in response to the police crackdown downtown, little old women with bent spines were out in the streets within minutes, building blockades with branches and rocks.[18]

And it won. Within seven days the Banzer government withdrew the contract from Bechtel and introduced a new system for the distribution of water controlled by the mayor and an elected committee.[19] The new organisation was built from the water committees that proliferated in the area. Marcela Olivera, a leader of the water movement, stresses that these committees were not formed in the January days.

> Many people have attributed the origins of the autonomous practices adopted by the water committees to the Inca empire... The result is that the water committees are often seen as contemporary expressions of ancient communal practices. In his 2001 article 'State and autonomy in Bolivia, an anarchist interpretation' Carlos Crespo explains that in Bolivia autonomy is 'not an ideal to be pursued but a day to day practice of people, communities and affinity groups.'[20]

The Cochabamba action was a triumph; for the first time a protest movement had beaten back a multinational company through independent action. The state had been forced to act by a movement from below.

It was also a detonator. Protests proliferated across the country. While the battles were raging in the streets of Cochabamba, a militant police strike erupted in La Paz over levels of taxation, and across the country communities blocked highways with their own barricades. In El Alto, water privatisation also brought the largely indigenous population of the city into direct confrontation with another multinational water company, Suez.

Cochabamba was the turning point at which mass actions at the grass roots became determinant in resisting neo-liberalism. It provided a new model of struggle. It was not a matter of the combativity of those who took to the streets – the whole history of the country is peppered with examples of heroism and determination in the face of the forces of the state. Rather it was the unity and coordination of different organisations that marked a new stage, as well as its increasing politicisation. The demonstrators, like the anti-capitalist protesters after Seattle, found that in a neo-liberal world every local issue led back to the global system. Equally significant was the fact that it was a politicisation that took place largely outside the framework of existing political organisations, even those of the left, and the discredited formal structures of the political system. It was a radicalisation whose rhetoric and references addressed several different traditions at once – the history of the working class struggle, the historic experience of the left, the complexities of community organisation, and also the strength of a resurgent indigenous nationalism. And it shared with the other movements arising in Latin America horizontal forms of organisation and a deep suspicion of formal political institutions and procedures. Here, resistance was its own method – its organs the local coordinating committees.

A Curious Blend: Water, Coca and Oil

The coca farmers of Chapare had played a central role in the Cochabamba coordination; their discipline and experience were the heritage of decades of revolutionary working class organisation in the Altiplano. Coca, of course, is a legal crop in Bolivia, sold from enormous sacks in the street markets. The tradition of coca chewing is part of the experience of life at high altitude, where food is often scarce and labour, hard and unrewarding. El Tío, the protective god of the mine, is offered coca every Friday morning, and the leaves form part of most communal ceremonials.

The huge expansion in heroin and cocaine consumption in the West, and the United States in particular, from the early 1970s onwards transformed the economies of Latin America. By the late 1990s cocaine represented 8 per cent of global trade. An apparently bottomless demand created the multimillionaires of Colombia, Peru and eastern Bolivia, not to mention the anonymous wealthy entrepreneurs who facilitate the trade north of the Rio Grande. Successive U.S. governments launched and relaunched eradication programmes against drugs through the 1980s and 1990s, attacking the origin of the leaf rather than the social causes of its massive levels of consumption within the United States. The 'war on drugs' began with Richard Nixon in 1969–74:

> Nixon's strategy – to browbeat foreign governments, militarize antidrug efforts and create the DEA, a multi-billion-dollar agency fighting the offensive in over sixty countries – defined U.S. policy for the next four decades. Nixon had absolutist objectives; he believed that with the right pressure, governments could obliterate drugs. 'Our goal is the total banishment of drug abuse from American life' he said in his 1972 campaign.[21]

As always, it was at the level of discourse that the trouble was defined as a problem of foreign governments rather than the United States itself. In 1988 agreement was reached with the Bolivian government to limit levels of cultivation to meeting local demand – unlike Colombia, Bolivia did not have to deal with blanket herbicide spraying, but it did have to accept the presence of U.S. Drug Enforcement Agency (DEA) personnel on its soil.

Under Banzer (1997–2000) – the same man who had made shadowy fortunes out of the drugs in the 1970s – the campaign against coca production was stepped up. The *cocaleros* themselves, however, were already on a battle footing, having joined with other peasant organisations in a coalition which, in 1999, became the MAS (the Movement Towards Socialism). Its leader, whose face had become well known in the earlier campaigns against eradication, was Evo Morales, who had led the *cocaleros* union for a decade.

The impact of the neo-liberal reforms launched after 1985 on the land was to restructure production around export crops and open the country to imports of cheaper food. For small farmers, the threat could be allayed to some extent by turning their land over to growing coca. The eradication programme, however, was a direct attack on their livelihood, and water privatisation would sound a death knell as production in the Chapare fell significantly. There had been a flow of aid from the United States and the European Union into projects designed to promote alternative crops, but these had rarely been able to offer an income comparable to the earnings from growing coca. More importantly, perhaps, U.S. aid has often been conditional on abandoning the established forms of communal organisation and replacing them with individual land titles – and that, in its turn, provoked resistance on cultural and ideological grounds.

The slogan of the *cocaleros* – 'Coca not cocaine' – pointed to the fact that the production of coca was more than an economic issue. It was a cultural reference for the indigenous peoples of Bolivia, a symbol of indigenous tradition and history. The fight for coca had intensified through the decade as the DEA's eradication programmes were supported by the state. From the United States the programme was presented in the context of a war against terror, weaving the coca farmers into a complex knot of terrorists and drug traffickers. But from Bolivia it was an imperialist intervention specifically directed against the Quechua-Aymara. There was, however, little agreement among the indigenous leadership on how to address the problem – after all, one of their leaders, Cárdenas, was a member of the Lozada government which enthusiastically supported the U.S. programme, though he had negotiated some restrictions. For the *cocaleros*, however, and for Evo Morales, the question of coca wove together several strands of resistance to the neo-liberalism, imperialism and racism embodied in the state.

Resistance to the consequences of neo-liberalism intensified. Civil servants, teachers and other state workers were the victims of a 50 per cent cut in state employment (the police, launched their own strike in 2000). The growth of the private sector in the areas they might once have worked in did not replace their jobs – by definition the multinationals were centrally administered outside the country, and were in any case invariably capital intensive. There were the students of the deteriorating state university sector, and especially the University of El Alto, whose prospects of finding work were minimal. And there were the pensioners whose state pensions after the mine closures often went unpaid because the state pension fund was shrinking as a new neo-liberal pension scheme directed money into private pension funds instead.

From February 2000 onwards, inspired by Cochabamba, the pattern in Bolivia of highway blockades, marches, protests, strikes and collective resistance evolved and developed. The defence of traditional water systems and of the collective forms of land ownership motivated a wave of activity among the Aymara nation of the Altiplano. Beginning in April it exploded again in September and October. There were now, as Webber notes,[22] three major fronts of struggle – Cochabamba, the *cocaleros*, and now the mobilisation of the CSUTCB under the leadership of Felipe Quispe. What was critical was not simply the multiplication of battle-fronts, but the combination of ethnic, class and economic resistance. That, no doubt, is why Hylton and Thomson saw the march on the capital organised for later 2000 as 'raising the revolutionary spectre of 1781.'[23] They were referring to the rebellion of Túpac Katari which had briefly held the capital, La Paz, under siege in that year.

This may well have been the fear that haunted the Bolivian bourgeoisie and provoked the repression launched by Banzer in response (though massacres, like that at Achacachi, punctuate the history of struggle in Bolivia). The mobilisations and highway blockades continued into mid-2001, as the organs of struggle began to consolidate into a unified leadership.

This series of revolts was racialised peasant class-struggle. The defenders sought to defend indigenous *usos y costumbres* (customary practices) in the communal management of water and land – under threat from privatisation laws. These were struggles for indigenous liberation. They were also anticapitalist, as peasants sought to defend communal customs against the blood and fire processes of capitalist expansion.[24]

In February 2003, a strike by the police against new taxes fired the wide range of discontents in the cities. The government sent the military against the striking police and against the other urban sectors – workers, students – who had risen in their support and in protest at the murderous repression launched by Lozada. It was obvious that the neo-liberal state had lost control of the situation, and that each new neo-liberal measure further inflamed public rage. At the same time, the expansion of indigenous struggles across the country and into El Alto itself drew together the threads of rebellion – the Aymara nationalism symbolised by *wiphala* banner now represented both anti-capitalism and indigenous nationalism, the very fusion that neo-liberal multiculturalism had set out to prevent. The presidential elections of 2002, in which the vote for Morales and the MAS came within just under 2 per cent of Lozada's was an unmistakable sign of a dramatic shift in the balance of forces, and heralded the insurrection of February 2003 in El Alto.

The Gas War

Traffic moves constantly over the black mud that covers roads and pavements; the sound of car horns mingles with Andean music, played on pan pipes or electric guitars, and the shouts of people buying-selling-complaining-bargaining. Hundreds of lorries prepare to dive into the bowl of La Paz or to haul themselves up the interminable mountain roads. This is El Alto, 4,100 metres above sea level, where the freezing air blows down from the snow-capped Cordillera. Its population has now passed 1 million, as more miners from the Altiplano were forced to move in search of work; they brought with them the Aymara (and Aymara-Quechua) language, and the traditions of communal organisation in the Katarista tradition revived, after 1996, by the movement led by Felipe Quispe el Mallku. 81 per cent of El Alto's inhabitants describe themselves as indigenous. The majority are poor, 20 per cent have no access to drinking water or sewerage, 75 per cent have no health cover and around 40 per cent are illiterate.[25]

Yet this is a highly organised population, gathered in a series of local and communal organisations which alone can guarantee their survival in such hostile and unforgiving conditions. Zibechi describes them in detail:

There are mothers' circles, youth and cultural associations, centres for immigrants from different regions, associations of migrant workers, family organisations that specialise in organising education, and COR, the Regional Workers' Organisation of El Alto which brought together groupings of small traders, artisans and sectoral workers. Since its creation in 1988 it has worked closely with Fejuve, the powerful federation of community organisations. It was their joint agitation, for example, which led to the creation of the public University of El Alto in 2001.

The 40,000 market stalls along the main highway through El Alto, for example, are not individually owned but are collective property allocated by the appropriate organisation. The provision of public services is decided for each area in public meetings and assemblies, while educational provision is the remit of the family organisations. Furthermore, the leaders of the organisations have to fulfil a series of conditions in order to be eligible – they cannot be speculators, nor traders, nor belong to any political party. According to Pablo Mamani, head of sociology at El Alto University, these organisations share features with the Andean communities in their structure, their control of territory and their forms of organisation. It was these organisations, and their horizontal networks, which were mobilised during the insurrectionary actions of 2003.

El Alto, the indigenous city of nearly a million inhabitants above La Paz became a new centre of popular resistance. Bolivia has 43 trillion cubic feet of reserves of national gas.[26] The decision by the Lozada government to sell Bolivian gas to the United States and Mexico, piping it out through Chile, lit the fire of rebellion again, first in Cochabamba and shortly thereafter in El Alto, where the Gas War began. The immediate issue was both nationalist and anti-capitalist; Bolivia had lost Tacna, its outlet to the sea, in the Pacific War of 1879. Exporting the gas through Chile was simply a reminder of a historic injustice, but beyond that it was another chapter in the surrender of Bolivia's natural resources to foreign interests. The atmosphere was already primed for confrontation as the rebellion had spread and intensified through 2001 and 2002. Though the movement was developing outside the framework of electoral politics, the vote for Morales and Quispe expressed the rising power of the movement – as well as the weakness and disorientation of the bourgeois state. The decision to export Bolivian gas to California might be interpreted as a provocation, but more significantly it was an instruction with menaces from the IMF.[27]

The beginning of the Gas War is usually located in October 2003; in fact it might be seen as a continuation of the confrontation that began in Cochabamba over two years earlier. Benjamin Dangl describes the mobilisation of 19 September 19 2003, called jointly by the Oscar Olivera of the Coordinadora, Evo Morales of MAS and Quispe's Pachakuti movement which was joined by over 20,000 in Cochabamba and 50,000 in El Alto. There were marches in the mining centre of Oruro, in Sucre and in Potosi. A few days previously, La Paz had been placed under siege by the population of El Alto – echoing Túpac Katari's eighteenth century action mentioned by Hylton and Thomson. The February rising in La Paz and El Alto had been less clear in its objectives and less well organised – but its largely spontaneous character did not lessen its consciously anti-neo-liberal tone. In the two days the protests lasted the cities were militarised and the military response to the police strike left a heavy toll of death and injury in what came to be known as 'Black February', though the protesters also made their rage felt in attacks on key buildings in the cities.

The Gas War of October, however, was very different and reflected a high degree of coordination across the range of social movement organisations in El Alto,[28] as the September siege had shown. The arrest of a community leader, Edwin Huampu, for murder was the spark that lit the fires of insurrection, together with Lozada's decision to export Bolivia's gas. From the Altiplano the communities marched towards El Alto to join the action. By 1 October El Alto was in the throes of a full scale insurrection. On 2 October, the COB convened an assembly in La Paz; these assemblies or *cabildos abiertos* (open town hall meetings) had marked the whole insurrectionary process, as expressions of a new kind of democracy. The COR, which represented the workers of the city, and FEJUVE, the coalition of neighbourhood councils, called a third general strike for the 8 October. Within two days, the barricaded highways stopped all traffic into the capital, blockading the airport which is located in El Alto and blocking supplies of food and petrol. The government had already responded with repression and the toll of deaths was rising. On 12 October the government declared a state of emergency and used tanks and helicopters in a full scale military deployment against the movement. One day later 100,000 marched from El Alto to La Paz led by the *wiphala*. The insurrection increased in numbers and in its geographical spread. The government began to fracture.

In the 2002 presidential elections, Evo Morales, leader of the *cocaleros* and candidate of the MAS, won 22 per cent of the national vote. This has to be set in the context of a political environment in which most political parties were essentially machines for government and/or apparatuses to advance the careers of power hungry politicians. The mass movements that had developed through the 1990s were linked by their common distrust of party politicians – or indeed politics of any kind. Oscar Olivera, leader of the Cochabamba movement, expressed that caution in a seminar in La Paz in June of 2000:

> For the true nation not to be supplanted by the market or the state, the working class, both urban and rural, and the marginalised and economically insecure of the nation – in other words, the overwhelming majority of society – must assume control over the wealth embodied in hydrocarbons. And they must do so through assembly-style forms of self-organisation at the neighbourhood, regional and national levels. The nation must enact a self-presentation – it must self-govern through autonomous structures of participation that socialise responsibility for public life.[29]

Olivera's description of the movement closely corresponds to what did emerge in the subsequent four years. But his words are imbued with a notion of mass organisation and resistance in isolation from the political life of the state – including involvement with the institutions of representative democracy. Morales's candidacy in 2002 exposed a tension at the heart of the movement. On the one hand, his support clearly came from those who regarded him as their representative, rather than of the party in whose name he stood – MAS – because Bolivian electoral law required that he stand on behalf of an officially registered political organisation. On the other hand, his entry into the electoral arena proposed an alternative dynamic, a different kind of resolution, to the kind of power enacted from below that Olivera was proposing. What remained unclear, and still does, is what the political expression of such a movement would be – and how it would address the continuing power of the state. The experience of 1952 had left little doubt as to the consequences of such an omission.

For the moment, however, Bolivia's political future was not being played out in Congress but in the streets – and in particular in the streets of El Alto; in February that year there had been major protests in El Alto and elsewhere against the government's attempt to impose an additional 9 per cent tax on income. The police joined the protest, and a number of public buildings were razed to the ground. On the Altiplano, the movement led by Mallku (Quispe) blocked principal highways in protest at a number of unresolved demands regarding land. The government responded with repression, and four peasant farmers were killed. Then, on 19 September in La Paz, the massive 500,000-strong demonstration demanding the return of Bolivia's gas reserves to public ownership also raised the call for a constituent assembly. When Lozada refused to respond, the organisations of El Alto combined to organise an indefinite *paro cívico*, a general civic strike. In Chapare the *cocaleros* barricaded highways, and other roadblocks began to appear around La Paz. As food began to run short, Lozada sent troops into El Alto. Seventy were killed in the confrontations that followed.

It was too much for Lozada. Unable to drive through the Hydro-carbons Law which would have ceded control of Bolivian gas to foreign multinationals, he resigned and fled the country on 17 October. The state had lost control. His successor, Carlos Mesa, promised a referendum on the issue of gas. But he had no intention of nationalising – he would not break existing agreements with foreign multinationals, he announced. Then, in March 2004, the Bolivian Congress passed a new law which added 32 per cent taxes to the 18 per cent royalties those companies paid. It was still far from what the movement demanded – but it was too much for Mesa, who tried to veto the law. Yet the Supreme Court, headed by Eduardo Rodriguez, declared all previous contracts null and void.

The political tensions which already existed within the movement itself were exacerbated by the confusion deliberately sown by Mesa. Morales's electoral success appeared to open up a possibility of answering the demands of the Gas Coalition without challenging the state. It was an illusion carefully fostered by Morales and sustained by many outside Bolivia – a promise of reform that flew in the face of the whole of Bolivia's recent history.

However, for the social movement, and also for Morales and the MAS, the key reference point was the wider Latin America situation. Lula had just been elected to the Brazilian presidency, Lucio Gutiérrez still pre-sented himself as the candidate of the Ecuadorean popular movement, Kirchner in Argentina claimed to speak with the voice of the Argentinazo of 2001, and in Venezuela, Hugo Chávez had survived two attempts to bring him down.

In fact, Morales had supported Mesa's appointment as Lozada's re-placement, but his growing moderation did not impress the rank and file movement; the 2004 municipal elections cut his vote by half, to 11 per cent nationwide. By May 2005, the mass movement had lost patience; mobili-sation was renewed with a clear and simple demand – nationalisation.

On 16 May, a symbolic encirclement of La Paz announced a new phase of the struggle. The COR called for another civic strike, which was launched in El Alto on 23 May. The following day, indigenous Aymara protesters from Felipe Quispe's movement came within yards of the Congress, before they were driven back.

El Alto was, again, at the heart of a national movement. But there were important differences from 2003. First, the level of participation was higher and the degree of coordination across the country was significantly greater. There were occupations in Cochabamba and Oruro, and actions in Santa Cruz province. In El Alto itself the indefinite strike caused serious problems of supply, particularly of petrol for the capital. Most significantly, perhaps, the indigenist movement had now moved into El Alto, which it began to describe as the headquarters of the Aymara rebellion. Thus organisations of workers in the mainly small workplaces in and around La Paz, the teachers' unions, Fejuve and the community groups, housing cooperatives and student groups were at the heart of a broad movement united around a single demand – nationalisation of oil and gas.

Mesa's resignation was now inevitable, and the role of Evo Morales became both more central and more problematic. On 26 May a brief truce opened a space for the Catholic Church to intervene with a proposal that linked issues of human rights, regional autonomy and the demand for a constituent assembly. This was clearly an attempt to reinforce, or perhaps more accurately to create, a middle ground of compromise that could pull back the movement from its revolutionary objectives. In this, the support of Evo Morales was critical. Announcing his electoral running mate, Alvaro García Linera, a supporter of Quispe and an ex-guerrilla of the Tupac Katari Guerrilla Army, Morales and the MAS set out to embrace and recruit to their project of compromise and reform the increasingly militant indigenous movement.

But events were accelerating away, though it has to be acknowledged that the intervention of MAS and the Church produced a kind of hiatus as well as some confusion. On the face of it, the demand for a constituent assembly may have seemed to differ very little from the call for a National Popular and Indigenous Assembly. In fact, the constituent assembly was a body whose elected delegates would function as a bourgeois parliament until and unless the bourgeoisie – reeling now under the impact of the mass popular rising – could find ways to reimpose their institutional order which, for the moment, was irredeemably corrupted and incapable of functioning.

It became obvious in June, by contrast, that the model already being constructed at a local level was for a very different kind of assembly, a form of mass democracy recalling the great popular decision-making gatherings of the nineteenth century – the *cabildos abiertos*. These assemblies enshrined the project for a future that could not only carry through the nationalisation of oil and gas, the immediate demand, but also establish the existence of a new kind of power – democratic, accountable, and controlled by the producers.

Mesa's resignation on 6 June was a victory for the mass insurrectionary movement. He had threatened to resign twice before in the face of protests over price rises,but in the absence of any alternative, the bourgeoisie had kept him in power for a further three months. For Evo Morales, his departure opened a space he could clearly see himself filling – and he rushed to present himself as the saviour of the Bolivian state. His running mate, the sociologist and one-time guerrilla leader Alvaro García Linera, gave a fascinating interview at the time, which was explicit in its aims – the creation of a strong Bolivian capitalism.[30]

> *Linera:* Socialism is not a viable project in Bolivia, because it can only be built by a strong working class base. The socialist utopia emerges from the extreme maturity of capitalism. In Bolivia there is no capitalism; 70 per cent of urban workers are in small family businesses. You can't build socialism out of small business, but on the basis of advanced industries, and we don't have that in Bolivia. You can't build socialism where 95 per cent of the rural population live in traditional communal economies.
> *Interviewer:* So what kind of society is MAS trying to build?
> *Linera:* A version of Andean capitalism.

Linera goes on to discuss the problems MAS is having in its negotiations with other organisations – with Felipe Quispe the Aymara leader, with Jaime Solares of the COB, and with the leadership of the coordinating organisation of community groups, Fejuve. It is hard, he argues, because everyone wants to be part of the electoral slate.

Yet, the promise that Evo Morales represented echoed the rhetoric of Lula in Brazil and Lucio Gutiérrez in Ecuador. Linera is quite clear that MAS's hope lay in an alliance with Lula, Chávez and the other new populist regimes in Uruguay and Argentina. Leaving aside the discredit into which the Lula government was already falling, the programme for a revitalised and strengthened alliance of capitals did not challenge the neo-liberal project. On the contrary, it merely offered the prospect of a government that would mediate between global capital and the mass movements that had carried each to power. A Morales government would clearly function to restore a Bolivian state vying for a place at the banqueting tables of Davos and the WTO.

The fundamental irony of all this is that global capital, and the U.S. government, only tolerated such regimes because of the strength of the mass movement – and only until that strength was sapped, or the movement weakened or diverted.

What became incontestably clear in the first five years of the new century was that the Bolivian mass movement was anti-capitalist in its spirit and its demands. It was an insurrection that challenged, not simply the conduct of successive governments, but their strategy. The privatisation of resources – their transformation into commodities bought and sold on a world market by private capitalists – was the object of their rage and their resistance. It is true that there was a debate about whether a higher level of taxation of foreign corporations would be enough, but that demand was first suggested by the now rejected Mesa, and only later taken up by Morales and the MAS for their own purposes. And while in 2004 that was echoed across the movement, its radicalisation since then had left the argument for 50 per cent taxation as the demand of the moderates, while the central policy of the combative majority of the movement in 2005 was for the nationalisation of Bolivia's gas and oil resources. Used for the general good, they could transform the Bolivian economy – but not in the context of a neo-liberal market.

The alternative was a transformation that fully realised the demand for democratic control over the economy enshrined in a new state. The people's assemblies that developed in the May/June days were the embryonic expression of a new kind of power. As yet, that experience had not been embodied in an equivalent national organisation, though it had been proposed and argued for in the local gatherings. In part, that was the result of confusion about the demand for a constituent assembly as an electoral forum – in part it was also a consequence of the lack of political coordination and agreement within the movement.

The analysis put forward by the miners' union (FSTMB) argued that the task was to 'forge the political instrument of the working class',[31] the revolutionary organisation capable of unifying and giving strategic political direction to the many forces that had waged such a heroic and successful struggle against the state over the previous five years. No one on the left would disagree with that as a general and abstract proposition. But the reality is that the COB, which had played that role historically in Bolivia, no longer fulfilled the conditions. The definitive crushing of the miners in 1984–5, and the rapid decline of the tin mining industry that followed it, marked the end of the era when mining was Bolivia's central industry. In fact, of course, it had long ceased to be sufficient to sustain the economy, yet until that moment there was an uninterrupted tradition to refer to in the political debate.

Where is the working class in Bolivia today? It is dispersed across the country. In Santa Cruz it is the oil workers. In the mining areas it is the small cooperatives working to extract metal under terrible working conditions in the now declining and increasingly dangerous mine workings, in addition to the shrinking body of underground miners (now less than 15,000). In El Alto and La Paz the COB's influence was largely restricted to teachers and health workers. The manufacturing and productive units in the region were for the most part small workshops producing consumer goods – the workplaces rarely employed more than ten people – organised by the COR, a regional trade union federation rooted in El Alto. More importantly, these organisations were essentially concerned with developing a militant trade unionism – a syndicalist position which does not pose the question of state power, but is seduced by notions of political spaces autonomous of and separate from the state.

That working class is also indigenous – 81 per cent of El Alto consider themselves to be Indian (Aymara and Quechua), and the same is true among the *cocaleros*. The figure would certainly have been lower two decades earlier, so it is a mark of the qualitative development of the movement that Quispe's indigenous peasant movement has become active in the urban environment as well as in the highlands. It is also evidence of its continuing authority. In the past, in 1952 for example, the demands of indigenous communities were largely marginalised – they were seen as anachronistic and inhibiting the modernising project represented by the working class movement. In the context of the late 1970s and early 1980s, however, it was these communities that fought the state and developed forms of mass confrontation which have certainly informed and shaped the more recent mobilisations. For nearly 20 years, communal resistance was the centre of the popular movement in Bolivia.

The fact that other sections have now emerged to take on the state is a great leap for the movement, but the ideas of the indigenistas are still powerful. Community and territorial unity are still central, even in the urban struggles, and the suspicion of political organisations among them reflects a real experience of manipulation and opportunism by political leaders in the past. Many of the communal organisations, for example, do not allow members of political parties to stand for leadership positions.

Between March and June 2005 the Bolivian mass rising crossed an important frontier. Its confidence and determination grew out of the successful challenge to Lozada, the renewed struggles around gas privatisation that began in February that year, and Mesa's subsequent bluff in March. The tactic backfired on him, but it both deepened the conviction of the resistance and exposed the rifts within the ruling class itself, particularly between the Santa Cruz oligarchs and the powers centred in La Paz.

The effect was to radicalise the movement even further and to propitiate an emerging unity of the many forces in struggle. On 16 May, while 100,000 people besieged the parliament in La Paz, the miners began a march towards El Alto and the teachers' union launched a strike. Inexorably, the movement's actions moved towards 9 June, the high point of this phase of the Bolivian Revolution of the '21st century'. On that day a powerless government faced a mass popular movement that was resolute, coordinated and proposing alternative forms of power.

Yet within days it seemed that the unity was fracturing and their confidence, faltering.

The new president, Rodríguez, was a transitional figure – he immediately proposed presidential elections for December. This opened up the possibility of a solution to the deep crisis the country was facing within the structures of the existing state. And it won the instant approval of the MAS, whose candidate, Evo Morales, would be the likely winner of such a contest. Thus within a matter of two days the political focus was shifted back towards an electoral solution and a restoration of the system, and away from the revolutionary demands for a different kind of power and the suspicions of the electoral process voiced just days earlier by the people's assembly. The government side was strengthened too, by the tantalising promise of a recognition of Aymara national rights in a new constitution.

The Bolivian mass insurrection was extraordinary for its absolute determination, its courage in struggle, its insistent collective impulse, and its combination of many different demands. In 1952 that most powerful of instruments, the COB, made unity a class issue, and drew peasant and indigenous struggles behind a working class leadership that could have been capable of challenging the state. Yet indigenous struggles were subordinated to class politics rather than fused with them. The demise of the COB – for both material (the decline of mining) and political (the internal divisions that were in part the consequence of defeat) reasons – had left the movement with no coordinating, centralising force. There are some left groups influential within the COB today who might claim that they do lead the movement. That is simply not true, and nothing is gained from the pretence that a ready-made programme and a self-proclaimed directorate is all that is required to achieve leadership of this complex and varied movement. There is a dominant ideology, which is sectional, nationalist, communal and in many sections syndicalist. All of these currents have militated against the forging of a common politics whose purpose was the conquest of power.

3

Evo Morales in Power

The resignation of Carlos Mesa was the final crisis of the old Bolivian state. Its demise was the direct consequence of the insurrectionary character of the social movements who had expressed themselves in the Water and Gas Wars. Linera himself would describe this phase, 2000–3, as a period of dual power – defined as a period in which the old system can no longer rule in the old way and the subordinate classes will no longer accept the old way. New forms of organisation were emerging in the course of struggle which tested and contested the state. But more than simply modes of resistance, the neighbourhood organisations, the *cabildos abiertos* among them. were embryonic forms of a different way of organising society, a potential model for a participatory democracy.

In 2005, Evo Morales, an Aymara speaker born on the Altiplano who had moved with his parents from the mining area to the Chapare, was elected to the presidency of Bolivia. Before 2005 the state could continue to contain the movements as long as its repressive capacity was untouched; the strikes in the police had called its ability to turn to repression into question, as Mesa realised. He had publicly disagreed with Lozada, just before his resignation, over the question of state violence. The population, and especially the communities of the Andean region, were mobilised. The call for a Constituent Assembly echoed the popular demands of the past, and resonated with a mobilised and combative movement which – and this was crucial – had the victory of Cochabamba as its reference point. The Constituyente, it was argued, would be far more than a more advanced form of bourgeois democracy; among the array of revolutionary activists in El Alto, Webber comments, the Constituyente was seen as

> ... a body which would replace the existing legislative, executive, military and judicial apparatuses. On this view, the assembly would be a

process through which Bolivia would be fundamentally 'refounded' by, and in the interests of the poor indigenous urban and rural majority.[1]

Mesa's attempt to hold on to power fell on the issue of oil nationalisation; he had returned the law to congress unsigned, and then resigned from the presidency. The provisional president Edgardo Rodríguez signed it into law on 27 June 2005, with a clear intention of heading off more radical demands than the increase in royalties it laid down. On 18 December, Evo Morales was elected to the presidency with a majority of 54 per cent; it was the first time the leading candidate had achieved an absolute majority in the first round and the first time the victor was a member of an indigenous community.

Alvaro García Linera,[2] Evo's vice-presidential nominee, had been a member of the MRTK, the Katarista Revolutionary Movement. Arrested and jailed, though never charged, in 1991, he was tortured and spent five years in jail. He is a Marxist, originally a mathematics graduate who studied sociology in prison and taught it before being nominated as vice-president in the Morales government.[3] He is perhaps the most prominent intellectual voice of the new movement, though he has undoubtedly moderated, or at least adjusted, some of his Marxist ideas since the election. In his five-phase characterisation of the Bolivian movement, he described the period between 2003 and 2005 as a 'catastrophic equilibrium'. This was his re-articulation of Lenin's notion of dual power:

> a sort of stasis in the configuration of the class struggle, when neither of the major contending class blocs has the ability to establish its hegemony over the other, a situation that can endure (as García Linera says) for months or even years.

So much for the 'equilibrium'; the 'catastrophic' element refers to the essential instability of the situation. These are not two powers sitting on a scale but two hostile forces confronting one another, where neither has hegemony. In García Linera's vision, the concept of hegemony is absolutely key; it is derives from Gramsci and refers to a dominant force in society whose dominion is ideological, social and political, and invariably economic – bearing in mind Marx's reminder that 'the dominant ideas in society are invariably those of the economically dominant class'. García Linera might well wish to substitute the word 'bloc' for 'class'. The new state in whose construction he was engaged would be the expression of alliances both political and ethnic, what Webber describes as a 'left-indigenous bloc'. García Linera warned, however, that:

> It may be reversible. The catastrophic equilibrium is a phase in the state crisis, if you wish, a second structural moment that is characterized by three things: a confrontation of two national political projects for the country, two perspectives for the country, each with a capacity for mobilization, attraction, and seduction of social forces; a confrontation in the institutional sphere – it might be the parliamentary arena or the social sphere – of two social blocs shaped by a will and ambition for power, the dominant bloc and the ascendant social bloc; and, thirdly, a paralysis of the upper echelons of the state and a failure to overcome this paralysis.[4]

In his periodisation of the Bolivian process, that original paralysis was reached in 2003, in the October days of the Gas War, though the outcome of the Cochabamba Water War was without doubt the inaugural act of the revolutionary process. The insurrection of El Alto was an equal and equivalent moment, the fusion of the two, not simply in terms of mass mobilisation but more fundamentally in the forging of the left-indigenist force, a project with 'the capacity to mobilise, attract and seduce social forces'. The alternative was the 'old' Bolivian state, ethnically white, oligarchic and, it would be argued, anti-national (Lozada's American English accent when speaking Spanish was symbolic). They had in García Linera's words 'lost the capacity to define public policy in a stable and straightforward way'. It may be more accurate to suggest that that capacity had been *taken from them* – which was the historic significance of Cochabamba.

This was clearly a crisis of the neo-liberal state, that concept and strategy rooted in the idea that global capital was the engine of development, exports the only route for participation in the global market for Latin American countries, and 'governability', the successful combination of different and sometimes conflicting interests through negotiation. That model was in crisis, but its alternative was not yet articulated through the movement and by it. That responsibility fell on García Linera. His membership of the La Comuna group of intellectuals and strategists[5] had certainly prepared him for the task, since part of the group's writings focussed precisely on the crisis of the state. His notion of 'a point of bifurcation', when the two competing strategies diverged, may have been illustrated by Evo's election, but in fact it may be more helpful to look at a stretched point defined by the continuing conflicts with the eastern bourgeoisie and the battle over the Constituyente and the new Constitution.

In the period of catastrophic equilibrium between the social movements and the state, two logics and two potential futures confronted one another, two forces each with a power in their hands, the one dominating the institutions, the other controlling the streets and the public terrain. This was dual power in the flesh. But this equilibrium was by definition unstable and temporary; the confrontation would have to have an outcome at some point, a victory for one side or the other. The Gas and Water Wars of 2003 and 2005 in El Alto were definitive.

Carlos Mesa did not belong to the eastern bourgeoisie as Lozada has, but he was equally committed to a neo-liberal strategy, though he had distanced himself from the state repression in El Alto. In the end he came to power as a direct result of the mass mobilisations; perhaps for that reason he proposed a Law of Hydrocarbons which raised the level of royalties paid by the oil corporations. It was on the basis of that proposal that the MAS, and Evo Morales, supported him in the presidency until his decision to refuse to sign the law on its submission to Congress. Until then he claimed to have located himself in the political centre ground, which won him the support of the MAS and some credibility among the mass movements. The MAS itself was divided, between a right current which devoured the negotiations with Mesa and a left, which was highly critical of Evo, and argued against it and in favour of the full nationalisation of oil and gas. The fall in MAS's vote in municipal elections to 18 per cent in 2004 sent the clearest message possible from the movement on MAS's support for a soft, neo-liberal option, and it returned to street and highway blockades. Evo eventually withdrew his support from Mesa in March 2005, as a second water war was developing in El Alto over a contract awarded to a subsidiary of the multinational Suez, Aguas de Illimani. The new Hydrocarbons Law eventually emerged from Congress in early May, though it fell far short of even the moderate expectations of the right-wing of MAS, which had argued for 50 per cent royalties. The law proposed 18 per cent (and 32 per cent taxes). The Media Luna, however, had campaigned against the law in Congress.

The movement prepared new mass demonstrations. One march was organised by the right-wing of MAS, while the movement prepared a range of actions which included highway blockades and a march from El Alto into La Paz. The central demand, nationalisation, was the movement's clear response to the new law. Mesa continued his attempts to hold a middle line, but while Evo argued against the radical call for full nation-alisation, the closure of Congress and a Constituent Assembly, the ranks of the revolutionary masses held to their key demands. In the event the new law was passed on 17 May 2005.

Hylton and Thomson are unequivocal in their assessment of the role played by MAS, through Evo Morales, in these critical days.

> The MAS never lost sight of its objective of winning office through elections. To do so, its strategy since 2002 had been to present an increasingly moderate face to the urban middle class. Winning the 2007 general elections was a long term objective, and when elections were rescheduled for December 2005, the immediacy of the project took precedence over all else. Thus MAS played a part in the mass-mobilisations of May and June (2005) but ultimately acted as a dam, helping to prevent a revolutionary flood from washing away the reigning power-structures of Bolivian society.[6]

On 1 May 2006 , wearing a white helmet bearing the logo of the state oil and gas company YPFB, Morales announced the 'nationalisation' of Bolivia's oil before several thousand supporters:

> The time has come, the awaited day, a historic day on which Bolivia takes absolute control of its natural resources.[7]

Symbolically, it was an enormously significant moment, echoing the declaration of the 1952 revolution but also the concept of the historic day (*pachacutik*) when the Aymara nation would recover its birthright. The resonances were unmistakable. But like Dangl, I have placed the word 'nationalisation' in inverted commas.

> Far from all-out expropriation of the industry, the decree simply gave the state more power over the gas and oil business, and aimed to generate more income for the government through increased prices, taxes and royalties.[8]

It was a renegotiation of the terms of Bolivia's relationship with the oil multinationals; it would generate considerably higher revenues – but it was not a revolution, and fell far short of the demands advanced by the movement that had challenged the state across the whole country during the Gas War.[9] The activists who spoke to Benjamin Dangl seemed clear that there was much more to be done. 'The 54 per cent majority gave Morales the presidency,' one said, 'but it isn't a blank cheque; it's a loan.' Nevertheless, there was a clear political agenda embedded in Morales's inaugural speech and his declaration at the San Alberto oil facility. It conceived the state as the subject of the process that began with his election, or at least it was the projected protagonist.

Reform or Revolution

The state was still inhabited by the old functionaries, but according to Linera this phase of the Bolivian revolution began with the assumption of government 'by the insurrectionists'. It would have been more precise, in fact, to say that government had been taken by MAS in representation of the insurrection. With La Paz under siege by the mass movement, power had passed into its hands. But the movements had no strategic project for the state – indeed they had by and large rejected the notion of seizing the state in favour of creating alternative and independent forms of self-government. Faced with the collapse of the existing state, MAS had severed its links with Carlos Mesa. There were two contradictions in those critical months; the class confrontation between the new government and the old ruling class and a second within the historic-popular bloc between two kinds of power, two political logics.

Morales now declared his to be 'a government of the social movements'; this could of course mean two very different things. Either the government was composed of the direct delegates of the social movements, elected by them and accountable to them; or the government was run by the *representatives* of the movements. These were two different and opposed concepts of democracy and the central contradiction of the pink tide.

The period between 2006–9 would be the time in which the balance would be tipped and the location of state power definitively determined. The dominant class, the capitalists of the eastern lowlands, had lost control of the government which until then had defended their interests at the expense of the majority of society, and which in its imposition of neo-liberalism had widened that gulf and concentrated wealth and power further in the hands of the capitalist class. What followed was a battle for the state between the historic-popular bloc represented by the MAS, the indigenous majority, the peasantry and the working class, and the powerful capitalist interests of the provinces of the Media Luna (the Half Moon) of the eastern lowlands who had held power for the previous 30 years since the decline of mining and the *rosca* – the tin barons, the eastern bourgeoisie, controlling much of the oil and gas industry as well as export agriculture had replaced the *rosca* as the dominant force in the national economy. The state had been their state, and they were now prepared for a fight to hold on to it.

García Linera described this as the 'Jacobin moment' of Bolivia's revolution, the passage to open class war. The catalyst was the demand for a Constituent Assembly, which had emerged from the left-indigenous bloc in October 2003. It was conceived as an extension of the social movement, an elected delegate congress where the future political shape of Bolivia would be discussed and determined by the spokespersons of the movement itself. For the dominant classes, too, this was a critical moment, and the Media Luna launched its campaign to prevent or undermine the Constituent Assembly. It mobilised its forces in the eastern lowlands, including shock troops of young men prepared to attack supporters of the MAS and violently prevent the land occupations and highway blockades by the indigenous peoples of the region, who were now organised and exercising the right to occupation of unused lands set out in the previous constitution. The confrontations, the assaults and the killings were not simply designed to terrorise government supporters. They had a deeper, explicitly racist underpinning among the predominantly white urban middle classes of Santa Cruz and the Half Moon provinces.

Much of Bolivia's oil and gas was in the eastern provinces, as were the main engines of Bolivian capital – export agriculture, cattle-raising, industrial production and increasingly, the distribution and trafficking of drugs. The bourgeoisie here was largely immigrant and white and overtly and fiercely racist. The main city of Santa Cruz was an alternative focus to La Paz, and the Brazilian and Argentine capital behind the expansion of the soya and cattle-raising industries established their relations with Bolivia there. The importance of the region had grown with the opening of a major highway from the Andean sierra in the 1950s. At the same time, the region had not been immune to the mass mobilisations of the late twentieth century. The lowlands indigenous communities had forged their own organisation, CIDOB, and had occupied unused lands, as the Constitution allowed, throughout the decade, often confronting the violence of the big landowners. And in the context of a Bolivia which was now explicitly assuming an indigenous-nationalist character, the economic as well as the cultural implications of the *buen vivir* included in the new constitution, proposed a model directly contrary to the globalised capitalism to which the Media Luna owed its prosperity.

The Constituent Assembly met in September 2006, in Sucre, the national capital located in the Andean highlands. Within the Assembly itself another tension prevailed. MAS, having defined itself as the government of the social movements, established new criteria for Assembly delegates. It was decided that only organised political parties could send representatives, but not the social movements. This was an enormously significant move, reinforcing the widening gulf between MAS and the mass movement that had carried it to power and consolidating MAS's hegemony.

> MAS refused to open the constitutional assembly to the full spectrum of voices [...] that refusal began the effective closure of the revolutionary process.[10]

It was only in April 2009, and as a result of mass agitation, that social movements were allowed to present candidates.

The Media Luna provinces of Santa Cruz, Tarija, Pando and Beni launched a separate, and unconstitutional, campaign for secession or autonomy, with the explicit support of the U.S. ambassador to Bolivia, Philip Goldberg. Their arguments were both reactionary and overtly and explicitly racist, mobilising the predominantly white population, as well as including the defence of free market capitalism and the right of the Media Luna provinces to retain the oil revenues rather than the central government.

In December 2007, the new Constitution was to be approved by the Assembly, but after violent attacks on some of its members, the vote was postponed as opposition activities continued to escalate. In May the governors of the Media Luna region organised a referendum on a statute of autonomy which was rejected as illegal by the Constitutional Court. On 10 August 2008, Morales submitted himself to a recall referendum, emerging with a majority of over 67 per cent but it also confirmed in post six of the eight state governors of the Media Luna region. Nine days later, the six prefects called a 'civic strike', in support of their own statutes and in protest at the transfer of oil revenues to central government. The campaign became increasingly violent, and a paramilitary force called the Union of Youth of Santa Cruz (UJC) began to attack government supporters and buildings. The six governors threatened to interrupt the flow of oil, and several attempts were made, with at least one explosion in Tarija. In early September some oil and gas installations were occupied by the opposition. On 11 September, a march of government supporters – the majority indigenous – was attacked by state police and paramilitaries outside the remote town of Porvenir in Pando province. At least 30 indigenous protesters were killed and 100 more were 'disappeared'. Morales then declared a state of emergency in the province; the provincial governor was arrested and troops sent to guard the airport and government buildings.[11] A revised version of the Constitution was passed by the Assembly in October. In January 2009 the Constitution was approved in a referendum by a 61 per cent majority, though protests and confrontations continued in the Media Luna.

At this point, the governor of Santa Cruz scaled down the violence. In the meantime, Morales had agreed to hold elections in December 2009 and not to stand again in 2014. After Morales's decisive victory in the December 2009 presidential elections, the Media Luna moved to a campaign of obstruction in the parliament and ended its street confrontations. In fact, Morales had met with eastern leaders before the referendum to negotiate an agreement which acknowledged MAS's political domination of the state and gave undertakings to respect the economic interests of the Media Luna.[12] This calls into question the characterisation of this phase of the Bolivian revolution as 'Jacobin'. It appears much more as a coalition-building exercise, in which private and public interests could coexist with relative ease.

The emphasis in Evo Morales's first speeches was on indigenous identity, and in 2006 he was named Mallku of the Aymara nation, whose nationhood was formally acknowledged in the new Constitution of 2008. Support for the new government came from the indigenous communities, the peasantry and the working class, won over by a left discourse which acknowledged indigenous culture and history.

According to Linera, Bolivia had now entered his fifth and final stage, characterised by what he described in an extremely influential essay as 'creative tensions' or to put it another way, contradictions that could be resolved within the framework of the current state.[13] Bolivia is a complex society in which class and ethnic identities interweave with gender and geography. Morales' successful ascent to power certainly had to with a charismatic personality, but that is not sufficient explanation of his continuing authority. In many ways García Linera, despite his Marxist trajectory, had developed a new theory of revolution which was highly personalistic, so that he and others now spoke of 'Evoísmo' – an echo of Chavismo. What Evo combined in terms of background and experience, was his Aymara identity, his trade union background derived from the mining industry and his later deployment of that experience as leader of the *cocaleros*, where he applied the lessons of trade union struggle to farmers who came from a similar background. These features became active at the moment in which the collapse of the Bolivian state provided the vacuum of authority into which he was able to step. In the debates leading up to the 2016 referendum, for example, in which the proposal to be voted on would have allowed Evo to stand for the presidency beyond the second term limit established by the new Constitution, Linera warned of the dangers of losing the leadership of the 'father of the nation'.

Linera himself and others have claimed that neo-liberalism has been defeated in Bolivia and that the economy has passed into public control. The nationalisation of the primary industries has been offered as evidence. The reality is more complex and more contradictory. The nationalisation of 2006 took back into public ownership some companies privatised during the 1990s. Under the new hydrocarbons law the state took a leading role in the primary industries, but it did not take full ownership or expropriate the oil and gas companies. Instead it increased its stake and renegotiated the relationship with foreign corporations, raising taxes and royalties on private capital. In the context of the commodities boom, driven largely by China, between 2006 and 2014, Bolivia's revenues rose dramatically. Direct investment by the state was largely in major infrastructural projects on the one hand, and in welfare and anti-poverty programs directed at the poorest sectors on the other. As a result the level of poverty fell from 64 per cent of the population in 2002 to 36.3 per cent in 2011, and extreme poverty from 37.1 per cent to 18.7 per cent in the same years. Ten years earlier, Bolivia was the poorest country in the region, so these statistics represent a real achievement. But the economic model envisaged a dynamic private sector which would both generate jobs and consumer spending – manufacturing, agriculture, construction and tourism for example – in which the state would invest directly. There are no limits to private sector imports and the fiscal responsibility that has won Bolivia praise from the World Bank and The Economist among others has resulted in very low inflation. Surprisingly perhaps, given the radical discourse, foreign direct investment increased from $278 milion in 2006 to $1.18 billion in 2013, and maintained its relative weight within the economy. The overall result until 2014 was a respectable annual increase in GDP of around 4-5 per cent, an increase in the country's foreign reserves, and the 'Bolivianisation' of the economy. What that signifies is that domestic capitalist production has steadily increased, but that its growth has also expanded the capitalist class, particularly in the indigenous communities, with the emergence of a new layer of small and medium capitalists who form a guaranteed part of Morales's social base.[14] Ironically many of these new capitalists function on the basis of employing the cheap labour of Bolivia's poor, for example in the cooperative mining sector.

None of this reflects a qualitative change in political terms; there is a continuity, as Webber and other analysts point out, between the neo-liberalism of the past and the present. This is not to deny the realities of growth, of course, nor the social benefits that have improved the lives of many of Bolivia's poorest citizens, which together explain the continuing popularity of the Morales administration. Nonetheless, state investments were largely directed at major projects financed by foreign investments and loans.

These projects raised a central question about the character of the Bolivian revolution. The constitution rests on the claim that the process is directed at the achievement of *buen vivir*, a concept that has informed Evo's high profile in the international debate around the environment. Perhaps this had seemed convincing because outside Latin America *buen vivir* has been conceived fundamentally as a cultural revolution, the adoption of features of indigenous culture in regime discourse, in the forms of public institutions, state ceremonial and so on. There is no doubt that the Bolivian revolution has placed indigenous civilsation at the centre of its discourse, and redeemed the five-century-long oppression of indigenous communities. The political consciousness of today's Bolivians is left-indigenous, combining the language and ideas of socialism and of indigenous culture and history, in contrast to their absence in the racist rhetoric of the bourgeoisie and the Media Luna. The first nation popula-tion of Bolivia is today included fully in the institutional democratic order of the plurinational state. But *buen vivir* is not merely a cultural and historical practice; it is an economic one – an alternative to capitalist development. It is environmentally conscious and consistent in arguing for a harmonious development that balances economic democracy with conservation of resources, sustainable energy use with the production of use values, a society no longer dominated by the market but rather by the expressed, organised and organic needs of society as a whole. It is in this sense that it interprets the relationship between humanity and nature. The individual consumption which is the heart of the neo-liberal model of market capitalism would be replaced by the fulfillment of collective needs. The problem is that this is simply incompatible with large scale, expensive and environmentally destructive projects, as a glance at neighbouring Brazil would make dramatically clear. Projects like the cable car linking La Paz with El Alto are socially responsible, but as the incidents at the TIPNIS National Park in 2011 clearly showed, the economic strategy of the MAS contained profound contradictions.

TIPNIS

TIPNIS proved to have been another of the points of bifurcation that García Linera anticipated in his discussion of the Bolivian process. But it was a signpost on a journey *away* from revolution, a contradiction that was neither creative nor progressive but which exposed the real tensions at the very heart of what he chose to call Evoismo. The causes and implications of what happened on the march from TIPNIS to La Paz have been fully narrated by Jeffery Webber, to whom I have turned often in this account of the pink tide. His account is clear-sighted – and devastating.[15]

In 2009 Evo Morales was re-elected with an unprecedented 64 per cent majority. By then. the secessionist ambitions of Santa Cruz had been largely overcome, in part through the internal divisions within the opposition ranks as a result of negotiations with Morales, the new Constitution was approved, and the new national-popular state was established with a discourse of left indigenism, encapsulated and symbolised in the person of Evo Morales, Mallku, trade unionist and president. Evo and Linera called this the 'government of the social movements', yet the nature of the relationship between the two was ill-defined. The indigenous, peasant and working masses had brought down a bourgeois state through their mobilisations and the exercise of their collective power, and had carried Evo to the presidency. Yet they had been excluded from the Constitutional Assembly and denied a role in the new Bolivian state.

Between August and October of 2011, less than a year after his re-election, Evo's popularity ratings were halved, fading as a demonstration of mainly lowland (but some highland) indigenous movements marched the 600 kilometres from Beni to La Paz to protest at the government's decision to permit the construction of a highway between Villa Tunari (in Cochabamba) and San Ignacio de Moxos in the eastern province of Beni. The highway would pass through the indigenous territory of the Isiboro Sécure National Park (TIPNIS). The marchers were stopped en route and violently assaulted by the national police sent by the Minister of the Interior, Sacha Llorenti.

The response from indigenous groups, labour unions and the community organisations of El Alto and Cochabamba was immediate and enraged; all the more so when government spokespersons denounced the marchers as 'primitives', 'savages' and 'anti-modern', the slanders so often repeated wherever indigenous communities fought back. Only this time they were delivered by the representatives of the 'government of the movements'! When many of the movements abandoned MAS in protest, they were denounced as traitors. As it proved:

> The TIPNIS conflict is the most recent, and in some ways most intense, expression of the class contradictions – or 'creative tensions', as government functionaries prefer – underlying the development model introduced by the Morales government after its assumption of power in January 2006.[16]

The revolutionary process that Bolivia had lived through between 2001 and 2005 had brought a mass movement onto the historical stage, shaping events and in its practice, laying out new priorities and values, an alternative logic to the neo-liberal agenda that had prevailed until then. Because of its particular history, however, it did not have a project for state power, nor a broader vision that could translate the logic of their struggle into a social transformation. Into that vacuum stepped MAS, translating that energy back into the language of electoral politics, taking over the administration of the state without transforming it. It was one of the many contradictions of the early part of the Morales administration that it did not challenge the eastern bourgeoisie, then at its weakest as Hylton points out, but instead preferred to pursue a policy of alliances with the racist and ruthless capitalist bourgeoisie of the Media Luna, who used the opportunity to regroup, and to murder peasants at Porvenir, the small town whose name, ironically enough, means 'the future'.

...between the time the Assembly was designed and concluded, the government showed its reluctance to rely on direct action from below and its willingness to make backroom concessions, to the right. As the massacre in Pando – the circumstances of which remain murky – demonstrated in September 2008, such caution did not restrain the racist violence of the right, or prevent bloodshed, although the right-wing rampage may well have hastened the failed coup plot of October 2008, and the popular ratification of the new Constitution in January 2009.[17]

By 2009, however, Morales had prevailed over the enemies to the east, though only by according them a degree of autonomy in practice denied to them in the Constitution. But he was seen to have beaten them back, and his support, even in the eastern provinces, rose dramatically.

A more important test of the meaning of a 'government of the movements', however, was the economic model that it was building. The core demand of the movements had been nationalisation of oil and gas. In reality it was a nationalisation of a limited kind that left a great deal of room for foreign capital to continue to invest. The elements that responded to the movements, however, like agrarian reform or public services, were underfunded and in the case of land reform, which was presumed to address the needs of small farmers, the backbone of support for the MAS, was largely neglected in favour of consolidating large private landholdings. The central question is how the model related to, or transformed, the relationship between Bolivia and the global capitalist market. Very simply it reinforced and deepened it by expanding the production of primary materials at the expense of alternative development. It is true that the Morales regime diverted investment to private capital, domestically, creating an emerging class of indigenous entrepreneurs who now employ poorer propertyless Bolivians at low wages. Ironically, Webber reports, this sector is now pressing Morales to open new avenues for export and international trade. And while small-scale peasant farming has declined as a proportion of the national economy, the agro-export sector (in the east) has also grown with state support.

It is against this background that TIPNIS has to be understood. Who were the beneficiaries of a state-subsidised highway?

While opening up Bolivia's northern savannah region to further capitalist expansion, the TIPNIS highway would also crucially provide an integral link in an international north east to south west trade corridor, allowing Brazilian commodities from the western expanses of that country to reach Pacific ports in northern Chile, via Bolivia.[18]

Brazilian capital is a major investor in the capitalist expansion in the eastern lowlands. In fact, the highway project was to be partly financed by the Brazilian Development Bank on condition that a Brazilian company was given the contract to build it! That expansion of extraction and agro-export enterprises eats into lands occupied by poor landless peasants who live on crafts, small-scale agriculture and the use of forest resources. They are indigenous communities like the Mojeños-Trinitarios, Chimanes and Yuracarés, who are increasingly driven into semi-proletarian labour by the aggressive growth of big capital in the region. When their march began they were accused of being the puppets of imperialism and as Linera himself put it 'NGOism', who had been encouraged to occupy lands to embarrass the government. In fact these communities had been occupying lands since the 1980s, as they were permitted to do by the Constitution, then and since. It was interesting that not long before the attacks on the marchers, Morales had announced the government's commitment to 'communitarian socialism', a ringing phrase eagerly taken up by networks of supporters around the world. The slogan must have seemed less inspiring to the marchers outside La Paz.

The reaction of the social movements was immediate as thousands joined the marchers. The Minister of Defence resigned in disgust and after some delay, the project was suspended. In 2017, it was announced that it would be resumed. In the meantime the organisation of the lowland Indians has been expelled from the government's Unity Pact.

It is simply untrue to argue that the direction of travel of the Bolivian process is, as Linera suggests, towards use value and away from neo-liberalism.[19] Elsewhere he was franker. It may be the aspiration, Linera argued eloquently in his 2013 speech to the European Left Conference, but it is far from the reality.[20] In fact, Linera was clear that what is being constructed in Bolivia is 'an Andean-Amazonian capitalism' – a process that may take 100 years. Evo disagreed; the project, he said, was for a 'Bolivian state-capitalism'. There is no disagreement, however, that the model is capitalism, and a capitalism embedded in a global, neo-liberal market.

The economic model, as Molina[21] shows clearly, rests on the continuing and expanding production of oil, gas, and minerals. The arrival of Japanese and Chinese mining enterprises on the exquisite Salar de

Uyuni (the salt flats of the Altiplano) searching for lithium is the latest 'gold rush' following the copper boom. It is only the most visible example. Over the ten years since the declaration of 'communitarian socialism' the evidence points in a negative direction. The agrarian reform has not resulted in the redistribution of land to communities, but rather in the allocation of large extensions of land for export agriculture. There are, of course, within the Andean world, different and competing demands. The defence of coca production by Evo has been perhaps the most successful advocacy of indigenous practices, but it has involved concessions to eradication programmes in exchange for an agreement to continue and defend limited legal production on small plots and in designated areas. The remote area of Yungas has been less willing to accept the provisions than the Chapare, where the influence of the state holds sway, for example. And most importantly of all, the growth of the major capitalist concerns in the east has continued apace. Many of the huge agricultural holdings there belong to Brazilian and Argentine interests – soya and cattle production for example – and the highway through the TIPNIS park was designed to facilitate the transport of oil among other products. The Water and Gas Wars sent a very clear message from the grass roots – that the commons are collective property that cannot and must not be alienated or commodified. Yet today, Bolivia continues to expand the exploitation of its natural resources for the external market. The 'Dutch disease' which assumes that oil flows effortlessly from the ground to be exchanged for consumer goods and services has not been addressed in Bolivia; and nor has the corruption that has proliferated, with the assistance of Odebrecht, throughout the continent. The scale of the corruption is exactly proportional to the scale of the infrastructure projects and their finance; and it is in the public sector, where the tenders for these huge projects are offered together with equally enormous 'commissions', where corruption has proliferated. Unfortunately corruption in Bolivia appears to be little different from elsewhere. Extractive industries are not just one more industry like any other. They are the centre of a model of social and economic relations, which reproduces market capitalism at its fiercest and most corrupt. The idea of *buen vivir* is to provide an alternative. It will not happen overnight, of course, but the preparation and anticipation of it must inform any society and any state which makes a claim to be constructing a socialist future, in which use-value, social justice and grass roots democracy will prevail.

In 2016, for the first time, Evo Morales failed to win a majority in a referendum for a proposed constitutional amendment to allow indefinite re-election for the president and all other public officials. Participation was low and the number of spoiled votes and abstentions significant.[22] There is some debate as to why it happened, but by 2016 there was a noticeable slowing of Bolivia's economic 'miracle'. The fall in the oil and gas prices internationally meant a decline in state revenues which was compensated from its reserves which are considerable, but falling – from $15 billion to $10 billion between 2015 and 2017. Imports in the same period fell by 20 per cent, suggesting a decline in both industry and consumption. One result was a fall in the levels of investment in the private capitalist sector with an immediate consequence in a contraction of the labour market and a fall in the value of wages, as a higher proportion of the jobs available became temporary or transitory. It seemed that Bolivia was as vulnerable to the variations in the global market economy as it ever was. The 'plural economy' had, as Medina puts it, revealed its 'Achilles heel' – its continuing dependence on primary extractive industry as the boom began to fail.

In June 2018 the recently established Electoral Tribunal announced, using some questionable constitutional arguments, that it had reversed the 2016 referendum result to allow public officials, including Evo, to stand again for the presidency. In the context of the Bolivian process this is a betrayal of the revolutionary impulse. The deliberate flouting of a democratic decision in this way raises important questions about democracy, especially where the vote was clearly delimited and defined. But it is much more than a matter of legalities. The movement that brought Evo to power and supported him throughout was characterised by a radical democratic practice. The participatory democracy embedded in those practices was fundamental. The perpetuation in power of one person or group represents a limited bourgeois conception of democracy directly contrary to its significance for socialists.

Yet García Linera argues, with his usual skill and eloquence, that the separation between state and society has been overcome; it has become an 'integrated state', and therefore the internal contradictions within society are 'creative tensions', transitory in their nature. The state-as-society can resolve them internally through processes of dialogue and negotiation without succumbing to the external enemy – neo-liberalism. But the social movements that became revolutionary through the epoch of the Water and Gas Wars have been excluded and marginalised from the dialogue. The higher levels of consumption that have marked recent years in Bolivia are expressions of a society of competitive and possessive individuals rather than the collective in which each is responsible to all, as is expressed in the *ayllu* and the traditions of the indigenous community.

What has happened to the combined opposition consciousness Webber speaks of? The 'creative tensions' in the state it seem not to have been resolved and that is because the universal state that can deal with all its contradictions internally must now produce an explanation for renewed internal opposition. Hegemony under such circumstances can easily become domination and control.

To anticipate a familiar criticism, this is not a critique from a position of ideal situations or utopian possibilities. To speak of a participatory democracy in Bolivia is a reference to a living and a lived experience; the organs and the practice of self-emancipation exist in recent memory. A revolutionary leadership would be actively and urgently engaged with that mass movement in developing that potentiality and in debating and preparing the foundations of a different social order. It would be challenging, and defying neo-liberalism, rather than re-entering its terrain at its most exposed point. Extractive industries lead in one direction only; they do not produce new opportunities for diversification and production for need. On the contrary, they destroy them. To be forewarned is to some extent to be prepared, and to have the opportunity to deepen the argument about what an alternative, humane and egalitarian model – it might even be a communitarian socialism – would look like. The difficulty for those who have seen the end as taking state power, from which all benefits flow, is that they must now increasingly defend that state against those in whose name they occupied that power. If creative tensions and catastrophic equilibrium underpin the transitory nature of any kind of dual power, it is significant that all talk of transition or transformation has ended. In a curious repeat of past errors, Evoismo now argues that the only guarantee of change is its own continuity, while those who fought the old state and brought it down are enjoined to wait the hundred years or so it might take for Andean-Amazonian or Bolivian state capitalism to run its course.

4
Ecuador and the Battle for Yasuni

The Rise of Rafael Correa

Rafael Correa was elected in 2007 as president of Ecuador by a very narrow margin, winning in the second round. His election followed the removal from power of Lucio Gutiérrez who, three years earlier, had taken the presidency with the support of the indigenous movement. Gutiérrez had positioned himself carefully in the wake of the removal of the previous president, Jamil Mahuad, who was forced to resign in 2000 after dollarising the economy. Gutiérrez, an army colonel, then presented himself as the champion of the anti neo-liberal cause; indeed three indigenous representatives joined his government. Within a short space of time, however, Gutiérrez in his turn bent to IMF pressure and imposed the same policies. His removal, however, was not the consequence of a renewed indigenous mobilisation; he had divided the movement and his conduct of government provoked both anger and resentment within the indigenous communities. It was a broad movement of the middle class, a 'civic movement'[1] that removed Gutierrez, in a reaction to his personal corruption and his privatisation of public assets like the electricity and telephone companies. The movement was equally hostile to the measures of 'reconstruction' imposed by the global financial institutions. In this sense, it was a reaction perhaps closer to the Argentine movement of 2001, expressing a disillusionment with politics in general rather than advocating an alternative programme.

> Three important actors have emerged in recent decades: workers, whose strength was undermined by the neoliberal model; indigenous peoples, who, despite their impact, have been weakened by various internal dynamics; and the new citizens movement, which represents a broad-based and heterogenous range of interests and whose main objective is 'political reform'.[2]

Correa became Minister of the Economy in the government of Alfredo Palacio that replaced Gutiérrez, but was forced to resign when he announced that part of the country's oil revenues would be devoted to social spending. In the election that followed, Correa positioned himself and his organisation, Alianza Pais (AP), firmly within the anti neo-liberal camp, exploiting the political cynicism of the civic movement by presenting his organisation as an alternative to political parties. His opponent, the billionaire banana magnate Alvaro Noboa, clearly represented the oligarchy, and although he won in the first round, there was sufficient feeling against his conservative policies to allow Correa to win in the subsequent round, when Gutiérrez, who stood again despite his reputation and still gathered over 20 per cent of the vote, stood down. Correa was an economist and academic who, although U.S. trained, was critical of the strategies of globalisation. An early experience as a missionary meant that he spoke Kichwa, the main indigenous language, as well as French and English. His policies and discourse were populist and in tune with the radical mood of the social movements at the time. Correa turned his lack of any direct involvement in political activity to his advantage, presenting himself as an outsider – *un forajido* – like the supporters of the civic movement. In 2007 he called a Constituent Assembly to revise the Constitution, a move that won him more credibility and the support in Congress of an alliance of left parties including Pachacutik, the MPD (a Maoist party with particular influence among teachers) and the Democratic Left.

The Constituent Congress was enormously popular. The new Constitution, approved by 64 per cent of votes cast in a referendum in 2008, transformed the National Assembly with the participation of indigenous and Afro-Ecuadorean delegates. In 2008 Correa was re-elected with a first round majority of 52 per cent. He announced the deepening of the 'Citizens Revolution' (the *forajidos* as Correa had baptised them) and echoed Hugo Chávez's commitment to twenty-first century socialism. The Constitution itself was radical in several ways; its environmental provisions were extremely advanced and included a commitment to 'good living' (*sumac kawsay*), a concept of living in harmony with nature and community which had its equivalent in several of the constitutions of the pink tide, in particular Bolivia and Venezuela.

And yet, despite his public identification with Chávez and the Bolivarian revolution it very quickly became clear that there was a gulf between Correa's public rhetoric and his actions as president. The 2008

Constitution pointed to a sea change in the racialised and oligarchy-dominated politics of the country. In fact the major transformation in the political culture had come earlier and had nothing to with Correa. In 1986 the major indigenous nations of Ecuador formed a joint confederation, CONAIE. At its foundation it rejected electoral politics in its fight for recognition of indigenous rights and for the restoration of the original territories. It advocated a form of direct participatory democracy, and adopted direct action methods from the outset. Its original programme was a comprehensive list of demands for recognition of land rights, for bilingual education and state support for cultural and community activities. Its first dramatic intervention into public politics came with mass protest in Quito, the capital, in 1990, in defence of indigenous rights. Like other indigenous communities across Latin America, they used sheer numbers to blockade major highways as well as the streets of the capital, though their demonstrations would often include cultural expressions like dance. CONAIE's political horizons were wider, however, as it opposed imperialist interventions like Plan Colombia and the economic strategies of neo-liberalism. It was instrumental in bringing down the government of Jamil Mahuad in 2000, for example, when he announced the 'dollarisation' of the Ecuadorean economy and attempted to impose the IMF's austerity measures. Its support for Gutierrez, however, produced significant disorientation and disappointment among its members and the organisation was not a major force in bringing about Gutierrez's fall.

Correa's adoption of plurinationalism and *sumac kawsay* in retrospect seems like classic opportunism. The advanced environmental provisions of the Constitution promised, first and foremost, a redirection of the economy away from its dependency on oil and extractive industry, in line with Correa's avowed hostility to neo-liberalism. Immediately after the 2009 elections, however, he shifted his political ground to the right. His sudden attack on the indigenous movement and its defence of *sumac kawsay* for its 'infantile leftism, environmentalism and indigenism' was a comprehensive abandonment of the policies that had won him the presidency.

Two years earlier he had launched the Yasuni-ITT project. The Yasuni National Park, in the Ecuadorean Amazon, is possibly the most biodiverse region on earth, having escaped the Ice Age. It is also the location of 40 per cent of Ecuador's oil, which had been exploited by Chevron-Texaco and other multinationals under the preceding oligarchic administrations. In fact, Chevron had ceased production there early in the decade and left behind it devastation, pollution and poisoned rivers and river banks. The corporation refused to accept responsibility for the environmental damage. An Ecuadorean judge found the corporation responsible for the contamination and fined it $9 billion. Unsurprisingly, this was rejected in the U.S. courts. In response to a global campaign against the resumption of oil extraction, Correa launched his initiative, challenging the international community to provide the equivalent revenues, some $3.6 billion, in exchange for which there would no further extraction in the area. Various Hollywood celebrities offered major contributions and some social-democrats considered adding their weight too. Germany also offered a contribution, though Angela Merkel subsequently withdrew, citing Correa's relationship with Hugo Chávez as an obstacle. The financial crisis of the following year undermined the appeal in its turn. The initiative was scrapped in 2013; only $336 million had been pledged (and less than $14 million delivered) against the $3.6 billion that was required. Correa then announced that drilling would be resumed in the region, though the government claimed that it would be conducted under strict controls, and that there would be no resulting damage to the environment, though there were many informed people who cast doubt on that possibility. In fact the high profile campaign concealed a very different reality. By 2009 the entire Amazon region of Ecuador had been divided into concessions to various oil and mineral companies, with only Yasuni unattributed until 2014. Drilling was resumed there at the beginning of 2018 under Correa's successor, Lenin Moreno.[3]

Correa's denunciation of 'indigenism' was his response to the demand that the agrarian reform, promised in the Constitution but not implemented, should be carried through. It remained a paper undertaking. From the presidency, Correa began to attack the indigenous movement. The protests over communal land ownership in Cuenca and the collective resistance of the Shuar community were criminalised and their leaders imprisoned. The factor that drew together all these elements was Correa's continuing commitment to an economy based on oil and mineral production, subordinated in the reality of globalisation to the demands and dictates of multinational corporations like the Canadian mining corporation, Corriente Resources, among others.[4] Luis Macas, the presidential candidate of the Pachacutik movement in 2006, explained to Jeffery Webber that the attack on the indigenous movements was not just racism for racism's sake, but because their movements were the principal enemy of the neo-liberal model, which rests on the maintenance of the extractive industries under the control of global capital.[5] Correa also announced a series of redundancies in the public sector and attacked labour activista, particularly among teachers.

Yet he nurtured his reputation as a pink tide president through his decision not to renew the lease for the U.S. military base at Manta, his continuing denunciations of neo-liberalism and his very public association with Hugo Chávez. Though he declared his support for the concept of twenty-first century socialism that Chávez had announced in 2005, his enthusiasm did not extend to a commitment to the participatory democracy which was announced in the 2008 Constitution and which CONAIE had fought for since its formation.

By 2010, the political situation had returned to conflict between the grass roots movements and the state. When ALBA convened a presidential summit in the Andean city of Otavalo, the indigenous organisations were not invited; they organised an alternative 'Plurinational Parliament' in the streets, which was attacked and repressed by the police. Yet within the conference the presidents continued to discuss indigenous rights.

Economic Realities and Economic Myths

The defenders of Correa on the social democratic left point to Ecuador's sustained economic growth and the increases in social spending; yet as a *proportion* of GDP they remain stubbornly at the bottom of the Latin American scale.[6]

Ecuador had experienced four economic booms based on exports. In the early twentieth century it was cocoa, and mid-century, banana exports floated the economy. In the mid-1970s oil exports drove the economy, and by the 1980s cut flowers were added as a major contribution to its export income. Mining and oil production were permanent features of the national economy from the 1970s onwards, and production expanded with the Chinese-led commodities boom. Canadian multinationals occupied a central place in the extractive industries of Ecuador.[7] The beneficiaries of each of these phases of expansion were the oligarchy, whose stronghold was the coastal city of Guayaquil, and the foreign capital that exploited Ecuador's natural resources for its own benefit. The indigenous population were held in poverty.

Correa's electoral victory in 2009 was described by Marc Becker, whose writing is essential to any understanding of Ecuador, as 'an unequivocal victory for the left tide'. Correa's programme certainly justified optimism, on the face of it. He had beaten back both the banana millionaire, Noboa, a powerful member of the oligarchy, and Lucio Gutiérrez, who had the insolence to present his candidature again and who still enjoyed broad support from some indigenous organisations, with the backing of both evangelical and catholic groups. Nonetheless, Correa's campaign promises won him an absolute majority of 52 per cent, and he assumed power without a second round run off.

Correa was an independent candidate in a society whose political life had been characterised by endless squabbling between parties and by the frequent premature ending of presidential terms. He had proposed increases in social spending in his brief sojourn as economics minister under Palacio. He had promised a 'citizens revolution', appealing to those sectors whose scepticism about politics had driven Gutiérrez from office in 2005. And he had been responsible for the establishment of the Constituent Assembly which produced the new Constitution.

> Correa promised to construct a government based on five revolutions: an economic revolution that re-established the government's redistributive role; a social revolution that favoured equality for Ecuador's different social sectors and ethnic groups; a political revolution that would reverse the privatization of state structures and enhance participatory democracy; a revolution for Latin American integration; and an ethical revolution to combat corruption.[8]

He later added two more, relating to the environment and judicial reform. In the immediate aftermath of his victory, Correa began to align himself with Chávez's notion of twenty-first century socialism, though he redefined its meaning. On a trip to Cuba, for example, he spoke about 'the dogmas history has defeated', which included 'the class struggle, dialectical materialism, the nationalisation of all property, and the refusal to recognise the market.' It seemed a curiously inappropriate place for the expression of those particular ideas!

His first measures from the presidency were conditioned by an unfavourable parliamentary arithmetic. He had made a great deal of his independence from party politics, and insisted that his AP organisation was not a party but a broad front that contained several currents. The congressional elections left AP just short of a controlling majority, almost certainly as a result of his confrontation with CONAIE, which had announced that it would not vote for any presidential candidate.

Nonetheless his early measures did produce economic improvements, new investments in healthcare, education and poverty reduction programmes. He also announced a refusal to pay the country's foreign debt or to renew the lease on the Manta air base. These were both popular and populist measures.

It was clear that many of the measures were directed at his urban support base to the detriment of the rural and indigenous populations. Urban poverty was reduced in his first term by 17 per cent, but in the countryside the figure floated around 50 per cent.[9] It was clear that he was committed to minimising the power of the indigenous organisations, which had defined Ecuadorean politics since 1990, and above all their capacity for independent action. The intention was that indigenous demands should be channelled through the state, but this would be against a background of an agrarian policy that favoured large scale development over the interests of small farmers or collectives. This clearly acted against the interests of the indigenous movements. Pablo Dávalos, an economist who had worked with Correa in the Palacio government, argued that Correa's aim was 'to neutralize the ability of the indigenous movement to organize and to destroy it as a historic social actor'. His subsequent clashes with, and denunciations of the indigenous organisations, certainly confirm that analysis. Monica Chují, who belonged to the Shuar community and had been a key figure in Correa's first administration, resigned from the government. 'Like all neo-liberal governments, we Indians represent an obstacle to development,' she said.[10] Most significantly, several of Correa's key allies, including Chují and the ex-president of the Constituent Assembly Alberto Acosta, distanced themselves from him, arguing that he was increasingly arrogant and authoritarian. And indeed the new Constitution had significantly strengthened executive power, allowing him to act directly without reference to the National Assembly through decrees and enabling laws.

Correa did not emerge from the social movements; unlike the other presidents of the pink tide, Evo, Chávez, Lugo of Paraguay, Mujica in Uruguay or even Ortega in Nicaragua, though that relationship was different in each case. But Correa had no links to movements of resistance. Neither did he have a historic political base, like the Kirchners in Argentina. Becker's highly optimistic assessment of the implications of his presidential victory is understandable in the context of his professed commitment to twenty-first century socialism. And in 2009 he took a series of steps which seemed radical, even though he systematically evaded any definition of what he understood socialism to mean. He defaulted on the foreign debt, confirmed the closure of Manta, and refused to recognise Lobo, the leader of the coup that had ousted Manuel Zelaya in Honduras[11] until those responsible had been punished, when even Venezuela had agreed to recognise the Lobo regime. He also joined ALBA, the Bolivarian Alliance promoted by Chávez, with whom he clearly had a very warm relationship.

Yet even then there were warning signs. The confrontation with the indigenous and Afro-Ecuadorean movements had been denounced by Monica Chuji and Alberto Acosta; they called into question the sincerity of his commitment to *buen vivir* and to an alternative concept of development. Acosta, a founder member of Pachacutik, was the author of the AP programme and president of the Constituent Assembly. He had also developed the alternative strategy for the Yasuni-ITT region based on alternative technologies, the protection of the region's extraordinary ecology and the development of its pharmaceutical potential. It was Acosta who proposed the launch of an international fund to finance the alternative development programme. Acosta's resignation was a sign of his disillusionment with Correa; this was not, he would later say, twenty-first century socialism but '21st century extractivism'.[12]

Correa was seen by the 'citizens movement', for all its lack of clarity, as the person who would clean up Ecuadorean politics and its political system, the twin evils well represented by his opponents in the 2009 elections, Gutiérrez and Naboa. In many ways, that part of the Correa project was successful; the state, which as Chuji argued, Correa identified with himself, arrogated control of the economy, denouncing all those who criticised the centralisation of power that directly contradicted the constitutional commitment to a participatory democracy, particularly the leadership of the indigenous movements. But his confrontation with them was not only about his authoritarian project. It was already very clear that, despite the Yasuni Initiative, Correa was committed to maintaining the centrality of the extractive industries for the national economy. Yasuni had produced around 40 per cent of Ecuador's oil production, but a number of multinationals had land conceded to them elsewhere in the Amazon region. Mining, especially of copper, was largely under Canadian domination – the result in part of the direct intervention of the Canadian government through its embassy. One of largest companies, Corriente Resources, operating in the centre of the country in Cuenca, faced massive local protests over its contamination of water supplies. One of the leaders of the movement, Jose Tendetza, was killed on his way to denounce the company's activities at a conference on Lima. The company withdrew, its ownership passed into new (mainly Chinese) hands and it has now resumed operations. The indigenous movement was clearly, as Chuji had said, the main obstacle to the extractive strategy, not only because their territories were the location of many mining operations but because the development philosophy of *buen vivir* was in direct contradiction to neo-liberal capitalism whose concept, in Acosta's words, developed nothing but the machinery of profit.

There were major actions, including blockades of the principal highways in 2009. Correa argued that the continuity of these industries was essential in providing the revenues for increases in public spending. He promised a 'socially responsible' extractivism, under state supervision – but this did not mean nationalisation, a solution he had already dismissed in his interview in Cuba in early 2009. In 2010, the demonstrations outside the ALBA presidential meeting in Otovalo were met by the police and key leaders of the indigenous movement were arrested. In the same year, a police strike led to the kidnapping of the president; the issue was a new wage regime which affected police bonuses.

What was Correa's project? In the first place it involved a stronger state, interventionist in its method and, as some critics argued vocally, clientilistic – creating new organisations from the state to rival and undermine the existing social movements. Becker quotes René Baez:

> Correa advocates a statist model of development that allows for no real popular participation. His actions are a violation of the new constitution. Workers, teachers, indigenous organisations and ecologists have no say in this government.[13]

In effect, Becker argues, Correa was closer in his political strategy to Lula in Brazil or the Concertación in Chile than to his ostensible political allies in Venezuela and Bolivia. His policies were clearly directed towards a state-capitalist model with political reforms that would ensure a social base of support for his government. His victory in the 2009 election did wrest power from the old oligarchy and transform the political culture of Ecuador. But Becker's claim that it was a victory for the pink tide raises some key questions.

If participatory democracy was, as Chávez had argued, a central element of twenty-first century socialism, then Ecuador cannot be seen as an example of it. In his foreign policy, and in particular in relation to Latin America, Correa adopted a critical position reaffirmed in his withdrawal in 2012 of Ecuadorean participation from the programme of the School of the Americas. Correa was also an enthusiastic advocate of the new regional formations like ALBA, Unasur and Celac. He was clearly committed to regional integration (one of his five 'revolutions') but that did not represent a challenge to neo-liberalism let alone global capitalism. It represented a renegotiation, a diversification of markets and investors, but Correa continued to work with the United States as well as opening the country to large scale investment from China, accepting a $3 billion loan which was certainly not conditional on the deepening of a citizens' revolution.

By 2013 Correa was openly confronting the indigenous and environmentalist movements , and persecuting their leaders. The alternative Yasuni project had been abandoned and oil production was scheduled to restart. He continued his attacks on the indigenous organisations and public sector employees, including teachers. At the same time Correa was opening avenues to the business sector, especially after signing a free trade agreement with the EU, which was interpreted across the left as neo-liberal.

On the other hand, Ecuador's GDP grew at a steady 4 per cent per annum between 2007 and 2014. Although Correa's second presidency, beginning in 2013, was marked by an intensification of his conflicts with the indigenous movement and public sector unions and the increasingly authoritarian character of his regime, economic growth and the fall in levels of poverty, (from 37.6 per cent in 2006 to 22.5 per cent in 2014) held the popularity of his regime steady. But the optimistic picture began to reveal cracks in 2015 as the economy felt the combined impact of the fall in oil price and the exchange value of the dollar. The realities would emerge slowly. Despite declarations to the contrary, the public debt had risen from $10 billion in 2009 to $43 billion in 2017. The debt to China stood at $10 billion in 2017. Permanent employment fell from 49.3 per cent of the economically active population to 42.3 per cent between 2014 and 2017. The value of wages also fell. Industrial production was stagnating and the contribution to exports of oil and minerals was rising. This was highly significant. In 2017 it also emerged that the concentration of wealth remained at earlier levels and that the major corporations, like Eljeri and Nobis, paid only 2.3 per cent of their earned profits in tax.[14] It made a nonsense of the tax protests in June 2015. In August that year, a mass demonstration organised by the indigenous organisations and supported by the range of anti-capitalist movements, converged on Quito. Taken together the two demonstrations marked a return of both the left and the right; though neither was in a position to mount a challenge, it was a sign that Correa's position was weakening. The right, for its part, was showing a different face. It was not the oligarchy who had taken to the streets; it was a more middle class movement, social sectors who had benefitted as consumers from the years of modest but continued growth. The economic environment was changing, but in addition there were increasingly persistent allegations of corruption within the state, reinforced by Correa's attacks on his critics of both right and left and his accusations that the August march had been organised by the right. The new right, for its part, showed a more moderate face, a disposition to dialogue within a framework of soft neo-liberalism.

In his analysis of what he calls 'the Ecuadorean impasse', Jeffery Webber discusses Gramsci's concept of 'passive revolution' as it applies to Ecuador:

> ...a set of changes distinct from the preceding periods, but these changes ultimately guarantee the stability of the fundamental relations of domination, even while they assume novel political forms.[15]

The result of this process, which can combine restoration with a discourse of transformation 'gradually [drains] the capacities for self-organisation and self-activity from below.' The crises of the period of neo-liberalism, from 1990 to 2005, reached peaks at which the political system seemed to have ceased to function and the future was being determined on the streets and highways. The extractive model advocated by the conservative forces was in jeopardy. And it was Correa who re-established it through mechanisms combining co-optation and repression of the movements from below. The August 2015 march may have seemed to confirm the return of the indigenous movements to the centre of the political stage, but that was an illusion. They were certainly mobilising again, but Correa was still popular among his urban base, though his popularity declined in the course of the year. And there was a consensus on the state capitalist project across the right while the struggle between the state and the movements continued.

If the central feature of the pink tide was this fundamental contradiction between what Acosta called the logics and practices of transformation and those that defended capitalism and its neo-liberal expressions, then despite the demonstrations it seemed that the balance had tipped to the right – not against Correa, but with him. If he was succeeding in containing popular resistance it was not simply physically, by jailing its most prominent leaders, but also in winning an ideological battle – despite the confusions inherent in the discourse of twenty-first century socialism. He had, by his very vagueness, created an interpretation of the project as the restoration of a state capitalism with elements of social responsibility – the reduction of poverty for example – under a new set of political arrangements and a diversification of economic partnerships, but which rested on a resumption of the neo-colonial relationship with foreign capital. For extractivism was not just an economic practice – it was also profoundly ideological.

The presidential election of February to April 2017 (it went to a second run-off ballot) was won by Lenin Moreno, the choice of Rafael Correa, who had announced that he would not stand again just a few months earlier. Moreno's opponent in the run-off, Enrique Lasso, was a major shareholder in the Bank of Guayaquil and the candidate of the right.[16] From his new home in Belgium, Correa argued that the old order had returned. One commentator wondered how profound a transformation it could be that allowed the old order to be restored in three months? Moreno's team included members of the Correa administration, some of his critics and technocrats from the business sector. But his first act was to open a dialogue with both the left and the right. He returned the headquarters of CONAIE, which had been taken from them, with a 100-year lease, a gesture that Correa denounced in the social media as a sign of 'mediocrity'. Moreno then turned to the owners of the principal private media outlets with a proposal to allow them greater freedom and to slowly dismantle the mechanisms of control and censorship set up by Correa. He went on to release indigenous and environmentalist leaders whom Correa had jailed. Shortly afterwards he questioned Correa's final statement that he had 'left the table laid'; the state of the economy, he said, was not as optimistic as Correa had claimed.

Moreno announced that there would be freedom to criticise and alluded very directly to Correa's persecution of his critics and opponents and his criminalisation of protest. His second undertaking was to take on corruption and the clientelism that had characterised the latter part of Correa's regime, and to pursue those who had made fortunes out of public projects through bribery and corruption.[17] More than half a dozen

senior officials of the Correa government are currently under investigation for the $42 million paid to them by Odebrecht in connection with
public infrastructural contracts worth $4 billion. (Many of the projects
remained, and still remain, uncompleted). The most prominent of these
figures is ex vice president Jorge Glas, who was later dismissed by Moreno
and jailed. Moreno's third undertaking was to publish the public accounts
and expose the massaging of data, above all the reality of debt, and the
grandiloquent claims made for the economy. That in turn would bring
him face to face with the members of Correa's administration still in
powerful positions. He has called for a public consultation in 2018 on two
issues: the possibility of indefinite re-election and the dismantling of
what was called the Council of Public Participation and Social Control,
which had the right to nominate and remove the members of key state
institutions. The decision on re-election was clearly made with an eye
to Correa's continuing political ambitions. The consultation will also
address a political ban on those found guilty of corruption; new rules
on sexual offences against minors; the prohibition of metal mining in
protected and urban areas; the withdrawal of a Surplus law that
taxed speculation in land which had led to a reduction in building; and
the reduction of the area of permitted oil exploration in the Yasuni
National Park. The measures proposed are populist without doubt,
and the environmental provisions have been questioned by the social
movements for their perceived ambiguity.

The proposals are indicative of an urgent need to confront the economic reality and assign blame for its condition.[18] Correa's figure for the
public debt was 27.7 per cent of GDP. Moreno's team has suggested that it
is in fact 59 per cent, surpassing the upper limit established by Correa
himself. The fall in the price of oil has exposed other areas of debt.
In 2014, Ecuador quietly returned to the World Bank/IMF fold, having
denounced both in previous years. But its principal creditor today is
China, whose loans are more short term, more costly and linked – as everywhere in Latin America – to the most aggressive extractivist projects. As
of 2018 that debt to China amounted to $10 billion. Moreno has proposed
further savings by restricting the pay of upper level civil servants, cutting
back on external assessors and luxury spending while taking measures
to reactivate small and medium production.

There has been significant criticism of the measures; for some left commentators, the measures are mainly symbolic and designed to apportion
blame to the Correa administration for its economic mismanagement.

Correa has denounced the programme as reflecting the interests of big capital, but at least in the early stages it appears to contain no austerity programme as such, nor cuts in public spending. But the most obvious and important absence is the lack of any alternative to extractivism that will allow the country to break its dependency on oil and mining.

For Alberto Acosta and John Casas Guijarro,[19] the project that Correa was defending up to 2017 and before his decision not to stand for the presidency was a neo-liberal programme, or as they put it 'a neo-neo-liberal programme'. The evidence was the expansion of the oil fields further into Amazonia, and in particular into Yasuni, delivering oilfields and mines to foreign capital, especially Chinese, supporting agricultural corporations at the expense of agrarian reform, and privatising health and parts of the education system.

Lenin Moreno was a fairly colourless figure, but he was Correa's nominee. His public criticism of Correa since his election has provoked an enraged response from Correa who has condemned him as a prisoner of the right. By the beginning of his second year of office that increasingly seemed to be true. Moreno's original proposal for open dialogue with left and right has weakened under intense pressure from corporate interests in Ecuador who now have three representatives within the Moreno government. But the reality is that the clear neo-liberal direction of his government is not a break with Correa but a continuation of his policies. The one difference, it would seem, is that those policies are no longer masked by a socialist discourse.

Moreno's first economic plan, as we have suggested, offered some reassurance to small businesses and left social spending relatively untouched at the level it had reached in early 2017, which had already fallen short of Correa's original projections. But his second plan, in April 2018, withdrew increased taxes for big business and the rich and turned away from support for small farms. His new Economics Minister, a representative of a corporation, returned to the podium a month later to amend the plan. The clearest sign of what is to come, apart from the measures already taken by Correa prior to 2017, was the minister's statement that the ceiling on external loans would have to removed and that it was important 'not to stigmatize' the IMF and the other international agencies. Together with the rising indebtedness to China, and the low level of taxation on big business, it is hard to see how this can avoid the neo-liberal label.

The example of Ecuador, like the others we have discussed, illustrates one thing above all – that the discourse of twenty-first century socialism and the pink tide slips easily off the tongue of eloquent and charismatic leaders like Correa. But the content of their actions belies the rhetoric. Correa may have addressed the political and economic crisis in which Ecuador found itself before his entry into the presidential palace. But his solution has restored neo-liberalism at the expense of those who opened the way to an alternative kind of development and for whom he may briefly have seemed like a leader who would echo and support that objective. The constitution he proposed in 2008 resonated with the promises of the other governments of the pink tide; yet his actions in power contradicted its provisions. We will return to the general issues that the Correa regime raises in relation to a project of genuine transformation. For the moment, for all they may have quarrelled, Correa and his nominated successor are driving the country backwards, and opening wide the gates to those global interests who not so long ago were denounced and exposed as enemies of progress and justice.

5
Venezuela: Decline and Fall

Dancing While Rome Burns

19 May 2018. On the eve of the postponed presidential elections, Venezuela teeters on the brink of a crisis of gargantuan proportions. It is impossible to deny that that the Bolivarian revolution inaugurated by Hugo Chávez Frias on his election to the presidency in 1998 has collapsed. The facts and figures are devastating. Yet there are those both within and outside Venezuela who persist in their denials, and still refer to the government of Nicolas Maduro as socialist. It makes a mockery of the very word.

In 2018 Venezuela, the world's second largest oil producer, is confronting the world's highest inflation figures: 4250 per cent annualised for 2017, and 5065 per cent for the cost of food. It has occupied this unenviable spot for four years.[1] Hyperinflation barely begins to describe its social and economic consequences. Translated into real lives, it signals a collapse in living standards for a rising proportion of the population – declining meat consumption, an average weight loss of 12 kilos as a result of a lack of carbohydrates and vitamins. Though official figures are absent, the most basic medicines are unobtainable – including anti-convulsants, aspirin, birth control pills, retroviral drugs and diabetes medication. There is a rise in infant mortality, and diseases that had disappeared – diphtheria, malaria, measles – have returned. The health system, meanwhile – both hospitals and local emergency and clinical services – has virtually collapsed. You are more likely to find armed men in the corridors than surgeons, and the most basic equipment has either been stolen or simply deteriorated beyond use.

The minimum wage, to which are added food vouchers (*cestatickets*) whose value is not included in the calculation of social benefits, pensions etc., is now increased almost daily yet never coincides with the rate of inflation. It is currently set at a little over 2 million bolivars; that will buy you two packets of disposable nappies, or two dozen eggs, or a kilo of pork. Meat consumption, which is basic for Venezuelans, has declined in the last three years by 22 per cent.

At the level of the national economy, GDP has fallen to a deficit of 15 per cent from a high point in 2004–5 of over 15 per cent growth. For the sixth year running there is a fiscal deficit – since 1990 Venezuelan fiscal receipts have fallen by 4.5 per cent per annum (as compared, say, with Bolivia, where they have risen by around 20 per cent annually).

All the available data – though the Central Bank has failed to provide regular updates on the economy since 2011 – simply confirm the economic disaster. The anecdotal evidence offers no respite. The pictures of the poor scrabbling among the rubbish in search of food are not fabricated; the regular incidents of looting of shops and supermarkets across the country are so commonplace that they are rarely reported.

And yet, as the lacklustre presidential campaign of 2018 proceeds to its probably inevitable outcome, Maduro and his wife appear singing and dancing before their carefully selected audiences at election rallies – always wearing red and exhibiting a cheerful confidence, which does not extend to genuinely open meetings. Maduro travels with well over 100 bodyguards, and he uses television as his main platform of communication – since it is controlled and state-owned.

But the question that every observer should be asking – but sadly is not – is this: Why is an ostensibly socialist regime overseeing a catastrophic decline in the living standards of its mass base, its health and well-being, and doing nothing about it – not even referring to the tragedy unfolding at the palace gates? More importantly, how has a country with the world's second highest oil and gas reserves reached a point where its monetary reserves are at their lowest for 20 years, bearing in mind that those two decades have seen the highest ever oil prices. In fact, the Central Bank has no liquid reserves at all – where did the $69 billion oil revenues earned between 2003 and 2012 go?

One thing is certain. The presidential elections – postponed by the Maduro government until the most favourable conditions existed – will produce neither an answer nor new directions. It is impossible to avoid the conclusion that both the right-wing opposition and the ruling Chavista group are content to allow the population to continue to suffer extreme hardship, their lives hanging by a thread, in the belief that the situation will favour them as long as the blame can be laid at the door of the other. The right-wing electoral alliance, the MUD or United Democratic Platform, is a band of warring groups who have been unable to come up with an agreed candidate or any kind of strategic plan. Their abstention in the presidential election covered the absence of any strategy or solution. They have literally nothing to say about the state of the economy, and seem to be adopting the attitude of Madame Defarge, who knitted while the guillotine fell in 1789. The candidate the right is likely to support, Henri Falcón, is an ex-Chavista city mayor and provincial governor who has some credibility among the majority population, who still consider themselves Chavistas, but is regarded as a deserter by others. His history means that he is unlikely to win very many votes from the bourgeois right either, cemented together by their bitter class hostility to Chávez and Chavismo. A third candidate, whose campaign has been heavily financed and well-organised, is an evangelical Christian, funded largely from the United States. This reflects a much wider right-wing operation which has already divided the Bolivian and Ecuadorean indigenous organisations and formed a powerful bloc in the Brazilian parliament. It is not coincidental, that the Amazon Basin has been a base of operations for the Pentecostals for years now, in addition to Central America. In Mexico, they have organised in Chiapas to counter the influence of the Zapatistas. Their message is hostile to collectivism, individualistic and socially reactionary, focussing on the question of abortion. Their slick campaign in these elections has focussed on the social issues that have affected the poor across the country, eroding the mass base of Chavismo, though it is hard to measure, at this stage, the extent of that influence. But disillusionment and despair provide a fertile terrain for evangelicals endowed with considerable wealth. Their penetration, however, is not limited to the anti-Chavistas. A number of leading Chavistas, at the very pinnacle of power, are evangelicals, including the recently arrested ex-Interior Minister, Miguel Rodríguez Torres, a military officer with a powerful base of support within and beyond the armed forces.

The candidate most likely to win, of course, is Nicolás Maduro. He represents, ostensibly, the continuity of Chavismo. He maintains the discourse and the symbolism of Chávez, and as foreign minister he was a key member of the Chávez administration for most of its duration. He makes enormous play of his working class background – he was a bus driver and a leader of their trade union. In his first election campaign after Chávez's death, in 2013, Maduro won, but with a majority of less than 1 per cent. He did so by relentlessly mobilising the name and popularity of Chávez. Anyone who arrived in the country during the electoral campaign would have been justified in assuming that Chávez was still alive, since his speeches and public appearances were endlessly replayed by the media, and Maduro never tired of asserting that Chávez was by his side – or on one occasion, on his shoulder in the form of a bird. There is little doubt that Maduro won because of Chávez's enduring charisma rather than because of any personal qualities of his own.

In December 2015, in elections to the National Assembly, Maduro fared still worse. The shortages of goods, the lack of medicines, the increasingly visible levels of corruption, and the sheer ineptitude of the administration took their toll despite the attempts to ascribe the deepening crisis to an 'economic war' waged against Venezuela by the national bourgeoisie on the one hand, and imperialism on the other. It was a crude device to simply locate the causes for the catastrophic decline of the economy outside the country in order to foster a fallacious unity under siege.

Yet there was some validity to Maduro's argument, though not in the way he presented it. The central question was not whether Venezuela was under siege and under attack – that much was obviously true. The long aisles of empty shelves in the supermarkets – or at least those in the poor and lower middle class districts – were impossible to hide, as were the huge queues that built up outside their doors in search of basic items. These were not bargain-hunters in search of cheap goods. They were queueing for sugar, corn flour, nappies, rice, eggs – the most essential items. And their patience often went unrewarded. For when the items did arrive, their price rose by the week. One result was the growth of a kind of parallel economy – the *bachaqueo*, referring to the lines of large ants (*bachacos*) engaged in an infinite series of journeys carrying things to the queen. New unofficial networks of distribution were built up through which products were available at lower than supermarket prices – sometimes goods bought there in the first place by organised teams of professional queuers. Other items came via the back door of ministries and official institutions or through a vigorous cross-border contraband traffic.

Despite voluble declarations of concern and the creation of innu-merable ineffectual commissions, nothing was done by government to effectively control prices or ensure distribution to those in urgent need. On this even the supporters of Maduro reluctantly agree. There was a Law of Fair Prices, a campaign against corruption which claimed some 200 mainly middle level functionaries. Eventually, in 2016, the CLAPs were introduced. These were packages of basic goods, at guaranteed controlled prices that would be delivered directly to people's homes. In fact, distribution was placed in the hands of the government party, the PSUV, with the inevitable result that they would be allocated as political rewards; and in fact the CLAPS quickly became commodities in another circuit of illegal trade, being resold at higher prices and often delivered, where they reached the intended consumers, with their contents partially stolen. In the meantime the only minister of consumer affairs who actually attempted to implement a fair prices policy, Eduardo Samán, was twice fired from his job within two weeks. He was replaced, and as was to occur elsewhere with growing frequency, by a relative of Maduro.

As ministers were changed at dizzying speed, it was becoming clear that their real functions and power were decreasing. Power was concentrated in a small inner circle of the PSUV. As the crisis continued to deepen, there was no strategy in place to address the problem, no attempt to restrict or control the widespread corruption, no measures taken to ensure access to food and basic goods. At least none that had any effect. The Chavista party, the PSUV, appeared to be merging with government; cabinet meetings were substituted by weekly meetings of an inner core consisting of Maduro, his wife Cilia Flores (whom he dubbed 'la primera combatiente' – the first fighter – though she had never fought for anything outside the courtroom where she had operated as a lawyer) and Diosdado Cabello, a military officer who had been vice president under Chávez, Minister for Infrastructure, president of the National Assembly (as had Cilia Flores before him) and who is, in my view, undoubtedly the real power behind the throne. In attendance too was Vladimir Padrino López the new minister of defence. Somewhere in the shadows were representatives of the Cuban government, whose influence permeates the regime, in particular in areas of intelligence, policing and social control. It is scarcely credible, but true that the Venezuelan civil register in its entirety is in Cuba.

Is there then an economic war? Steve Ellner insists that there is, but agrees that neither Maduro nor his government have offered any concrete evidence. The U.S. administration has been relentlessly hostile to Venezuela, even before Trump, dissuading U.S. investors by various means from investing there. Venezuelan capitalists have sent their money abroad, the flight of capital smoothed and facilitated by the chaotic exchange system and the enormous opportunities for corruption it offers.[2] But there is another reality which Ellner does not discuss – the external investment and loans coming from China, now the region's second largest investor. It is hard to imagine, however, levels of investment that could compensate for the enormity of funds corruptly removed from the country by both capitalists and Chavistas.

Perhaps the most disturbing aspect of this whole situation is the silence that has attended it internationally and internally. As so often happens, the solidarity movements establish their relationships with states and governments, believe their rhetoric, and join the chorus of denunciations for betrayal that meets any criticism. To question is, it seems, automatically to ally with the bourgeoisie. The same message has been disseminated within Venezuela, though it is sustained, as I shall argue, by more then mere credulity. There are complex reasons why the majority of the population has not responded to the disaster. There are less complex reasons for the scandalous complicity of yesterday's radicals, whom the comfort of government has transformed in so many cases into playing in the orchestra on the Titanic. It is only in very recent times that some cautious questions have been raised, beyond those who have consistently argued a critical left case – like Edgardo Lander, Roland Denis, Manuel Sutherland and a small number of others.

A Backward Glance

It was a regularly quoted achievement of the Chávez regime to have reduced poverty levels dramatically in its first phase. The 60+ per cent of the population reduced to poverty and extreme poverty by the austerity measures of the 1990s were the first beneficiaries of Chavista largesse, and by 2012 the Venezuelan government was congratulated for the scale of its poverty reduction. Yet a study by four Venezuelan universities in 2015 argued that 73 per cent of households had fallen back into poverty.[3] Looking back, it is clear that the high price of oil enabled the Chávez regime to fund social programmes from the state which were largely responsible for the reduction of poverty levels. The same was true for Bolivia, Ecuador and even Peru, whose government was under neoliberal domination in those years. This is not to take away from the real and tangible improvements that this implied for millions of Venezuelans. At the same time, the fluctuations in the oil price produced pronounced variations in annual GDP, which hit its lowest level in 2003 during the *paro patronal*, the 'bosses' strike', which virtually paralysed the oil industry between December 2002 and February 2003. The following year, GDP rose to 8 per cent as oil production resumed. The variation meant that oil revenues fluctuated between 65 per cent and 95 per cent of export earnings.[4] The economic model that Chávez was working with was not especially radical at this point; while the new Bolivarian constitution proposed the nationalisation of Venezuelan oil (which finally happened in 2005) the immediate decision by Chávez was to win the argument for controlling production in OPEC (the organisation of oil-producing countries) and to raise the level of royalties on sales of its oil (principally to the United States). Rising revenues would then finance social programmes in education, health, housing and in other forms of subsidy. These would be organised by the Missions, which were not only social programmes but organs for mobilising communities at the grass roots to carry them through.

What was immediately apparent was that state spending would be wholly financed from oil revenues, which were abundant during the commodities boom of 2005–13. The assumption was that the surplus from those revenues, after public spending commitments, would also be used to encourage local production and diversify the economy to move away from the dependence on oil. That, for example, was the course that Bolivia would follow after 2006 and which, briefly and not very successfully, Venezuela would also pursue through financing small business and social production enterises (EPSs). But Venezuela's model remained what Leonardo Vera[5] calls 'distributionist' though 'assistentialist' may be a more familiar term. The distribution of services by the state to the poor produces another layer of consumers but does not generate productive activities. When oil is plentiful – or even better apparently infinite – and prices high, it is easier and cheaper to buy your goods abroad than invest in production at home. It is what is known as 'the Dutch disease'. Though in this early period, Chávez relentlessly provoked and challenged both capitalism in general and Venezuelan capitalists in particular in his public speeches, he did not move against private interests until 2006.

2006 was a watershed year in the story of the pink tide, and no less so for Venezuela. The April 2002 coup had demonstrated the loyalty of poor Venezuelans to Chávez and that was underlined by the sustained public spending to their benefit after its failure. But the oil revenues were also spent elsewhere; the use of the mass communications media was a feature of Chávez's government, and that also absorbed public revenues. Chávez also launched, at various times. major infrastructural projects. Steve Ellner notes that:

> Under the Chavista governments, they moved into imports and performed local public works projects for which they had a mixed

record, but failed to develop a viable financial and industrial capacity or the capability to carry out mega projects. As a result, for many of the large-scale and complex projects, the government switched from traditional partners to new ones abroad. The Brazilian company Odebrecht, for instance, received contracts for a diversity of undertakings including such mega projects as the construction of the second bridge over the Orinoco River, extensive work on the Caracas metro and rail systems and an offshore oil tanker loading terminal in Jose, Anzoátegui.[6]

It appears that Steve Ellner may be the only person in Latin America to be unaware of Odebrecht's business methods and their implications. Had it been 2008–9, the bonanza of new loans, often short term and at very high interest, might have seemed unproblematic. But by 2015, when this article was published, the extent and depth of Odebrecht's corrupt dealings across Latin America were known – and not just in Brazil. There is no reason to suppose that the construction giant's dealings were any different in Venezuela from everywhere else.

Chávez also distributed largesse among his military colleagues,[7] whose support – especially after the coup – was essential to the consolidation of his regime. It was, after all, a civic-military alliance, though the arguments for the special social consciousness of the Venezuelan military might be questionable without the specific benefits of close association with the state. Diane Raby, for example, asserts that 'what saved the revolution was the civic-military alliance. Troops were "workers in uniform".'[8] They always are, of course, and the issue is under what circumstances they may break with their commanders and act as members of their class.[9] It was, in my view, wildly utopian to go on to assert, as she does that 'the conventional army had been in large part transformed into a revolutionary army', as subsequent events have unfortunately demonstrated convincingly.

In November 2006, Chávez stood again for the presidency under the new constitution, and won with a convincing tally of 62.8 per cent of the votes. Early in December in one of his Sunday morning broadcasts, he announced the formation of a mass party – the United Socialist Party of Venezuela (PSUV) – and called for all Venezuelans to join. It was a critical moment in many different ways, and it appeared to mark the implementation of the 'twenty-first century socialism' he had announced in Porto Alegre a year earlier at the World Social Forum.

The proposal was extremely controversial but the sheer weight of his authority was sufficient to convince nearly 6 million people to join the new party within weeks. There was no indication, nor clarity, however, as to the nature of the party, its organisation, its programme, its conditions of membership or its relationship to the state. All that was known was that it would be socialist (though Chávez's original announcement of his vision of socialism had been very imprecise), and that it was to be a mass party. But to be consistent with the constitutional promise that Venezuela would be a participatory democracy, it would have to be open, its structures transparent, and allow within it the coexistence of the different currents of thought and political positions that were included in the ill-defined framework of 'Chavismo'. The sudden announcement caused great confusion, and a number of political groups divided on the question. The main Trotskyist party, for example, split into two organisations; one elected to enter the PSUV as a critical current, the other to maintain an equally critical independence. The problem was that in terms of sheer numbers the PSUV had become a mass party overnight, and for socialists working with the mass movement there was little real choice but to join. But active and organised revolutionaries were a tiny proportion of the numbers who entered the party. The majority of the new recruits will have had some involvement in local grass roots organisation as part of the popular movement that had grown up in the *barrios* and communities, but have had limited experience of political parties and their organisation.

What was the model for the PSUV? In some sense, though its revolutionary credentials were extremely questionable, the Mexican PRI might have been one point of reference. It was created in its first manifestation in the aftermath of the Mexican Revolution of 1910–17 as an organisation built from above to integrate the different social sectors into the state machine; in another sense, Venezuela itself had already experienced the creation of a party of this type, the political expression of the state *for* but not *of* the masses, in the shape of Acción Democrática, the architect of the puntofijista agreement that dominated Venezuelan political life for 40 years, and which was much closer to the Mexican corporate model. My own view, however, is that the major influence in the creation of the PSUV was Cuba, whose influence was pervasive under Chávez and whose highly centralised Cuban Communist Party might have been seen as an effective tool of political integration.

That seems all the more plausible in the light of two developments. Despite an assurance of internal democracy in the PSUV, two four-person groups were nominated by Chávez to draw up the programme and the organisational structures of the party. There was no prior consultation, and the internal elections to the party's first conference a year later were controlled from above by appointees. The second development was the publication of a Development Plan written by Planning Minister Jorge Giordani, a member of the communist party. Between 2007 and 2009, Chávez moved into a second and more radical phase of nationalisation and state intervention in the economy, on the one hand, and on the other into the active construction of the Bolivarian Alliance for the Americas, ALBA, a proposal for the economic integration of. Latin America.

The plan drawn up by Chávez and Giordani involved the nationalisation of strategic sectors of the economy. Enterprises in electricity generation and distribution, telecommunications, cement, aluminium, steel, banking and mining were taken over in 2006–7. They have been described as expropriations, to give them a more radical character than they actually had. These companies were not expropriated – they were bought by the state, often at inflated prices. The purchase of the Bank of Venezuela, for example, cost the government a billion dollars for around 51 per cent of its shares. Santander had, in fact, bought the bank earlier and had paid $300 million for over 90 per cent of its shares. Two-hundred and fifty of the nationalised enterprises produced food or dairy products. Other factories were old, abandoned or technically obsolete, yet the state paid out in all over $23 billion to their bourgeois owners. That money then flowed into what was becoming the biggest and most profitable industry in the country – financial speculation on imports. In the event, the much trumpeted process of nationalisation stopped in its tracks with the advent of the 2008 financial crisis. Some companies were expropriated later, but only when they were threatened with closure – and their owners were compensated.

Venezuela imported technical products, machinery, consumer goods and food, among other things. In 2003, imports were valued at $14 billion; by 2012 the figure had risen to $80 billion. In 2012, 70 per cent of imports were destined for industry, yet there was no increase in production. Between 2003 and 2013, imports by the public sector increased by 1033 per cent. The statistics are astonishing – but in some sense they simply serve to confuse. The general picture is one of waste and inefficiency and increasingly of corruption. But the central problem is best illustrated by looking at the currency system. There was an official dollar exchange rate which floated at that time around ten bolivars. But the unofficial rate,[10] illegal but widely used, was perhaps 100 times the official rate. Importers and businesses who applied to the Central Bank bought their currency at the official rate. The goods they imported, however, were sold at the unofficial rate – which represented an instant 1000 per cent profit. Although this systematic fraud was a matter of public knowledge, bribery and the complicity of the state allowed it to continue and expand, since everyone involved made a great deal of money from it. Sutherland gives the example of meat,[11] imports of which increased by 17,000 per cent between 2003 and 2013; yet in the same period meat consumption fell by 22 per cent. The only explanation is that either the meat never arrived or that it was (as was the case in many areas) diverted to the Colombian market. The reality is that many of the dollars provided for imports were banked in the United States or in turn used for speculation. It is important to underline the fact that, despite the increasingly radical rhetoric in the period, both the bourgeoisie and Chavistas exploited the speculative opportunities – while denouncing one another in public. No capitalist, nor any member of what came to be called the *Boliburguesía,* the newly created Chavista capitalists, will invest in productive activities whose rates of return are infinitesimal compared with the profit on speculation. Imported food, which by 2015 represented over 90 per cent of what was consumed, also sold at black market prices, and the regular disappearance of items from supermarket shelves was simply a device to raise prices further.

In the case of medicines, which are also largely imported, the scarcity of pharmaceuticals became very serious over the period, leading to the current situation in which the most fundamental and the most important medications are simply unobtainable. It is no coincidence that infant mortality rates are no longer published, that diphtheria, malaria and measles have reappeared. Yet I can testify that a chain of pharmacies owned by a relative of a leading Chavista official, the ex-president of the oil corporation PDVSA, has a number of branches in Colombia, where all the absent medications are available off the shelf.

This speculative frenzy is a feature of oil economies, accustomed to importing all their needs with the bottomless product of the oil wells. Any socialist, or indeed developmentalist strategy must rest on the diversion of oil profits towards productive activities, diversifying the economy, expanding the domestic market, providing jobs and lessening the dependency on oil. The fundamental problem of Venezuela is that Chávez's project, despite endless declarations to the contrary, rested on the continuation and deepening of that dependency, renegotiating only its conditions. The nationalisation of PDVSA did not alter that; the corporation became, instead a sort of shadow state, not amenable to the public audit or oversight as the state, however imperfectly, still was. Oil revenues were increasingly channelled through a fund, Fonden, directly under presidential control, as well as over twenty other funds linked to Chinese investments for which there were no accounts.

Edgardo Lander, a highly respected independent academic, and a long time critical supporter of Chavismo has written recently on the crisis of the extractivist model[12] in relation to the Arco Minero project in the Orinoco Basin, to which I will return below. He offers one interpretation of the 2005–6 moment; until then, he argues, the base organisations that carried and supported Chavismo were driving the process forward; its radical and participatory character at that point came from a history of grass roots mobilisation, albeit without links to political parties. It was a rich experience of popular democracy on which the Chavista project could build; that movement is the subject of Carraciolo-Maher's oral history *We created Chávez*.[13] In 2005, however, things began to change. The model implicit in the 2006 Economic Plan and made explicit with the creation of the PSUV was a 'socialist' model in the sense that it reproduced the Cuban conception of the state. The Cuban political structure is highly centralist, authoritarian and admits no serious critical oppositions; most delegates to the (infrequent) Cuban Communist Party Congresses, as well as the lower level state and party institutions have been, and still are, nominated from the party leadership. That is the central contradiction in the Chavista process that Lander identifies – between a bottom-up construction of a new, open democracy and a top-down authoritarian system. And as the political structure is, so too is the economy. Expropriation is the defining process of a state-led system; and a centralised, top-down structure mirrors the expanding control of the economy by the state. Steve Ellner, by contrast, presents it simply as a radicalisation, a logical phase in the Chavista process, rather than a deviation from the declared nature of the society towards which the Bolivarian revolution was purportedly moving. That alternative would have implied a much greater level of grass roots control, the establishment of economic and social priorities through mass democratic participation and above all, a public debate about the priorities that should govern a socialist, redistributive state moving away from dependency.

There were left-wing intellectuals and activists within or around Chavismo who raised these issues in the period before 2006. The creation of the PSUV effectively silenced them, since all political debate was channelled through the party in a downward direction. It was at this juncture too that the system became increasingly corrupt, fuelled at first by speculation and later, in addition, by the infrastructural projects driven from the state; it was an inevitable consequence, too, of the concentration of power and the lack of transparency that followed the establishment of the PSUV. I visited the Alcasa aluminium factory in 2008, for example, which was emblematic in the Chavista strategy. I found it more or less inactive, with the workers complaining that raw materials were not reaching the plant, which was mostly idle. They asked why the state was importing a million Chinese bicycles while the aluminium producing complex was at a standstill. I didn't have an answer.

Price controls and anti-corruption initiatives were regularly announced. But the reality was that there were huge increases in state expenditure on expensive and ill-conceived infrastructural projects, on wasteful schemes that rarely came to fruition, on vanity projects like the sugar refinery in Barinas province that never opened. In the meantime, leading Chavistas were enriching themselves at the state's expense. But the thought processes that go with an oil economy still shaped government decisions. Thus, wasteful and unproductive expenditure was compensated for by short term foreign loans at high interest rates – on the presumption that the oil would keep flowing and its price keep rising. By 2011 the service on the foreign debt amounted to $15.5 billion per year – 20 per cent of the total value of exports. At the same time, Venezuela's internal tax revenue was less in 2015 than in 1990, while Bolivia and Argentina had increased their tax revenues by 20 per cent and 18 per cent respectively in the same period.[14]

The point to be made here is that while Maduro's administration of Venezuela has been and continues to be disastrous, the roots of the problem lie in the Chávez era. While Maduro has none of personal qualities or political consciousness of Chávez, and has a proven family involvement in corruption, the well-deserved criticism of Maduro must take us back to the flaws in the Chavista project itself.

Madurismo

The circumstances of Hugo Chávez's death in March 2013 are at best obscure. No details of his medical condition have ever been provided. He had clearly been ill for almost two years and he carried the visible signs of cancer chemotherapy in his last years of life. Chávez's final testament was the Plan de La Patria 2013–19. It opens with a combative reaffirmation of the project for 'socialism for the twenty-first century' that Chávez memorably announced at the Porto Alegre World Social Forum in 2005:

> This is a programme for the transition to socialism and the radicalisation of participatory democracy. We should not delude ourselves – the socio-economic form that prevails in Venezuela remains capitalist... This programme is aimed at the 'radical suppression of the logic of capital' and a continuing transition to socialism. For new forms of planning and production for the benefit of the people to emerge requires 'pulverising' the bourgeois form of the state that is still reproducing itself through its abominable old practices.[15]

It was in many ways a confession of failure, a recognition of the unresolved contradictions of the Chavista period. Its final call for a *golpe de timón,* a sharp turn of the rudder, became the watchword of the Maduro government that followed his death, a slogan repeated endlessly in the permanent need to seek legitimacy for Maduro's policies and decisions in Chávez's authoritative words. Chávez has also been elevated to the status of 'eternal supreme commander', with its disturbing echoes of Stalinist authoritarianism, to place anything that claimed to express his will beyond criticism.[16] At the same time the *golpe de timón* was cited, for similar reasons, by the critical currents that emerged as the crisis deepened over the next five years. The problem, however, is that Chávez's revolutionary final declaration contradicted the reality of Venezuela's development in the final years of his life; the radical discourse has persisted after his death – though it is often cynically employed to veil failures and deviations.

Maduro was designated as his successor by a dying Chávez in Havana, where he was receiving treatment for his cancer, in the presence of his children, Maduro, Diosdado Cabello and Cilia Flores, Maduro's wife. As I suggested above, these three, together with Minister of Defence and vice-president Vladimir Padrino López, are the real power in Venezuela in 2018, controlling as we shall see, the military and much of the economy under Cuban tutelage – though it is Cabello who controls the key components of the power structure.

In April 2013, Maduro was duly elected to the presidency but with a majority of less than 1 per cent over his opponent, Henrique Capriles

Radonski, the governor of Miranda province and a key leader of the right-wing opposition. He is a member of one of Venezuela's wealthiest families. There were protests, and street barricades or *guarimbas* mobilised by the right made a brief but violent reappearance. The campaign of the bourgeoisie had mainly moved into the streets after 2006, with large demonstrations dominated at first by students, mainly from the private universities, and the regular use of barricades. In 2014 their reappearance was marked by much greater violence. Clearly the right was encouraged by the unexpectedly low vote for Maduro, especially given the outpourings of genuine emotion that followed Chávez's demise. But Maduro was not and is not Chávez, however much, during his first year of office, he tried to mimic his style and reran his speeches and public appearances in the media. Rising prices and increasing shortages of goods were undermining the Chavista regime too, and Maduro's explanations left many people outside the diehard Chavista ranks increasingly sceptical. In 2011, Chávez had formed the Polo Patriótico, broadening the political base of his support and distancing himself somewhat from PSUV, whose credibility was waning. That suggested an increasing discontent among the Chavista base, though it was unlikely that they would ever turn their vote over to a right-wing whose leading figures, like Radonski, María Corina Machado and Leopoldo López, were all members of the country's wealthiest families. Chávez's personal charisma might have persuaded his mass base to control their frustration – Maduro could not. And Maduro never recovered that base.

The right-wing opposition obviously gained confidence from the result and came together under the banner of the MUD, the United Democratic Forum. The new Voluntad Popular (People's Will) organisation, however, led by Machado and López, called for continuing direct action. Their rhetoric was inflammatory and their methods confrontational. On 12 February 2014, huge, mainly-student demonstrations erupted in all of Venezuela's major cities, with the largest numbers in the capital, Caracas. Their initial demands had to do with the situation in higher education, but their slogans were mainly anti-Chavista, and they quickly expanded to embrace economic issues – inflation, scarcity and the relentless rise in prices. The barricades became permanent fixtures and were progressively more violent, as balaclava-clad protesters burned tyres, engaged in occasional acts of terrorism against government buildings and spread oil across main roads.

López had been arrested early on in the protests (and remained in detention for three years). He became the focus of a relentless right-wing campaign which represented him as a martyr. His wife toured the United States to reinforce the point, one of the group of white, middle class and good-looking spokespeople who became the image of right-wing resistance to Chavismo. CNN ran a non-stop campaign of denunci-ation of Venezuela, based on interviews with representatives of Voluntad Popular, and blurred mobile phone footage of unspecified acts of violence which were assumed to be the actions of government sup-porters, though in fact the most violent scenes involved supporters of López's group. The Chavista base was, as it always had been, racially mixed and predominantly working class – an image which Maduro carefully nurtured too. It played well to the Chavista social base, and fanned the loathing of the middle class towards 'the hills' (los cerros) where the poor lived.

The protests were clearly intended to make the country ungovernable – inhibiting traffic flows, creating artificial shortages and generally in-timidating people in the street. But there was a peculiarity about the demonstrations and the barricades. They were almost entirely restricted to middle class areas. In the past the guarimba had always been the method of protest of choice of the marginalised barrios that surround every Latin American city – and Caracas was no exception to that rule. They were a feature of the Caracazo and the chosen weapon of the pi-quetero movements of the unemployed in Argentina and the indigenous movements in Bolivia, as well as the protests against the World Cup in Brazil in the same year, which brought them to the streets of Rio.

By mid-May there were over 40 dead in Venezuela and close to 3000 arrests, at least half of them students. Responsibility for the deaths was pretty evenly balanced between the police and the National Guard and the random violence of the barricades. On 15 May the tent cities set up on a couple of Caracas's main avenues, obviously inspired by the Occupy movement, were forcibly removed. The government consistently described the protesters as 'fascists'. Although there is little real evidence of any organised, ideologically coherent, anti-working class movement, the hostility of the U.S. government and the powerful Venezuelan financial lobby in the United States was palpable. And Voluntad Popular was ideologically on the extreme right of the political spectrum.

The protests caused the Maduro government some difficulty. It could not condemn the barricades when many of its members had long histo-ries of bus burnings in the demonstrations against previous regimes. And every interview with a government person reiterated every Venezuelan's constitutional right to protest. The deeper issue was that the protests continued to be very big, and included massive numbers of students but also significant numbers of the middle and lower middle classes. Their protest was centrally economic. Rampant inflation, already a major problem in previous years, rocketed through 2013 and into 2014. Essential goods disappeared from supermarket shelves for weeks at a time and then reappeared at higher prices. Public services, particularly hospital provision, as well as education, deteriorated rapidly; every bureaucratic procedure was achingly long, unreliable, and usually attended by demands for money, be it getting birth certificates, ordering a car or getting your pension. The system of exchange, particularly for acquiring dollars, was corrupt and opaque. The economy seemed to be careering towards collapse, while the government announced all manner of economic measures and reassuring (if often incomprehensible) figures about the provision of housing, the regulation of prices, the penalising of speculators, the upward trend of the economy in general and action against corruption. Once announced, the measures rarely seemed to produce any visible effect. In reality, reliable official data on the economy from the Central Bank of Venezuela stopped being available in 2011.

Finally, the rising levels of violence across society left people living in fear of crime, robbery and hijackings. Urban life changed as people stayed at home, restaurants and theatres closed early and the levels of private security intensified. And they were right to be concerned. After several years during which no figures were issued, in 2013 it was announced by an independent monitoring agency[17] that 25,000 people had died violent deaths that year, making Venezuela one of the most violent countries in the world. This undesirable distinction still belongs to Venezuela in 2018. So the protests reflected very real problems faced by the middle and lower-middle classes, as well as their apprehension that Chavismo, as one poster put it, 'wants to make paupers of us all'. Rhetorically, at least, the attitude of Chavismo towards the middle class changed from 2006 onwards, as the regime moved in apparently more radical directions. The Chavista style now become uglier and more threatening, in a kind of parody of working class culture. The emblematic figure was the journalist Mario Silva, whose late night television programmes mainly consisted of insults and threats. Diosdado Cabello took over his role under Maduro with his programme 'Con el mazo dando' (Hammer blows) in which he singled out individuals for public denunciation. This was something very different from the articulation of a politics of working people and the poor which was set out in the Plan de la Patria of 2013, and bore no relation at all to Chávez's extremely effective Sunday morning 'meet the people' sessions.

The *barrios* were experiencing the same problems, but they were partly attenuated by the subsidised food programmes (Mercal and PDVAL) and the provision of medical services and educational opportunities in the *barrios*. But the food programmes were erratic and corruptly run, and the crisis in the health service was intensifying. Armed robberies inside hospitals were frequent and the scarcity of medicines and equipment were to bring the hospital sector to its knees. Barrio Adentro, the grass roots health system was equally affected by shortages of medication. But the key issue was food. Agricultural production was at its lowest ever levels, mainly through lack of state investment, neglect by the large landowners, and by the shortage of fertiliser whose price had become prohibitive for many small farmers and cooperatives, despite the fact that it was a leading Chavista, Elias Jaua, who had a virtual monopoly on its production. In any event, food imports had risen to over 90 per cent of national consumption on the one hand, and on the other, the large suppliers, like Lorenzo Mendoza's Polar company, had moved production of many items out of the country (like the staple for all Venezuelans, Harina Pan) – a clearly political measure. In their turn, distributors were hoarding and releasing products to ensure that their prices continued to rise.

Concentrated Economics

The core of Chávez's programme was to achieve state control of the oil industry, negotiate for an appropriate level of royalties, and use that income for social and economic development. PDVSA, the national oil corporation, was taken into state control in the wake of the bosses' strike of 2002–3 and the Organic Hydrocarbons Law of 2005 defined the industry's new role. As Rafael Ramírez, the president of PDVSA, put it at the time:

> With the social distribution of oil income, invested now in the welfare of the people, its human capital, its social and economic advancement, and by investing it in infrastructure, services and investments to increase national production, oil income will then take on the role of transforming the terrible social inequalities and imbalances that are, paradoxically, one of the features of oil-rich countries of the planet.[18]

By mid-2014, production was static at 2.5 million barrels a day at most, while Ramirez had earlier reassured the public that by 2015 production would reach 5 million barrels daily. Increasing technical problems reflecting the lack of investment in plant and infrastructure put even that level of production in jeopardy, especially after a serious fire at one of the key plants, which was rumoured to be the result of sabotage. What investment there was was a result of 'associations' with external investors which often carried conditions even more onerous than the 'operating agreements' made with oil majors during the 1970s. The Rafael Urdaneta gas pipeline across the Gulf of Mexico, for example, is run jointly by a cartel of companies including the Spanish Repsol, the Russian Gazprom and the U.S. Chevron Corporation. PDVSA's debt leapt from $3.75 billion to $78.5 billion by 2012. The Chinese investment (a debt of around $5 billion currently) is paid for in oil (currently around half a million barrels a day, but the figure will rise) at an undisclosed price; 1 million barrels are sold in the United States and Cuba receives over 250,000 daily, also at an undisclosed rate, which it then sells on to earn foreign currency. What the figures show is an income of around $90 billion annually, with a net profit of around $60 billion.

And yet production, agricultural and industrial, is at a virtual standstill. The state-owned industries – including iron and steel, and aluminium production based in Bolívar province around Ciudad Guayana – are paralysed by the lack of spare parts for machinery, the absence of raw materials and the failure to invest over time. Some $312 million assigned to the Guayana Corporation by Chávez in 2012, for example, never arrived. The supply of bauxite, the basis of aluminium production, dwindled to a virtual halt because the six massive extractor vehicles bought from Belarus were all damaged and there were no spare parts. The huge Alcasa Aluminium Factory in Puerto Ordaz, conceived as the first socialist factory under workers' control, is not functioning. The construction industry is crippled by the absence of cement and steel rods. Land expropriations, which were to be the basis of a new socialist agriculture, declined in 2013, and the agriculture minister announced in 2017 that some land might now be returned to their original owners, the same people who have regularly employed armed men to attack peasant occupations.

Auto production, which employed 80,000 workers, is barely functioning – the number of cars produced in a week is what would have been produced in one afternoon a few years ago. In 2007, 472,418 units were assembled; by 2015, 18,300 were produced and in 2016 only 2694.[19]

In the area of pharmaceuticals, national production has ceased. At a conference in 2017, Eduardo Samán, whose three tenures as minister of consumer affairs ended abruptly when he went after speculators and closed establishments that were overcharging, argued, in a well-informed speech, that Venezuela could produce its own generic drugs instead of importing them at a huge mark-up. The conference was well attended by press and media who recorded the ministerial speeches; Samán's contribution, however, was not even alluded to.[20] Prestige projects, like the oil production plants on the Orinoco or the sugar refinery in Barinas province, involved huge spending but have never started production. The full list of such projects is too long to include in this short chapter.

There is a pattern here. Chavismo never had a long- or even medium-term economic plan. The improvisation and pragmatism that characterised Chávez's presidencies fascinated and amused external observers. But the consequence in half-completed projects, disinformation, sheer inefficiency and above all corruption is only now coming to light to its full extent. The very foundation of the Chavista project, the deployment of oil wealth for the general good, is now systematically undermined. Barrio Adentro, the iconic Mission run by Cuban medical personnel, has no drugs or medicines and can only offer advice. The emblematic Gran Misión Vivienda, building social housing, is regularly presented as the shining example of Chavista success. Every Thursday, Maduro appears on television, delivering houses somewhere in the country and throwing out figures in the hundreds of thousands – but the reality, again, is very different from the extravagant claims made for the programme. In fact, house building fell by 66 per cent between the same period in 2013 and 2014. In April 2014, Maduro announced the plan to build 220,000 houses – without mentioning that this was a reduction from the original target of 380,000. And where Chávez's vision of a social housing project included schools, sports facilities, business and community facilities, the present projects are limited to the physical buildings, many of which remain unfinished. The administration of these half-built towers has, in many cases, been left to local criminals who buy and sell 'spaces' – not rooms or flats – under the benevolent indifference of the state.

Whose Economic War?

The question is, where has the oil income gone? Why are so many projects incomplete? Where are the dollars handed out to importers for goods that plainly have not arrived? In fact, the distribution of dollars on terms too byzantine to understand has covered a large-scale flight of capital which never returned at all. Jorge Giordani, the minister of planning, recently announced that $20 billion had 'disappeared' from the Treasury in 2012 and that 40 per cent of dollar allocations in 2013 had gone to *empresas de maletín*, phantom companies created to launder money. He claimed to have a full list of them, though it has never been published. Those dollars – the official estimate is $190 billion – are presumably now nestling in bank accounts in Panama, the United States, Russia and elsewhere, and in one case, in Andorra.

The beneficiaries of this secret commerce are not just the old ruling classes, the Venezuelan capitalists who run the 35 per cent of the economy still in private hands. The new Chavista state bureaucracy running government agencies and nationalised enterprises has grown personally wealthy in the exercise of state power. Infrastructural projects, absorbing vast amounts of state funds, are delayed or abandoned unfinished. The Brazilian engineering giant Odebrecht suspended operations until the financial future of the projects is clarified,[21] though that was before the floodlights were turned on its own activities. The house-building programme financed by what is called the Chinese Fund, the fund drawing money from PDVSA and the Central Bank of Venezuela for major projects, provides no accounts. Yet the budget for materials, like cement, has been allocated and spent in each case.

How should we characterise this economy? It is clearly capitalist, as Chávez himself acknowledged, and run by a layer of bureaucrats acting in concert with private capital, or indeed as profiteers themselves. The picture internationally confirms that it is currently operating joint enterprises, especially in oil, with China, Russia, Belarus, Spain, Iran and others, none of whom have any interest in altruism or building a socialist economy.

The economic project articulated by Chávez and Ramirez, and repeated by government spokespeople as a mantra, has gone into reverse. The state, which Chávez wanted 'pulverised', has grown in size and penetration and has accrued to itself greater and greater powers – from oil to communications, from currency agency to direct importer. It has also expanded from 16 to 32 ministries and quadrupled the number of vice-ministers, providing opportunities for the kind of nepotism[22] that was the defining feature of the Fourth Republic which preceded Chávez. The Missions, meanwhile, and the direct democracy they were to represent, have withered on the vine. They exist, and Maduro announced in

2016 that more would be created and all placed under the control of a single new ministry. Like the *consejos comunales* and the *comunas*, they are administrative arms of the state with neither autonomy nor political or economic independence.

The important thing is to understand the global picture. Two explanations for the situation have been offered by Madurismo and its supporters around the world. The first is to attribute the crisis to the fall in the price of oil. The first thing is that the Chávez government's budgets were based on an assumption of a price of $60 a barrel, yet through the decade 2003–13, the price reached peaks of well over $100 and held generally at prices close to that. On that basis the reserves should have been more than sufficient to ride the crisis, if it was simply a temporary fall. In fact, as Edgardo Lander argued in an important article in 2016,[23] the price fall is a sign of deeper and more enduring changes.

> Technological transformations permit the extraction of oil from the depths of the Arctic, from the pre-sal in Brazil, from the Canadian tar sands, fracking not only in United States but in other countries as well. All this means that today there is an overabundance of oil and that's not going to change.

In addition there is now increasing investment in alternative fuels, like ethanol, and alternative sources of energy, gas principal among them. As we have seen, there was no strategy for addressing this widely-predicted change. In fact the overspending of oil revenues left the economy with virtually no reserves and an astronomical level of debt when the crisis began. If there had been any serious commitment to 'pulverizing the bourgeoisie' – in other words, to ending its economic system, capitalism – ending the extractive economy and the dependence on it would have been a first priority. Instead, as we have shown, the reverse happened. Alternative economic sectors collapsed through lack of investment, and the Chavista leadership, while proclaiming the imminence of twenty-first century socialism, participated in the speculative frenzy draining the national economy to enrich themselves.

The most powerful and disturbing evidence of the absence of any thought of an alternative to capitalism in Chavista thinking was the announcement by Maduro of the commitment to the Arco Minero project. The second explanation was the endlessly repeated denunciation of an 'economic war' (*la guerra económica*). It was never clear who was mounting that war. For an anti-imperialist, the hostility of the United States to what was happening in Venezuela was obvious. If it was a reference to the Venezuelan bourgeoisie, they had opposed and set out to undermine the Bolivarian revolution from the very first moment, consistently with their class interests. Yet there was no consistent action taken against them – expropriation was trumpeted but carried out partially and unevenly, and compensation was paid. Capital flight was a devastating drain on the Venezuelan economy, particularly after the failure of the bosses' strike – yet no measures were taken from the state to stop it. On the contrary, it was permitted through the exchange system. And after the 2014 disturbances, Maduro worked closely with bourgeois elements. Even in 2017–18, as the crisis reached unexpected depths, the state was providing liberal credit and loans to private capital, directly through the state bank and indirectly through the extremely favourable conditions it was offering multinational corporations in the Arco Minero. In 2013, Tarek El Assaimi, a member of the Cabinet responsible for the economy, announced that it would devote one-third of the national budget to the private sector in credits. His announcement was preceded by a $9 million loan to Nestle and $4 million to Santa Teresa Rum.[24] At the same time, poor Venezuelans were fighting over scraps in rubbish tips and looting supermarkets across the country with increasing regularity.

The Elections of 2015

On 3 December 2015, elections to the National Assembly produced a surprise result. The right-wing coalition won a two thirds majority of seats, which would have given them the power to block presidential decisions and the passage of laws. The Electoral Commission conveniently discovered questionable practice in five local elections, which brought the result below the two-thirds line. According to Julia Buxton

> In regions like Bolivar, Miranda and Caracas, the popular classes defected in large numbers to MUD, while the rural poor in areas like Guárico and Yaracuy remained loyal to the PSUV.[25]

In fact the election result was not a sign of any mass defection to the parties of the right; it was, rather, the expression of the deep discontent of parts of the mass base of Chavismo, 2 million of whom abstained.

Their disillusionment, however, was not addressed or acknowledged. Instead, politics became a battle between the Assembly and the presidency for control of power. Maduro immediately used his exceptional powers (the *leyes habilitantes* or enabling laws) to transfer power to the presidency. The opposition, for its part, also ignored the message sent by the voters and offered no proposals to address the urgent problems of scarcity, failed services, and a proliferating criminality and insecurity. They concentrated on the only issues that concerned them, then as now, the removal of Maduro and the release of those people arrested as a result of the violent street barricades of 2013. Their policy was always the return of power to those who had historically exercised it in the 40 years before Chávez, through the puntofijista pact. The fate and condition of Venezuela's poor and working class population was of little interest to them, nor had it ever been. But it is important to acknowledge that the opposition to Chavismo was not limited to the bourgeoisie. The middle and lower middle class were the bedrock of the opposition, though not its leadership. And they formed a high proportion of the student population who were the activists of the opposition.

The decision on the Arco Minero was definitive in several ways. The area represents 12 per cent of the national territory and holds a cornucopia of minerals, oil, and gas. Additionally, it is the country's principal source of fresh water. Chávez had rejected a development proposal some years earlier on environmental grounds, and in recognition of indigenous communities' human and territorial rights.

Maduro's announcement presented the return of the multinationals to the exploitation of Venezuela's mineral resources as a solution to the country's depleted reserves and declining GDP. In a sense he was right – but it was the nakedly, unmistakably neo-liberal solution, the return to a neo-colonial arrangement and the definitive abandonment of both sovereignty and developmentalism. It was, as one writer called it,[26] not simply 'accumulation by dispossession' but 'colonisation by invitation'. The creation of an autonomous, military-run private corporation, Cominpeg to oversee the exploitation of the region, reinforced the continuing state of emergency which suspended constitutional rights and militarised the region; the circle closed. Since it is an autonomous corporation, Cominpeg will not submit its activities for public scrutiny. Chávez's concern for the local communities, some 150 of them, was simply forgotten, and the eviction of some of the mining camps and villages began almost immediately.

Maduro invited 150 multinationals – from the United States, China, Russia, Belarus – to bid for concessions. And 'concessions' was the appropriate term. He made the first offer to Barrick, the giant Canadian gold-mining concern that had been excluded from Venezuela a decade earlier. After Chávez nationalised the mines, the company demanded hundreds of millions of dollars in compensation payments. As a gesture of his good faith, Maduro has agreed to pay this debt as well as offer a ten-year tax holiday and develop the regional infrastructure at the state's expense.

The environmental consequences of opening the region to the rapacious mining industry are there to be seen across the Amazon Basin – populations displaced, land and rivers poisoned, fragile rain forest and mountain ecologies destroyed.

The military thus become a uniformed sector of the ruling state bourgeoisie, with both political control and a central economic role. Half of the ministers and over half of the state governors are military, and hold powerful posts in the key sectors of finance, infrastructure and internal security. This bears no resemblance to Chávez's notion of a civil-military alliance in which the military would serve the interests of the majority. Rather, Maduro has turned to the military in hopes of protecting his power. The PSUV reinforces that role, especially since the creation of the 'Patriotic Card', without which there is no access to state benefits.

All that remained was for Maduro to legitimise what is by any standards an authoritarian state. The tame Electoral Commission threatened to dissolve the National Assembly, leaving only presidential rule by decree, until Luisa Ortega, who had been Chávez's attorney general, denounced the attempt. In its place, Maduro called a Constituent Assembly under strict conditions of control. Five million voters were excluded from electing delegates, and there was no preceding referendum. The representation in the meeting was skewed towards the rural where Chavismo had the advantage in earlier elections.

The gubernatorial elections in late 2017, postponed from a year earlier and then called at very little notice, produced a majority vote for Chavistas. Steve Ellner expressed surprise at how high the vote was, omitting the fact that something like 5 million voters from 2015 did not cast a ballot two years later. It goes without saying that every proposal at the Assembly was passed by acclaim. The new Anti-Hate Law allowed the arrest of mass leaders (250 of them) and the persecution of dissent. Most disturbingly of all, the government-supported armed gangs; the Peoples Liberation Organisations (OLPs) were given free rein in the *barrios*, leaving between 500 and 1000 dead.[27] In July 2017, there was a wave of insubordination in the military barracks and hundreds were arrested. In 2018, before a dutifully cheering, hand-picked crowd, Maduro was elected to the presidency, as was to be expected.

Maduro has his defenders, internally and externally, though after the elections some cautious, measured criticisms were made by insiders. Their call for reform, however, has no bearing on the march to socialism that, according to Ellner, Maduro is embarked on. Participatory democracy remains only as a grotesque parody, the consent that even bourgeois democracy requires at some level is the silent consent of a hungry, terrorised, but ferociously angry population. Most importantly, Maduro's first post-electoral response was to invite the bourgeoisie and the business sector to a dialogue. No invitation was issued to the grass roots organisations, the community councils, the trade unions, or others – they had already been captured, co-opted, and silenced. The new bureaucracy in the state, uniformed and otherwise, may well be negotiating already with the institutions of global capital as well as the multinational corporations. They are, after all, travelling the same road now.

Roland Denis has been a revolutionary activist all his life, an uncompromising defender of a democracy based on the self-emancipation of working people. He is a fierce critic of the direction that Chavismo has taken, outspoken in his views, and fearless in articulating them. It seems appropriate to end the chapter with an extract from an extremely controversial article he published on the main critical Chavista website, apporea.org in 2015, entitled *Goodbye to chavismo*:

> Saying 'goodbye to chavismo' is saying goodbye to an extraordinary dream that has turned into a nightmare before our eyes, into a kind of curse for which every revolutionary tendency proposes a solution at least once a day. Some are more principled, others more pragmatic, others have the courage to distance themselves from the official political command structure. And yet day by day this situation becomes more senseless, because Chavismo lost its meaning as it became pointless to suggest solutions when its essence had been consumed by the gangsterism that governs the government, controls its base, and the massive pillage that it has allowed.[28]

6
On the Margins of the Pink Tide: Mexico, Brazil, Argentina

Mexico

Poor Mexico. 'So far from God and so close to the United States.'
(Porfirio Diaz)

Despite the key role that the Zapatista rising had in the emergence of the new social movements in Latin America and the beginnings of the pink tide, Mexico has continued to be 'too close to the United States'. The launch of the neo-liberalisation of Latin America was briefly interrupted by the Zapatistas in 1994, whose rising was timed to coincide with the official announcement of NAFTA. But Mexico was already on the way towards integration into the global market well before 1 January 1994. Its financial markets, for example, had been globalised a year earlier as part of the general abandonment of state subsidies and protections in conformity with the conditions imposed by the WTO. From the perspective of 2016, James Petras summed up Mexico's role in the neo liberal order:

> Mexico is the most favored imperial client in both foreign and economic policy. It supports NAFTA (integration with the U.S.); its security forces are subject to U.S. oversight; it has the lowest minimum wage in Latin America (even below Honduras); it is privatizing the strategic petrol sector firm PEMEX; it is a major 'labor reserve' for cheap manufacturing workers (especially in the auto industry); it has the lowest effective tax rate; it has joined the U.S. war on drugs and war on terror by militarizing its domestic society. Few countries in Latin America can match Mexico's submission to Washington and few regimes would want to!

The 'perfect dictatorship' of the Institutional Revolutionary Party (PRI), with its pervasive machinery of patronage, lasted effectively from 1926 to 2000. It employed a discourse of revolutionary nationalism which celebrated Zapata among others, though the organisations that bore Zapata's name had been systematically repressed. But in 1968 a mass student-worker rebellion challenged the perfect machine on the eve of the Olympic Games, mobilising hundreds of thousands in mass protests and demonstrations. On 3rd October that year, a mass meeting of students in the historic Three Cultures Square (Tlatelolco) in the city was raked with gunfire from surrounding buildings and army helicopters. 500 were killed, though the government denied it, and repression intensified as the Olympic Games unfolded.

The left radicalism of the movement expressed a resurgence of socialist ideas throughout the decade, and 1968 and Tlatelolco remain the touchstone of critiques of the PRI's institutional dictatorship. In June 1971, a new student movement arose, this time during the presidency of Luis Echeverria. He had been minister of the interior in 1968 and almost certainly gave the order for the massacre. Troops again confronted demonstrators in 1971. Yet at the same time Echeverria was presenting himself as a radical Third Worldist. He and all the presidents who followed were the beneficiaries of a controlled and corrupt political system, where electoral participation depended on both subsidies and approval from the PRI-controlled state. As a result the left was divided, all the more so since the strength of regional interests traversed the national political system. There were regular rumours of an internal left opposition in the PRI, and regular disappearances of their leaders. But in the late 1980s a new current emerged under the leadership of Cuauhtémoc Cárdenas, the son of the president who had nationalised Mexican oil and who was revered in Mexico as a symbol of revolutionary nationalism. Lázaro Cárdenas had also during his presidency (1934–40) distributed more land to the peasantry than any other president. At the same time it was Cárdenas who perfected the model of an integrated state machine that absorbed workers, peasants and the popular sectors into the party apparatus. It was under his successor, Manuel Avila Camacho, that Mexico moved in a more conservative direction and towards reconciliation with its northern neighbour. Cuauhtémoc split from the PRI to form the PRD, the Revolutionary Democratic Party, in 1988, in response to rising tensions in Mexican society around neo-liberalism and attacks on the standard of living of the majority. Cárdenas's strength lay in being seen as the inheritor of his father's revolutionary nationalism, so deeply embedded in the national imaginary. And for the first time, a leading politician stood on an openly reformist platform and exposed the reactionary plans of both the PRI and the PAN. But the PRI continued to manipulate the electoral system to ensure its permanence in power.[1]

In 2000, Vicente Fox of the right-wing Catholic Action Party (PAN) won the presidency on a platform of intensified neo-liberal measures. There was widespread movement of resistance, which created an expectation before the 2006 presidential vote, despite a series of changes in electoral law pushed through to favour the candidate of the PRI and the PAN. The favoured candidate of the movements was Andrés Manuel López Obrador, ex-Mayor of Mexico City (sometimes seen as the second most powerful post in the country after the presidency) and the candidate of the PRD whose recent internal battles had produced a left majority in its leadership. Obrador was a hard-working candidate, and he spoke a populist language; his campaign, he said, represented a 'coalition for the common good, but especially for the good of the poor', against the background of a society increasingly committed to neo-liberalism, riven with corruption, and becoming more militarised (Mexico had previously taken pride in the non-political nature of its armed forces).

When the 2006 result was announced and the lacklustre Felipe Calderón was declared the victor, the capital erupted. Obrador had identified himself with the social movements and won 35.31 per cent of the vote, losing by 0.58 per cent. He refused to accept the result, remembering, perhaps, the 1988 presidential election when the electricity supply in Mexico City failed and there were widespread allegations that this was what gave victory to Carlos Salinas de Gortari over Cuauhtemoc Cardenas.[2] Hundreds of thousands from across the country rejected the result and set up a massive tent city along Mexico City's principal city centre avenue, Reforma, in protest against electoral fraud. This was a social movement, and it reflected the new level of militancy exemplified by the 2006 rising in the southern city of Oaxaca.[3]

The city of Oaxaca had been the scene of mass demonstrations by the powerful teachers union, SNTE, for over 20 years, over wages and conditions, and specifically over the provision of original language tuition for the three and a half million indigenous people of the state of Oaxaca. Forty thousand teachers gathered in 2006, as they did every year, in the city's central square, the Zócalo. They represented one additional demand this time – the destitution of the notoriously corrupt and repressive state governor, Ulises Ruiz, a member of the PRI re-elected in 2004. On 14 June the governor sent in troops to empty the square by force. Helicopters dropped teargas on the protesters while they were beaten and raped by the state police. The outrage of the local population brought 300,000 demonstrators on to the streets and out of their mobilisation there emerged a new organisation, APPO, the Popular Assembly of People's Organisations, which effectively occupied the city for six months in a cat and mouse game with police and troops.

In the end the tent city in the centre of Mexico City was removed by force, but Obrador built on the experience of his campaign to create a national electoral organisation run by local committees across the whole country. Although he saw himself as the obvious spokesperson for the social movement, Obrador was careful not to give his endorsement to the Oaxaca movement; it was perhaps too radical and too violent for his partners in his emerging political coalition. The Zapatistas, for their part, deeply suspicious as they were of the electoral process and in particular of the PRD, did not offer their support for his campaign. When, in 2001, the Zapatistas had marched to Mexico City in support of legislation to give legal recognition to indigenous communities, the PRD deputies in Congress had opposed the new laws. They had been equally slow to support the Oaxaca insurgency, for what appear to have been sectarian reasons. Marcos did not forget. And in 2009, the Mexican Supreme Court exonerated the paramilitaries who, in 1997, had murdered 45 people attending a prayer meeting in the Zapatista community of Acteal. It felt like a declaration of war and the Zapatistas began to prepare for it by emerging from their voluntary isolation and joining the public campaign against the rising levels of poverty in the country, the extent of neo-liberal privatisations, and intensifying repression.

In 2012, the PRI's Enrique Peña Nieto won the presidency, but this time there were no mass demonstrations. AMLO remained the favoured candidate of social movements, but neither Oaxaca nor APPO had been able to overcome the variety of obstacles placed in the way of building a national presence.

The Mexican state has been a faithful disciple of neo-liberal ideology and practice and has overseen with equanimity the disintegration of the social fabric and the drug-based violence that has accompanied it. The scale of privatisation in the country reflected the high degree of protectionism that had earlier allowed Mexico to grow into a major industrial nation within Latin America. The Zapatista rising, for example, revealed one aspect of the general globalisation of agriculture that emptied the countryside of much of its working population who, in common with their peers throughout the region, converged on the expanding slums and shanty towns around its cities, and especially the mega-metropolis of Mexico City with its approximately 23 million inhabitants. As globalisation encouraged and enabled the growth of the huge drug trafficking industry, Mexico became the principal route for drug distribution from Latin America to its principal market in the United States. As is always the case, this extraordinarily lucrative trade produced violent competition for markets and the concentration in fewer and fewer hands of the control of the third most lucrative area of world trade (after oil and arms) – cocaine.[4] The level of armament of the drug traders certainly surpassed the capacity of most small states, with the result that the narcotraders were able to match and even surpass the repressive machinery of the state, and in many cases to absorb its personnel into its own operations. The nationalisation of the oil industry in 1938 by President Lázaro Cárdenas was the maximum expression of national sovereignty and the foundational moment in the creation of the machinery of state power in Mexico. In 2014, the Congress finally enacted President Peña Nieto's Energy Reform Bill privatising the national oil company Pemex an equally significant symbolic act of de-nationalisation and privatisation. Polls during the previous year had shown 65 per cent of Mexicans to be opposed to privatisation.

The victims of these neo-liberal measures, in Mexico as elsewhere, were the poorer sectors – the workers who lost jobs, the peasant farmers who lost their subsidies, the agricultural workers expelled to the city slums or later to seek work across the Rio Grande, whose children Donald Trump now refuses to allow across the border. At the same time the number of billionaires in Mexico rose from four to 16 with a combined wealth of $141 billion according to *Forbes* magazine. They include the world's richest man, Carlos Slim.

Despite the violence and repression deployed by state and traffickers, sometimes in combination, across the country, the traditions of struggle survived in many places. The struggle in Chiapas encouraged indigenous communities to fight back, though the withdrawal into the *caracoles* created some confusion. The Zapatistas' critique of the systemic corruption of Mexican politics and politicians found widespread resonance, but the withdrawal from that politics spurned an important opportunity and encouraged a politics of autonomism which left the state untouched by the mass mobilisations.

In 2012, Obrador had contained his reactions to the electoral loss. Looking back, it seems that he was preparing his candidacy for 2018, building coalitions with elements of the political elite, seeking allies among the mega-rich (he met with Carlos Slim and his Billionaires Club) and widening the base of his campaign to include elements of the right in his new coalition, Morena (the National Renewal Movement). He led all the polls for the last year of the campaign by a clear margin. He faced three opponents; Meade for the PRI, Rodolfo Anaya for the PAN but supported by the PRD, and despite their abstentionist stand, Marichuy for the Zapatistas. Their confused position illustrates one of the contradictions of autonomism. Elections in a bourgeois society are central political events, an opportunity to make political propaganda in front of a wider audience than normal; they also provide an opportunity to test and develop political arguments. This is not the same thing as electoralism in which the pursuit of power within the state shapes and defines the global political vision. The revolutionary left, in the main, argued for a vote for the EZLN candidate, Marichuy, as part of the process of preparing opposition to an Obrador government which has already made clear it will continue the neo-liberal strategy. In fact the EZLN, while it called for abstention in the elections, ran a campaign with an excellent candidate – though in the end the difficulties of collecting 15,000 individual signatures across the country proved too difficult and she didn't present her candidacy. Unlike the others she did not have the party machine behind her that could fulfil all the institutional requirements.

Obrador's reputation went before him and newspaper reports across the border very quickly began to draw comparisons with Chávez, though they are very different personalities. The comparison was made to imply that Obrador was a dangerous radical who would introduce anti-neo-liberal measures into the most solidly neo-liberal economy in the region. The word 'expropriation' began to circulate, together with the menacing thought that he would mobilise the poor, the 50 per cent of the country for whom neo-liberalism had meant poverty, unemployment, destitution – and this in the country that contained the world's richest man and some 40 others who figured in the same general league.

On 1 July 2018 the campaign culminated with the election of Obrador with an unprecedented 53 per cent of the popular vote. Though he was originally a political insider he now stood outside the 'perfect dictatorship' (as the writer Mario Vargas Llosa had once described it) of the PRI – perfect because it controlled the machinery of political power at every level for 70 years, a new president would be elected every six years and every level of bureaucracy filled with his supporters. There had been occasional critical and dissident voices inside the PRI over the years, but they rarely survived very long. Obrador, however, stepped outside that arena, criticised the political and economic system fiercely and built on the reputation he had gained twelve years earlier as an honest politician with the 'public good' at heart. It would be hard to overestimate the level of public expectation his campaign generated, and the elation his clear election victory has produced.

Mexican politics has always been characterised by back door deals and corruption. It was well known that more than a year before every presidential campaign, negotiations over who would be the candidate had been completed among the system's power brokers – for many years the main one was the head of the Mexican Trade Union Confederation, Fidel Velázquez. That person, still unnamed, would be known as *el verdadero tapado* (the authentic concealed one). Their identity would then be revealed, to pre-rehearsed acclaim, by Velázquez at the annual Trades Union Congress. Until Fox, the PRI candidate would always win, and on the one occasion when that was in doubt, the country's lights went out for 24 hours.

Obrador has set himself against that tradition, arguing that Mexico's central problem is the endemic corruption whose costs, he says, would be sufficient to fully restore public sector spending. The pervasive violence throughout Mexican society is the second issue on the lips of most Mexicans. As Mayor of Mexico City, Obrador achieved a decline in levels of violent crime and he is reputed to have cleaned up the notoriously corrupt Mexico City police force. But again his response to the problem has been unusual in insisting that it is material poverty that is the ultimate cause of the drug problem and that it must be addressed there.

During the campaign, Obrador called Donald Trump 'erratic' (an understatement by any standards) and immediately before the voting began Trump announced that he was going to delay the endorsement of NAFTA, the neo-liberal regional trade agreement into which Mexico has been fully integrated since 1994. Yet it appears that Trump and Obrador had a friendly conversation lasting half an hour as soon as the result was known, in which they discussed the issue of Mexican emigration.

In itself that would qualify as diplomacy. But it appears that Obrador's journey to the presidential residence at Los Pinos has not been without deals and negotiations on the way. The author of his political programme, his Plan for the Nation, is Afonso Romo, director of a large corporation producing GM seeds which was recently bought by Monsanto. A millionaire businessman, Romo will be Obrador's chef de cabinet – his closest advisor. And he is not the only millionaire in Obrador's circle. His cabinet team includes two ex-presidents of the PAN, the right-wing Catholic party of Fox and Calderón. Among his first announcements were the assurance that there would be no expropriations and the fact that he would not be renationalising Pemex, the national oil company. The symbolic significance of that statement is profound, since the 1938 nationalisation of oil was the most emblematic act of national sovereignty. The explanation for AMLO's caution may lie here, in this comment from an article on his election victory in the web page of the Atlantic Council:

> The 2013 energy reforms are rooted in the constitution and supported by implementing laws passed by Mexico's Congress. These reforms cannot be changed by the executive alone. The president-elect has already said he will respect existing contracts. The build-out of the national gas pipeline system and national grid are projects undertaken by national regulators. The estimated $200 billion in new foreign investment in Mexico, new production coming online in ninety awarded blocks among sixty-eight operators, the opening of more than 1,700 gas stations by thirty new private operators, and the development of an unbundled, competitive retail power market will continue unabated.[5]

Ramon Centeno[6] traces a rightward trajectory over the years away from Obrador's slogan of twelve years earlier 'for the common good, but firstly for the good of the poor'. His current election propaganda has laid great emphasis on national unity. According to Massimo Modonesi:

> ...within the(Morena) party the political practices are still marked by personalism (caudillismo) and centralisation, a lack of open debate or participation. Party loyalty dominates, making it difficult to form non-instrumental alliances or approaches with organised and mobilised sectors of civil society.[7]

In a television interview, Obrador maintained that in Mexico, inequality is the result of corruption, not of the exploitation of the workers by the propertied classes. Thus the main emphasis of his campaign has been on 'honesty', which does have some resonance in a country of spectacularly crooked politics. It is to be hoped that this promised transparency will unmask all those responsible for the appalling murders of 46 young students in Guerrero, as one example among many. But it offers no solution to the yawning inequality in the country, and does not address neo-liberalism nor offer an alternative future. Mexico has confounded predictions many times, but in this case Obrador was unstoppable. He has a level of support which will enable him, in a country where the president has the widest of powers, to act decisively in key areas. Chávez's original programme, like Obrador's, reaffirmed liberal values, anti-corruption and social justice for the poor. Obrador's programme goes no further, but what the two men certainly share is their open hostility to the corrupt ruling bureaucracy embodied in the ruling party (the PRI in Mexico, Acción Democrática in Venezuela) to which Obrador (unlike Chávez) belonged for many years. Had his victory been conceded in 2006, it is likely that he would have taken a more radical direction. He was at the height of his reputation as an independent critic of the Mexican political system, he was advocating more radical welfare policies, and there were tens of thousands mobilised behind his campaign. It was also the year that the year-long occupation of Oaxaca by APPO and the popular movement began, in the final stages of his presidential campaign. In 2018, his campaign represented a coalition across the political spectrum, and did not have any supporting mass mobilisation behind it beyond the packed election rallies. It remains to be seen whether Obrador will represent a new pink tide. As things look in the latter half of 2018, Massimo Modonesi, the respected Mexican commentator, sees the dangers clearly but is encouraged by the emphasis that Obrador has placed on 'honesty' and by the first defeat of the right in many years, or perhaps ever.[8] Obrador's main promise is for an ethical transformation of Mexican politics; economically he is, says Modonesi, two steps behind the left governments of Latin America, which as we have seen here, does not leaves much room for an anti neo-liberal position. Perhaps Obrador's first task will be pacification, an end to the endemic violence Mexico has lived through in recent years; next to develop the productive economy to slow the haemorrhage of Mexicans across the northern border. Yet for all that, he seems more in tune with the pragmatism that has overtaken the pink tide than with its emancipatory origins; only time will tell.

Brazil

'Fifa go home.' (Street banner in Rio)

In many ways it is Brazil's extraordinary Movimento Sem Terra – the Landless Workers Movement – that deserves recognition as the progenitor of the social movements of the pink tide era. It was formally established in 1984 at Cascavel in Paraná state, just as the military regime ended. But its activities began four years earlier, when 6000 landless families occupied land directly in the southern state of Rio Grande do Sul. Some had been evicted from their homes to allow the construction of a dam – and they would be the first of many; others were members of indigenous groups removed from their homes in the Kaingang Indian reservation by the state Indian agency Funai. What was most innovative and dramatic about the organisation was its method; families would be mobilised to occupy unused land under a constitutional provision that permitted occupation in those circumstances. At that point, in 1980, 77 per cent of Brazil's lands were in the hands of landowners with huge estates at their disposal – and they employed armed thugs to evict or prevent the occupations. The families were the poorest in Brazil, who literally had nothing to bring but the black plastic bags in which they slept. While today the organisation has 1.5 million members and settlements across the whole vast land surface of Brazil, their militancy and courage has never diminished, though the quality of their work has developed impressively. MST leaders and participants are trained and educated at the MST's own university.

The struggle for land by landless peasants and workers has been central to Brazil's political history since the Ligas Camponensas of the 1930s, whose tactics were in some sense a model for the MST, onwards.[9] What is different today is their ideological formation. The Ligas were led and shaped by the communist party; the foundations of the MST, by contrast, are an amalgam of Marxism and liberation theology. Joao Stédile, a Marxist economist, was one of its founders as well as an organiser of the international Via Campesina organisation. MST's first occupations were met with ruthless military blockades and paramilitary violence, but the movement eventually won many of its demands, though always in the face of paramilitary violence.

The founding of the MST shared its moment with an emerging resistance movement between 1978 and 1980 against the military government, beginning with strikes in the auto plants of the ABC region of Sao Paulo province, in defiance of the military regime and its corporate trade unions. The activities of the ABC coincided with an Amnesty Law that allowed the return of many political exiles. Both the Workers Party (PT) and the MST were influenced by liberation theology, which had opposed the military regime and which, furthermore, actively supported the land reform movement, arguing that it was morally reprehensible that some should own such vast tracts of rural property while others were without land, and that the occupations were therefore justified. In this atmosphere the PT was formed in 1980. It was an extraordinary organisation that from its outset rejected Stalinism and the communist tradition for a more open and democratic interpretation of socialism. Its ranks included Marxists of many stripes, Trotskyists, as well as radical artists and educators and liberation theologians. It stood against the current, but it represented a far more open and democratic understanding of Marxism:

> Party leaders were forced to listen to branch activists in plenary meetings and votes, receive their numerous bulletins, flyers, pamphlets, and complaints, and court their support for internal and external electoral campaigns. It was this grass roots base that sustained the PT as a party of struggle in its first decade.[10]

But by the 1990s, its original radical critique of capitalism was shifting towards reformism and the pursuit of influence in the institutions. It still supported the MST – it had, after all, emerged from the same soil, and shared the PT's original broad tolerance of different critical currents. But it was from the outset, and remains, a one-issue campaign devoted to the recuperation of land for the landless by direct actions determined by the landless themselves. It had no truck with the main organisations that claimed to represent the interests of peasants and agricultural workers through legal channels – which were by and large controlled by the landowners or their satraps. The MST's actions always included the families of workers and their actions were characterised by the key role that women played, as activists and leaders of the movement. It has remained a democratic, grass roots movement, accountable to its base. In this sense it clearly anticipated the new social movements. It did so in another sense as well; based on bitter experience it insisted on the organisation's independence from politicians and political parties. But the PT had moved away from those ideas and was now operating as a political party within the political system – and very successfully so. In 1988 it won 38 mayoral elections and placed hundreds of city councillors. It thus became a party of professionals, shaped by the culture of deals and alliances and increasingly distanced from its political origins. It still denounced neo-liberalism but held back from involvement in the MST's mobilisations, concentrating on parliamentary and electoral politics.

Luiz Inacio Lula da Silva was born in 1945 in the state of Pernambuco, before moving to Sao Paulo with his mother and seven siblings when she decided to seek out his long absent father. The reconciliation failed and his mother and her children moved into a small room behind a bar in Sao Paulo where Lula was brought up. He had little formal education and went to work in a car parts factory, becoming an official of the local trade union and eventually president of the Steel Workers Union of the industrial towns of Sao Bernardo and Diadema. In 1980 he was a founder member of the PT.

Lula was and is a hugely popular figure, widely known because he was the PT's candidate in all presidential elections from 1989 onwards. His background, like Chávez's, was a key factor in his popularity; his life mirrored the experience of the majority of Brazilians, and his confrontations with the military regime reinforced that reputation. He brought together an experience of workers organisation with the new politics of the PT. The MST, whose growth ran parallel to the PT's, and with which it shared many ideas, focussed singlemindedly on the land and the landless, with a discourse that emphasised questions of ethics and social justice.

With that background, it might have been a reasonable assumption that Brazil would figure among the pink tide governments. And the ideas and methods of the MST certainly extended into new directions as neo-liberalism began to dominate through the 1990s. An urban movement of the homeless, the Movimento Sem Teijo – the Homeless – emerged through the late 1990s. And other social movements and NGOs took their ideology and their methods of democratic grass roots organising from the MST. Lula, meanwhile, stood as the PT's candidate in elections in 1994 and 1998 on a platform emphasising his opposition to the payment of the foreign debt. He was defeated in both by the candidate of the PSDB, the Democratic Party, the influential ex-Marxist intellectual, political economist and ex-minister of finance in 1993–4, Fernando Henrique Cardoso. Cardoso imposed a ferocious neo-liberal strategy, privatising state-owned enterprises in steel, mining and telecommunications and opening Indian reservations to claims of ownership by big landowners. He was an advocate and defender of neo-liberal strategies which resulted, in Brazil as elsewhere, in widening the income gap, deepening inequality, and turning against the analysis for which he was known – dependency theory – which argued that countries in the underdeveloped world were held in that situation in permanent subordination to the interests of the developed world. As president he reversed his position. It was widely anticipated that Lula would, in turn, reverse his policies and set in motion policies of redistribution.

But Lula had changed in the interim. He had distanced himself from the PT, and in 2002 stood in his own name. His election propaganda, as I saw at the Porto Alegre World Social Forum, made no mention of his membership of the PT, nor indeed of the policies he would undertake to implement. The poster simply showed his face and his name; it also showed that he had changed his appearance and image. His casual clothes and big beard were gone. His beard was trimmed and he wore a suit. In terms of his relationship and representation of Brazil's poor this was very significant and so too was the absence of any reference to the PT and the emphasis on his personal story, his childhood in poverty, his lack of education.

The decision had been made, by him or his advisers, that his campaign would be personalist and in some sense non-political. His 'Letter to the Brazilians' published on the eve of the elections was profoundly disappointing for the PT and its supporters. It made explicit Lula's intentions to continue with Cardoso's policies in order to maintain stability.

When I saw him arrive at the World Social Forum in Porto Alegre in early 2003, the elation with which he was received by working people was boundless. To the crowds in the streets who simply shouted his name repeatedly, he was the Lula of the previous decade, the worker candidate who understood their needs and represented them. The day after his appearance at the Forum, the newspapers published photographs of his arrival at Davos where he was to attend the World Economic Forum with the power elite of global capitalism. The crowds still identified him at that point with the PT and his own past as a trade union activist (he was in fact a union official). They still do. The anti-poverty programmes he announced as president – Fome Zero (Zero Hunger) and Bolsa de Familia (Family Basket) were cash transfer programmes directed at the poorest part of Brazil's population. The programmes were perfectly compatible with neo-liberalism – after all, Cardoso had launched similar programmes during his second administration; the programmes represented no structural changes at all. They were directed at individual families rather than creating general improvements in living standards, which might have had the additional effect of raising the level of confidence of the poor and the working class as whole. Instead each family became an individual consumer, while on the other hand capitalists were promised access to state credits and liberal tax concessions. An early dispute brought him into conflict with civil servants over their pensions; they had been promised an increase before the election but Lula refused to accept it as president. It was a limited dispute, but indicative of what was to come. And despite the PT's close association with the MST, it did not support the land occupations, which were mainly directed at the landowning class who the PT were courting from government. The reality was that they did not have a parliamentary majority and formed alliances with liberals and conservatives to the right of them to construct one. The parliamentary arithmetic inhibited any move to structural change. On the contrary:

> ...the MST argued that such programs did not address the underlying socio-economic problems and only dulled the poor's political consciousness and made them less likely to join those demanding fundamental change.[11]

The MST was also increasingly involved in invasions of farms using GM crops, as were Via Campesina, with which they were closely associated. Lula's close relations with agro-exporters explains his poor record then, and later, on environmental issues, despite the presence in his government of Marina Silva as his minister of the environment.[12] There were other clear signs of the direction that Lula's government was taking. The decision to send troops to the UN Peacekeeping Mission in Haiti, which was widely viewed in Latin America as a U.S. military occupation, was extremely unpopular. Lula was careful after that not to enter too fully into relations with the United States. But his political orientation was clear. And in 2005, the *mensalao* (monthly pay) scandal exposed regular payments made to members of all parties by the PT to guarantee their votes. The scheme was controlled by José Dirceu, Lula's chief of staff and other important PT officials were also involved.

Brazilian politics had always been notoriously corrupt, but it was part of the PT's appeal that its members did not come from the middle classes as most politicians had in the past, and that was reinforced by the party's emphasis on honesty and ethics. The MST had maintained its distance from the PT, though its members undoubtedly voted for Lula and would again. But the issue of ethical conduct was central to the culture of the organisation and their suspicions deepened. Standing again in 2006, amid a profound internal crisis in the PT, Lula introduced more redistributive policies, though Webber suggests that this was 'out of political necessity'[13] to hold on to power. The measures were cash transfer schemes to the poor and some job creation programmes, though these were largely unskilled and low paid. But Lula's allegiance to big business was unaffected, and he actively supported the agro-export industry producing soy and maize for ethanol. Infrastructural investment was neglected, which would show in subsequent crises over water distribution and highway construction. The economic model as a whole produced high annual GDP growth rates of around 10 per cent until 2010, but this reflected an increasing proportion of primary products in exports – oil and minerals together with soy and ethanol – and a declining share of manufacturing – which fell from 55 per cent to 44 per cent of export earnings.

The tide turned dramatically in 2011, when growth fell to 2.1 per cent. Lula's term had ended and his hand-picked candidate, his chief of staff, Dilma Rousseff, was duly elected on 1 January 2011. Her campaign was attended by an international list of celebrities and supported by a coalition of nine parties. Her background as a guerrilla in the VAR Palmares organisation, and her subsequent torture and imprisonment, gave her credibility. But she continued the policies that Lula had promoted, giving incentives to commodity corporations and agro-industrial companies. The fall in the price of all commodities – iron ore, soy, oil, and ethanol – as a consequence of the financial crisis and the Chinese slowdown, sparked a crisis. Dilma's response was to accept all neo-liberal measures. The level of production in manufacturing did not rise but the profits of the major banks did increase. And the spectre of corruption was already waiting in the wings. A new corruption scandal relating to the state oil company Petrobras erupted and, as we now know, the Brazilian company Odebrecht was paying millions in bribes in return for massive infrastructure projects, like the huge Belo Monte dam in the Xingu, which served the interests of Brazilian and multinational corporations at the expense of the local Kayapo population.

By 2013 new movements were emerging, like the Movimento Passe Livre, arguing for free public transport in Sao Paolo. The MPL proved to be the sign of what amounted to an urban rebellion against corruption, shortages and the impact of decreased public spending in favour of consumer credit on a massive scale (when the fall in commodity prices meant lower revenues from primary production). The massive street demonstrations of the following year denounced the building programme for the World Cup as a white elephant bringing enormous profits to construction companies, banks and foreign lenders – at the expense of public spending and services. The demonstrators were right. The World Cup and the Olympics were prestige projects to conceal a deep crisis in the economy. And corruption was rife, as the Petrobras revelations had shown. Dilma was not the highly skilled and credible political operator that Lula was, though he stood by her. But the poor and working class of Brazil still had a memory of what the PT was or might have been. In her 2014 campaign, Dilma drew on that tradition and presented a campaign that was militantly anti-neo liberal and committed to a kind of welfare state programme. This was her PT face, but that PT had disappeared long before, as soon as state power came within its grasp. It was a political machine for administering capitalism in crisis, not the grass roots party whose faint image could still be glimpsed in the MST – which had broken with it long before.

Jeff Webber makes the critical point that the 2013 demonstrations were multi class; on the one hand there were the protests of youth and the poor against the failure of public services and a crumbling infrastructure; on the other, mounting allegations of corruption attracted a new right. It was young, middle class, and extreme; the evangelical right were present in force. This was a new right that was emerging across Latin America with the same features. It was white, rarely older than their mid-thirties, not linked to the old militarists or the conservative Catholics. Many of them supported gender rights and same sex marriage, though the evangelicals with their extensive influence in Brazil, did not. But they were present, and political, attacking the left or their banners wherever they saw them. And students formed a significant part of their numbers, just as they had in Venezuela and the Bolivian Media Luna. This was a new right contesting the streets. The World Cup protests fanned the flames, denouncing the squandering of public finances and the extravagant waste the event brought with it. And then, in March 2016, came Lava Jato – the Car Wash as it was called – the investigation of the complex and apparently all-embracing network of corruption that penetrated every corner of the state.

The left was unable to lead the protests, because it was the left, the PT, that were accused of conspiring with Odebrecht and the other corporations brought to book in the investigation. Wealthy businessmen, finding themselves in prison, were quick to inform on others to save their skins. The corporate bourgeoisie was, of course, up to its neck in corruption. But in a strange sense it was what was expected of their class, but not of the representatives of the people. Dilma was impeached in the same year and succeeded by Michel Temer, a right-wing businessman of unequivocal far right credentials. Almost inevitably Lula was drawn in, his trips paid for by corporate capital exposed together with two houses it was claimed he had been given by Odebrecht.

In October 2016, in local elections, the PT formed coalitions with parties supporting Dilma's impeachment, and repeated the exercise for the elections of city council presidents early in 2017, supporting pro-impeachment parties in a series of sordid horse trading deals. The explanation for these events has to go beyond conspiracy theories or accusations that the right-wing and the bourgeoisie acted in ways that were entirely predictable and consistent with their class interests. It is not surprising that Temer introduced a decade-long programme of austerity. The origin of this politics lies firmly with Lula and the PT. Their popularity with the masses lasted far longer than their commitment to the masses or to a socialist transformation of Brazil. Corruption is not solely about the greed and self-interest of the individuals concerned. It is systemic. The coalition that Lula built, and which continues still between the PT and corporate capital, national and global, was achieved at a price. The rewards of power would be shared, but so too would the values and convictions of those who ruled. The organisations of the grass roots, which gave the PT its support, its votes and its reputation, were abandoned early; the glittering prizes were in the corridors of power. The persistence of that support has to do partly with the yearning for change that people invested in Lula and which he manipulated with skill. His most vocal support came from those who were smarting from their exclusion from the benefits of power. But they were already working with the far right. As Benjamin Fogel puts it:

The only way a state could be strong enough to achieve this difficult task is through forging – and maintaining – an alliance with a vibrant extraparliamentary left and a powerful union movement capable of wielding the disruptive power needed to put the fear of God in capital.[14]

Though Brazil did not participate in the pink tide, preferring to work to build its economy in the global market and compete there on terms, it is the lessons of the pink tide and its failure that will provide, not only the important weapons for the process of rebuilding, but also the understanding of how and why the process failed. There are patterns here, to be learned and avoided by future revolutionary generations.

Webber's conclusion is harsh, but accurate:

> The renowned 'realism' of the PT functioned well enough in a period of high growth and strong external drivers in the international economy, when the rich could get exponentially richer but the poor could also become less poor. Those pillars faltered in 2011, and the entire edifice has since come crashing to the ground. Political momentum has shifted to a new right-wing, antiparty populism, the PT is increasingly bereft of a social base, and the far-left and popular social movements remain fragmented and disoriented in the new terrain. In an unusually atomised field of political contestation, no alternative socio-political force is yet capable of replacing the hegemony that has slipped from the hands of the governing party.[15]

Argentina

'Que se vayan todos' – Let's get rid of them all!
(19 December 2001, Buenos Aires)

The decade that followed Carlos Menem's privatisation of most of Argentina's state-owned enterprises traced the same pattern as the rest of Latin America. The industrial heartland of the nation, Greater Buenos Aires, displayed the same landscape of abandoned factories and growing numbers of unemployed – somehow symbolised by the people wheeling supermarket trolleys around the street piled high with cardboard for recycling. The neo-liberal policies were not restricted to major cities, however, but affected every corner of this enormous country. The economic crisis deepened with the removal of public subsidies, unemployment benefit, and the dramatic decline in social services.

It was the organisations of the unemployed, the *piqueteros*, who fanned the flames of resistance. Their methods were dramatic and very public – they blocked highways and occupied public buildings demanding work or proper unemployment pay. But they had certainly learned their key lessons of organisation as trade unionists; even though their methods were now very different, outside the formal state structures, their combativity had its origins in that earlier history. Meanwhile the crisis deepened. There were regular strikes by trade unions, but the contradictions of fighting a Peronist government were divisive and debilitating. In fact, the recovery of the Argentine economy before 1998 won it praise in capitalist circles. Menem pegged the Argentine peso to the dollar, to all intents and purposes subordinating the Argentina economy to the United States, while opening it to foreign capital with low taxes and even fewer controls. Things began to go wrong in 1995, however, when the Mexican banking crisis caused panic withdrawals of foreign cash from Argentine banks, money invested in a strategy that had undermined local industry, doubled unemployment and reduced the value of Argentine wages by half. When, in May 2001, the economics minister in Fernando de la Rua's government, Domingo Cavallo, announced that cash withdrawals would be restricted to $1000, it caused a middle class riot, and a subsequent closure of the banks.[16] Much of the decade's economic growth was based on large scale borrowing, and by 2001 the government defaulted on what was the largest external debt of any country – $133 billion. The IMF held back its next loan and the situation exploded.

Que se vayan todos! was the slogan that united the wave of protests that erupted on 19 December 2001, the first day of what came to be called the *Argentinazo*. Claudio Katz, the respected economist and commentator on Argentine events described it:

> The revolutionary days of the Argentinazo mark a turning point in the history of popular rebellions, because of its extraordinary weight of numbers, the overwhelming victory over the repressive forces and the success in bringing down a government of hunger. They crowned a decade of intense preparatory struggles and they are the beginning of a new phase of more radicalized mass movements.[17]

His comments, written in the heat of the moment and of the excitement that many other commentators also expressed, prove with hindsight to have been exaggerated, The *potential* for the movement's development was huge, but its outcomes were not as Katz and others had hoped.

What distinguished the Argentinazo was the social breadth of the participants, and the creativity that the protests displayed in their methods of resistance. The first wave of protest, surprisingly perhaps, came from an enraged middle class whose bank accounts were frozen. But the impact of the banking crisis went far beyond individual account holders. In fact it is probably incorrect to describe it, as it is usually described, as a *banking* crisis. It was a financial crisis whose last act was the closure of the banks. But it had been preceded, for example, by the widespread abandonment of factories and plants whose owners had disinvested and taken their money out of the country over the years. By the time the final crisis erupted, unemployment was at 14 per cent, doubling the rates of a few years earlier. The situation in the industrial districts of the major cities was already grave. The trade union movement, which was among the strongest in Latin America, was itself affected by the huge rise in unemployment, which undermined their base. Poverty in the country – marked as those living on less than $120 a month – was at 44 per cent, in a country that, in the previous decade had been a model of successful economic growth. And as the last straw, public spending had been cut to the bone.

The first demonstrators on the 19 December converged on the Plaza de Mayo, the central square in Buenos Aires overlooked by the presidential palace, the *Casa Rosada* or Pink House. The government immediately declared a state of siege and prepared its paramilitary police for repression. But the demonstrators were not the usual suspects. The well-tried pot-banging protests emerged on the streets of Argentina in an immediate response. It was, by and large, the lower middle class who brought their pots and pans to clatter. What was bizarre was that the deployment of the repressive forces seemed to have little or no effect. It is worth recalling that this was a country that had lived through a murderous military dictatorship between 1976 and 1983 that had invested the word 'disappeared' with sinister meanings; it had murdered some 30,000 people through torture and disappearance. Although the dictatorship ended in the wake of the Falklands War, the trauma persisted through the subsequent years, as the first post-dictatorship government, under the Radical Party's Raul Alfonsin, let the torturers off the hook with his Punto Final and Due Obedience laws of the late 1980s. The symbol of those times was the Grandmothers of the Disappeared, the *Abuelas de la Plaza de Mayo*, who demonstrated every week, wearing their emblematic white headscarves and carrying photographs of their disappeared sons and daughters. They had done so in the face of violence and abuse by the state, and refused to demobilise until the guilty were brought to justice and their children – or their graves – acknowledged. In December

2001, they also joined the protests. The young men of the poor districts attended in numbers, as did the motorcyclists, the Hell's Angels of the city of Buenos Aires. The piqueteros joined a little later, although they had not, for once, initiated the actions. But what was remarkable was that the demonstrators appeared to have lost their fear of the police – it was a sign of the intensity of their anger. There was also a merging of social sectors – the young motorcyclists had become popular heroes as they risked their own lives to rescue the wounded – and 17 of them died there, as a plaque on the Avenida de Mayo commemorates today. The cry of *Que se vayan todos*, rose in a chorus of different voices; 'they' were the ministers and politicians who had lined their own pockets at the expense of the majority, who had colluded with the banks and financial agencies. Within days, four presidents had come and gone, and most of their cabinet colleagues had fled the wrath of the people. As Katz put it, they could not go for a coffee or do their shopping without being surrounded by hostile crowds.[18]

Two months later, Katz could write:

A popular rebellion now exists in the whole country. There are weekly demonstrations in the Plaza de Mayo, 'cacerolazos' (pot banging) at the doors of the banks, general assemblies in the Centenario Park, meetings in the barrios, and protests outside the courts. In the barrio meetings everything is open for discussion, from how to organize the weekly 'escrache' (besieging the homes of torturers and the military) to what to do about the foreign debt. The importance of street activities and the value of solidarity and collective action increasingly recognized. In the neighbourhoods there are people who organize discounts on electricity bills and others who organize to stop evictions or the closure of small businesses. The inter-barrio meetings are a sort of People's Parliament, attended by thousands of people who debate and discuss, vote, applaud, and reject proposals for hours at a time.[19]

These neighbourhood assemblies were open to interventions by *piqueteros* or workers on strike, but this did not mean that the organised workers or the left parties were in control. The organisations of the revolutionary left were present and active, but they did not have hegemony in any way. As one commentator, cited by Katz, put it 'the assemblies haven't been taken over (by the left), it's just that their slogans and politics are on the left.'[20] Their primary function was to resolve immediate material problems.

People with jobs were often not getting paid; the banks were closed; supplies of food were irregular. Medicines were often not reaching hospitals; food supplies weren't reaching the city. And there was no actual cash, so a variety of voucher systems and local currencies – the best known were the *patacones* – were created. Abandoned factories were taken back by their workers, who coordinated through the Recovered Factories movement.[21] And the *piqueteros* continued and expanded their activities.

There was no doubt that all these activities, and particularly the *asambleas populares* or neighbourhood assemblies, were expressions of social solidarity as well as an immensely creative solution to an immediate emergency situation. Historically, they have arisen before – wherever a power vacuum, however temporary, has allowed long standing traditions of community self-help and solidarity to re-emerge. Strikes and occupations of any length invariably generate community support and imaginative ways of addressing the material, social and psychological problems that arise. This is not to downplay this impressive and resolute movement. At the same time, however, they were redefined as 'autonomous' movements, with the implication that they were evidence of the rising of the multitude predicted by Hardt and Negri or the self-sustaining communities like Chiapas celebrated by John Holloway. There were certainly strong anarchist currents in Argentina, stronger than in any other Latin American country, that saw these movements as embryos of a different, anti-state power.[22]

They shared the characteristics of many of the other social movements arising across the region (and elsewhere) in their grass roots and democratic character – and in the absence of an organised left-wing party leadership. The absence of a revolutionary socialist presence (as opposed to the participation of individual revolutionaries) was a reality – it was a result of an exclusive concentration on the trade unions and the electoral process which led the left there, and in most other countries, to disregard and underestimate new forms of protest and the multiple ways in which exploitation and therefore class is experienced in the real world.[23] The grass roots or rank and file character of the movements is not an alternative to a Marxist understanding of democracy – on the contrary it is fundamental to it. The claim that this form of organisation contradicts Marxism or revolutionary socialism is simply wrong.[24] But what is true, and it is a terrible weakness of the left, is that the struggle between left groups for leadership in the movement has produced a sectarian view, and a sectarian practice, which is particularly grave in Argentina.

Why did the left not anticipate the surging discontent and class anger through the 1990s among the victims of neo-liberalism? Were the inhabitants of poor areas or the unemployed not members of the working class, both objectively and subjectively?

This discussion illustrates the problem with the concept of autonomism. In identifying the contradictions between electoralism and the politics of independent mass mobilisation it has contributed to the current debates. Similarly, the 'horizontal' or 'assemblyist' forms of organisation directly address the shortcomings of a 'vanguard' theory of politics which inhibits and sometimes represses the active and open participation which is the only real guarantee of socialist democracy. But most fundamentally, the discussion leaves untouched the question of power and the state. The issue is complex and I will return to it in the conclusion. But it is immediately relevant and a central problem in the discussion of the pink tide.

The political outcome of the Argentinazo as a wave of popular rebellion, and after a series of transient and inept governments, was the rise to state power of a hitherto minor Peronist state governor, Nestor Kirchner from the state of Santa Cruz. As Webber and Carr point out,[25] the autonomists all too readily announced the final demise of Peronism, as a number of its leading figures had proved unable to address the problems of Argentina in the aftermath of the December 2001 rising. Nonetheless, the vertical system of power, and its state, had survived what could not in any real sense be described as a challenge to the bourgeois state as such. The assemblies and occupations continued outside the bourgeois system but not against it. The absence of an organised and credible left within the movement meant that no strategy for the transformation of society in an anti-capitalist direction emerged across the movements. On the contrary, and unfortunately, that discussion continued to be mired in the internal squabbles within the left.

And there was a much deeper misunderstanding among those who celebrated the autonomism of the movements, which had to do with the nature of Peronism. Peronism was, from its creation, a system of patronage, which over time became an enormous and pervasive clientilistic apparatus that controlled the trade unions and the civic and state institutions, not just nationally but at the level of the individual states:

What the left called 'old' politics – that is, the politics of Peronism, clientilism and patronage – was far from exhausted. In fact it was the key vehicle for political recomposition since taming and harnessing social movements was a fundamental condition for stabilising the economy.[26]

In some sense, it was the only political force that was capable of mobilising the state's resources to restore a shattered capitalism, while convincingly articulating their actions in the populist language of a Peronism that retained, for all its tremendous contradictions, some degree of credibility among working people, and which therefore could allow a process of capitalist restoration to be represented as a programme of national restoration. The autonomous space was not empty of politics because of the absence of a socialist vision; it was filled, or rather refilled by a Peronist reformism which was able, through an experienced political operator like Eduardo Duhalde, to relaunch Argentine capitalism in the name of a national-popular project.

Can it therefore be placed within the frame of the pink tide? Duhalde's primary concern, as a political boss in the old mould, was to re-establish the authority of Peronism. His weapons were the manipulation of the political system and the class method of patronage; he created a relief fund, a cash transfer scheme which probably affected around 2 million people. The argument was that the unemployed would be primary targets for this aid, individually allocated and definitively not to be confused with any long term or structured programme of subsidies to the jobless. Furthermore, his devaluation lessened the cost of production, and indeed of the cost of wages for the capitalist class, and even in 2002 new businesses were emerging. All this in anticipation of the 2003 presidential election, in which the three Peronist candidates swept the board in the first round – one of them was Carlos Menem, the living embodiment of corruption, who still received 24 per cent of the vote before standing down in favour of the victorious candidate, Néstor Kirchner, who was Duhalde's personal choice. The most arresting statistic, however, as Webber and Carr underline, is the reduction to almost nothing of the number of spoiled papers, and the high levels of participation in the vote. Given the scale of the anti-political movement that emerged from the Argentinazo, many assumed, wrongly, that there would be large scale abstention. Part of the explanation lies in the Peronist machine, which extended deep into state and local administrations. The Families Relief Fund was a useful way of cementing clientilistic relations, as we saw in both Brazil with the Zero Hunger campaign and

Venezuela with the CLAPs, the food parcels distributed through the PSUV. While the unemployed were ostensibly the main intended target, only 10 per cent of the relief went to them, and in a highly selective way designed to drive wedges between the different *piqueteros* organisations. For their militancy was general, but they also held political positions which differed markedly, and reflected the same divisions in the wider movement. The favoured groups were those who saw their actions as ways of forcing the state to negotiate with them; several other groups were dominated by the revolutionary left who had no truck with negotiations but who stood candidates in elections, though their results rarely reflected their level of militancy and daring. A third sector were linked to the various autonomist movements who addressed local issues and refused any form of political involvement, especially with Leninist or vanguard parties. Peronism was not, strictly speaking, a reformist organisation – but it had plenty of experience in enacting reformist measures and winning support through them. In a sense it had the field clear, since their political rivals on the left had nothing to match the electoral apparatus of the Peronists, and no access to the 'assistance' that could allay some of the difficulties faced by ordinary people in the crisis. Whatever their ideological impact, it was their material interventions that won the day.

And the beneficiary was Kirchner. His victory did not reflect any advance for the movement. His administration was an arena of internal conflict, not based on ideology but solely on the competition for power in the state. There was no sign of progressive intentions in the economy, no job schemes, no raising of taxes for the capitalist class for whom Duhalde had lowered tax levels, not even an intention to suspend payment of the national debt. The piqueteros had not reduced their activities, despite Kirchner's ostensible sympathy for at least their reformist wing. According to Katz, Kirchner would have liked nothing better than to repress them drastically, but he feared the consequences while 3000 grass roots activists were sill awaiting trial.

Kirchner did take some decisions in response to democratic pressure, most importantly the resumption of trials against the military regime and a derogation of Alfonsin's laws that gave them impunity. The Naval Mechanics School (AIMA) in Buenos Aires, which was the worst of the torture centres, from which 3000 activists went to their death, was to become a museum; the Supreme Court and the Electoral Commission would be purged, but only to allow entry to other equally suspect incumbents. Nevertheless the rhetoric of human rights won some social democrats to his side, and gave him credibility abroad. Kirchner's overriding concern[27] was to replace the Duhalde mafia and its godfather with them; rather than abolish that machinery of power and manipulation, instead he took it over. His support for gay marriage simply veiled the new turn towards extractive export industry, with its accompanying contamination, and the export agriculture based on soy, maize and cotton that would produce deforestation on a massive scale.

He lined up, in diplomatic terms, with Castro and Chávez and Lula at the level of discourse, while implementing policies that contradicted his rhetoric, repressing the radical *piqueteros*, honouring the national debt to the IMF as well as embedding the economy in the new extractivism. In that sense, perhaps, his trajectory before his death mirrored the actual direction of the pink tide economies, though he had not arisen on the tide of popular protest as the others had, but to contain and suppress it. Yet at the same time he extended the anti-poverty programmes massively, dividing the unemployed workers movements as a result.

> Almost 40 per cent of households have come to depend on state relief programmes for their basic survival. Having a large number of voters depending on receipt of a public income, a public salary, a pension or a subsidy provides a huge advantage to whoever is in power. In this sense it is important to understand how Peronist power is constructed daily in the enclaves of poverty.[28]

Cristina Kirchner succeeded to her husband's presidency in 2007, and was re-elected in 2011, a year after her husband's death. An attempted constitutional amendment to allow her to run for a third term later failed in the Congress.

Under her presidency, Argentina maintained a close relationship with Chávez and with Venezuela, and continued the human rights policies originally introduced in 2003 by Nestor Kirchner. Over a thousand people involved in the dirty war have been brought to trial. The most notable feature of the last period of her presidency was the extraordinary rise of the women's movement and its success, despite Cristina's noticeable silence in winning the right to abortion.[29] On the eve of the 2015 elections, however, Argentina had achieved a minimal GDP growth of 1.1 per cent, and the government had accepted the repayment of the foreign debt having resisted it for several years, by dramatically diminishing the reserves. The decline in industrial production was reflected in the falling figures for exports. The other face of this de-industrialisation was the expansion of export agriculture and mining. The pattern was familiar – and expressed a turn back to the global market, as financial speculation and capital flight deepened the economic crisis. It was significant that the new, Argentine,Pope had been an accomplice of the military regime; he was now emerging as a world leader. In 2015, in Buenos Aires, the Forum for Emancipation and Equality heard Rafael Correa, once a Catholic missionary, denounce the campaign for abortion rights and gender equality. The extraordinary women's movement that emerged in Argentina did not have the support of Critisna Kirchner, herself a practicing Catholic.

Kirchnerismo had long since abandoned its place on the centre-left. A new ruling class was enriching itself even as the crisis began to bite; the government had turned back to export agriculture and extractive industry with all the usual impacts on the public sector. At the 2015 election, Cristina Kirchner's chosen candidate was Daniel Scioli. Mauricio Macri, the representative of a broad coalition of conservative forces, Cambiemos, was an unreconstructed neo-liberal; but it was almost impossible to detect the difference between the two principal candidates. Cristina Kirchner had a personal following, but her policies had impacted most negatively on the working class and the poor. As Claudio Katz put it, for example, 'no current pensioner can expect to receive what they are due…ever'. Unemployment remained obstinately high.

Macri embarked on a restorationist policy, privatising and cutting back mercilessly on social provision. But he maintained some traditions from the past – in particular corruption. By 2017 the capitalists he had enriched were busy sending their money abroad, as Macri turned to the IMF for an emergency loan which, he was told, would carry the usual conditions – the reduction of social spending, greater flexibility of work, a reform of the benefit system and its gradual privatisation, a drastic cut in provincial budgets and layoffs in the public sector:

> The management of the bomb dropped by the government will depend on memory and capacity for popular reaction… The intensity of the mobilisation will define who wins… Faced with the artillery prepared by the government, the IMF and the capitalists, we need to

build popular defences at top speed. As has already happened before, once again it is them or us.[30]

The struggle against neo-liberalism continues with greater intensity. The experience of the pink tide, not as government but as mass popular mobilisation, can yet shape the future.

Conclusion

In 2006, Jorge Castañeda, ex-foreign minister of Mexico and now a prominent conservative commentator on Latin America, made a distinction between the 'good' and the 'bad' left in a famous article in the journal 'Foreign Affairs', a concept which he later developed in his *Utopia Unarmed*.[1] In fact, the formula had come from an earlier piece by Teodoro Petkoff, the Venezuelan writer who had been a member of a guerrilla organisation before becoming responsible for implementing austerity measures in the mid-1990s, and then moving on to edit the newspaper *Tal Cual*, the voice of the anti-Chavista right. Right-wing commentators and newly minted ex-centrist conservatives seized on Castañeda's contribution in the spirit of 'the errors of youth', mainly to allow Castañeda off the hook. His argument, in truth, was hardly very profound; there are people on the left, he said, who have recognised that revolution is no longer possible since the fall of the Berlin Wall, that capitalism is triumphant:

> Chile's post-dictatorship governments was an archetypal example of modest social reform pursued within a broadly capitalist framework.[2]

The 'bad' or 'wrong' left was fiscally irresponsible, 'closed-minded, stridently nationalist, economically reckless, indifferent to democratic norms, and irrationally anti-American'. The exemplars of this authoritarian populism were Hugo Chávez and Fidel Castro. This then became the orthodoxy among the opponents of the pink tide.

In fact, the pink tide has far less to do with individual leaders than with the rise of combative social movements, not to mention the fact that Castro led a revolution that overthrew the notorious dictatorship of Fulgencio Batista. It remains in place just under 70 years after it began, albeit it much changed. The pink tide is more than simply an epithet to be used to denounce some authoritarians but not others. Where are Videla, Bordaberry, Pinochet, Somoza in this pantheon of tyrants?

It is a fundamental error, and not one exclusive to the right, to define and describe the pink tide by its leaders. The individuals Castañeda names were carried to power in one form or another by waves of resistance that had brought down governments and regimes of the right. That is, of course, extremely hard for the grand theorists of politics to acknowledge since history, for them, is made solely from above. On the other hand, those individual leaders indisputably had an important role in both interpreting and representing the movements. Chávez always identified himself with the *Caracazo* of 1989, though his own first direct entry into Venezuelan politics had taken the form of a military coup in 1992. After the right failed to remove him in 2002 from the presidency he had won in a perfectly legitimate electoral contest, the *Caracazo* in some senses came back from the hills to rescue him, and in doing so became the subject of its own history, at least for a time. In Ecuador it was the mass indigenous movements who changed the course of Ecuadorean political life with the creation of CONAIE, its first mass actions in 1990, and the rising of 2000, that created the conditions in which Rafael Correa became president. And Bolivia witnessed perhaps the most advanced popular insurrection in its history through the Water and Gas Wars of 2000–5 which brought down the last government of the 'old' state.

The same may be said of Lula in Brazil or Kirchner in Argentina, of course, though both were able to deploy very powerful political machines (the Workers Party and the Peronist Justicialista Party respectively) to reimpose their authority on the movements that had achieved the unusual feat of removing four presidents on one day in the Argentinazo. For this writer, at least, the 'pink tide' is that succession of waves of popular movements which placed very new priorities on the political agenda in Latin America for a dozen years or so. They are the subjects of this historical era, rather than the epiphenoma of their leaders. This is contradicted, of course, by the creators of the idea of 'Chavismo' or 'Evoísmo', as if that automatically defined a coherent body of ideas and their corresponding political method.

Chavismo in fact emerged out of the debates that arose when Chávez had won the presidency. His own programme was described as Bolivarian, though that was attended with as many ambiguities as the other -isms that emerged at the time. But if his reference point was Simon Bolivar, whose project for Gran Colombia was a model of post-colonial independent capitalist development, then it may be that the most significant component of that strategy as far as Chávez was concerned was its scale. The initial programme he offered as a candidate stressed rights and freedoms; it was an advanced liberal platform in that sense. Beyond that was a concept of national sovereignty within a global context. In real terms it is and was impossible to imagine an independent road of development for a single oil economy. That was why oil was described by Pérez Alfonso as 'the devil's shit' rather than the 'black gold' favoured by the oil magnates of the north. It brought untold wealth it is true, but that wealth was only accidentally produced within the territorial bounds of Venezuela, García Márquez's great novel *Leaf Storm* brilliantly describes how foreign capital arrives like a hurricane, carries all before it, and then moves on, leaving devastation in its wake – as it did, for example, in the Yasuni region of Ecuador. Oil can only serve the long term interests of the north, while the south receives its minimal royalties which will be used to buy the goods produced by the industry driven by oil.

Changing that relationship will be the first stage in achieving meaningful sovereignty, as Chávez, Evo and Correa, all the pink tide governments, discovered very rapidly. The initial promise was to raise the royalties and taxes and with the surplus fund the services that had disappeared during the 1990s under the neo-liberal assault. A high oil price enabled that to happen, but there was little attempt to divert part of that surplus into expanding alternative areas of production. Instead it was channelled into consumption. The new air-conditioned shopping malls in Venezuela, Bolivia and Ecuador tell their own story – like the glass tower blocks so inappropriate and wasteful for a city like Caracas, with average temperatures around 30 degrees.

From 2005 onwards, with oil revenues at an unprecedented level (until 2015), it might have been possible to escape incurring new foreign debt and avoid repeating the errors of the import substitution industrialisation period. The IMF and the World Bank were replaced by China in the frenzy of the commodities boom. Petras at one point describes trade with China as part of an anti-imperialist strategy, simply on the grounds that the money was not coming from the United States nor investment from U.S. companies. That has proved to be an extremely costly error. There is nothing remotely socialist about China's investments in commodities, nor are its high interest, short term loans any thing other than economic imperialism.

It was, however, a plausible part of Chávez's strategic view to develop regional economic blocs that might be able to develop policies of exchange of goods and services, and knowledge, outside the framework of globalisation. The Bolivarian Alliance for the peoples of the Americas (ALBA) was an important statement of intent, Celac and Unasur are each embryos of the regional alliances that Chávez envisaged. ALBA's first members were Venezuela and Cuba, with some of the smaller Caribbean islands. But beyond these bilateral agreements built around Chávez's distribution of oil at bargain prices [3], the other Latin American countries were slow to respond to the concept of integration. Venezuela contributed Cuban medical teams to Bolivia and exchanged teachers and teaching methods. But the Bolivarian dream was still a very distant one. The Latin American countries had very clear ideas about difference; the general umbrella term 'pink tide' hardly does justice to their extreme historical diversity, their ethnic distinctiveness. In a curious way, it is imperialism that has imposed uniformity, ideologically at least, on Latin America. The emergence of left governments affirmed difference and the specific character of each process. And within the Latin American bloc there were major ideological and political differences – for example between the three 'clusters' identified by Petras. Internal trading did develop, slowly, but beyond that there was little real interest in integration – which must have seemed like a surrender of national sovereignty. What was shared was a critique of neo-liberalism, anti-capitalism and anti-imperialism. For the radical nations at least there was agreement on the negative role of U.S. intervention – or was there? Chávez was emphatic and eloquent in his denunciation of U.S. interventions and the Washington Consensus – yet the United States was and continues to be the principal purchaser of its oil. Correa made the grand gesture of refusing to renew the lease on the Manta air base, and commendably withdrew the Ecuadorean military from the programmes of the School of the Americas, as did Chávez. But at the same time Correa continued to work with U.S.-based multinationals and quietly revived negotiations with the IMF. And Evo agreed to eradication programmes in Bolivia in exchange for permitted levels of coca cultivation in approved areas.

Opposition to neo-liberalism was also questionable. In the discourses of power it was a central thread. But in the practice of government and the disposition of state power the objective appeared to be the renegotiation of the terms of the relationship rather than the construction of a new economic rationality. It could not have been an overnight process, quite clearly – I anticipate the critical suggestion that that *is* what I am arguing. We are discussing processes here, tendencies, the direction of strategy. And in practice there is nowhere in the pink tide countries any evidence of the laying of the foundations of a new economic order. One possible framework would be *buen vivir* – but the realities appear to have flown in the face of any attempt to put it into practice.

Insofar as *buen vivir* reflected the accumulated experience of collective labour among indigenous peoples, or the protection of territories where that experience was embedded, the opposite developments seem to have occurred. TIPNIS in Bolivia may be the most dramatic example, though the environmental catastrophe that is about to happen on the Salar de Uyuni, in Bolivia, in the frenzied search for lithium, may yet replace it. Correa's attacks on indigenous activism as 'infantile environmentalism' are another example; in Venezuela the murder of Sabino and members of his family for opposing the expansionism of the state coal-mining company Carbozulia is a particularly disturbing one. The examples from outside the pink tide countries are, of course, legion: the expulsion of the Kayapo who stood in the way of the building of the Belo Monte dam in Brazil; the Chilean government's persecution of the Mapuche peoples; the murder in Honduras of the environmental and indigenous activist Berta Cáceres and members of her family in 2016, have resonated across the world. Today the development of the Arco Minero region by Maduro and his 150 multinational associates has meant the 'clearing', that is the violent expulsion, of whole indigenous communities. Accumulation by dispossession was one of the characteristics of neo-liberal land acquisitions to expand export agriculture. Yet it is pink tide governments who are now carrying it out on behalf of the global market, most destructively in Brazil, but also more recently in Argentina under Cristina Kirchner.

The examples are multiple and reappear through the narratives in this book. The expansion of mining and other extractive industries during the Chinese boom prior to 2015 has slowed, but only marginally – and it continues to be the strategy that unites the governments of Latin America wherever they sit on the radical spectrum.

The movements that set in motion the series of popular mobilisations that defined the early phase of the pink tide, in Bolivia, Ecuador and Argentina, were defined by their anti-capitalism, as Subcomandante Marcos's first Dispatches from the Lacandon Forest clearly showed. But very soon the nature of the Zapatista rising was changed, and redefined as an indigenous revolt; it was always that, of course, but placed in the context of the globalisation that was distorting their lives as well as the lives of peasants and workers across Mexico. The Cochabamba water war, by contrast, was exemplary in its social character; it included small farmers, indigenous communities, neighbourhood groups, factory workers, students, youth. And it became emblematic of the wider struggle, as well as playing a key role in the further developments in El

Alto. Indeed, water itself was becoming symbolic in the anti-capitalist struggle; its appropriation in a very short time across the world by powerful and aggressive multinational companies exemplified what neo-liberalism meant – the transformation of every aspect of human life and need into commodities. It did not simply mean that they were bought and sold as objects in the global market; it also meant that the commons were no longer of universal access, no longer belonged in the realm of the undifferentiatedly human. Commodification meant privatisation and in-accessibility. But as Winstanley, the leader of the seventeenth century Diggers movement had put it so eloquently 'no man has any right to buy and sell the earth for private gain'. That most fundamental principle was rearticulated and translated throughout the social movements without any prior knowledge of Winstanley's words.

The Cochabamba movement had this distinctive feature; it confronted the state as surrogate for multinational capital. It was no longer neutral and nor could it any longer represent itself as the reflection of the general inter-ests of society, or as the place where those interests could be negotiated and ultimately reconciled. It was in this clear sense that the movement in Cochabamba described itself as 'autonomous', a term that has come to have considerable influence in the period of the rise of the social movements.

There are various ways to understand what this autonomism may mean, but the prior question must be autonomy from what. The origins of the political use of the term come from the intense class struggles in Italy in the 1970s and 1980s. The argument was a complex theoretical one, but essen-tially claimed that labour was autonomous from capital. It was a response to a real phenomenon – the rejection by many workers of their trade unions and of the parties of the left. In the context of twenty-first century Latin America it has been used to describe a different phenomenon.

The social movements that gave rise to the pink tide emerged first and foremost from a deep social and political crisis set in motion by neo-liberalism. The political crisis was expressed in the collapse of the local state, as a mediator between the interests of the global market and the society as a whole. The first clear expression of the new role of the local state, as an agent acting on behalf of global capital came in 1973 in Chile, and was repeated in a second stage in Bolivia in 1985. This had profound political consequences, in that the organisations that claimed to repre-sent the interests of the working classes had been dominated by a conception of the conquest of the state. This assumed implicitly that the state was not an instrument of class power only, but a contradictory space in which class relations were acted out, and that those contradictions (or what Linera would later describe as 'creative tensions') allowed for a permanent negotiation between the interests of capital and those of labour. The collapse of Eastern Europe showed that even so-called socialist states existed to defend and advance the interests of capital. The very concept of socialism was discredited as a result.

The social crisis was the consequence of the economic restructuring that neo-liberalism introduced. Dispossession was a central feature, as David Harvey showed, as capital expanded spatially in its intensification of export agriculture and its relentless severing of Latin America's open veins. Millions were expelled from the countryside into a permanent marginality, decanted into slum cities or set on a road of permanent displacement in the transient labour force moving constantly across the planet. The labour market was transformed, as more and more workers were either redefined as 'autonomous' – that is without collective rights or permanence – or sucked into the precarity of contractless part time, short term labour. Many more became street traders, crowded on to the urban pavements of Latin America's cities where they sold the products of the most exploited workers of the third world which, by and large, mirrored the luxury goods whose market, paradoxically, was expanding in the same cities, even as inequality increased the numbers of the very poor while the rich became fewer... and richer.

Necessity produced resistance. The Zapatista rebellion was, in its beginnings, the defence of impoverished communities whose very physical survival was under threat. Indigenous communities across the continent fought against their displacement, for land and territory (which as we have explained signified different things) against the agro-export giants producing soya, maize (for ethanol not consumption) and cotton. The urban poor organised to ensure the provision of the basic stuff of life – water and food – for access to minimum services denied them by the state.

Their practice, sometimes shaped by traditions in the collective memory, more often by their common experience and the levelling impact of poverty, was 'horizontal' and democratic. These horizontal ties were sometimes unstable and shifting, and distinguished by social and cultural differences. When Zibechi argues that in these conditions 'social action undermined representation,'[4] he identifies another key common factor – the dissociation between these struggles and the leaders and organisations who had until then claimed to represent them. The movements were in that sense 'anti-political', rejecting political traditions that placed a self-appointed leadership above the democratic traditions of the grass roots. This is not to romanticise those traditions and cultures. The consciousness among the working classes, all those subject to the laws of capital, is uneven and often contradictory. This cannot be an argument for vanguardism or for a parodic Leninism of self-appointed elites. But neither does it deny or eliminate the need for organisation and coordination.

The Bolivian experience makes the point dramatically. Between 2003 and 2005, the scale of resistance, the numbers involved and the representativity of the movement across the country – organising peasants, workers, indigenous communities, men and women in urban and rural struggles, students, youth – justified the characterisation of this moment as 'revolutionary'. The movement's demands related to wages, public services, control of national resources, equality, and the battle against racism. The internal contradictions of the state rendered it impotent in the face of the insurrection of the masses.

But at that critical moment it was the absence of a common project for an alternative order, an alternative vision, that determined the outcome of this extraordinary moment. The state existed, no longer as an instrument of bourgeois repression, the iron fist of the last instance, but as an empty space. Power lay in the hands of a mass movement – that could not seize it. Enter the MAS and Evo Morales, who occupied the state and assumed the leadership role that remained unoccupied. Evo was familiar with the mechanisms of state, having worked with the failed president Carlos Mesa to negotiate a place for MAS in the running of the state. The organisation was preparing for scheduled presidential elections in 2007; the collapse of Mesa's government hastened the process. MAS only severed its relationship with Mesa at the very last moment, but it did have a project for administering the state within and on behalf of capitalism. Stability was the order of the day, but a bourgeois stability with new managers. It is in that light that we should see the decision to exclude the social movements from the Constituent Assembly unless they were represented by recognised political organisations.

When progressive parties assumed the mantle of state leadership, however, the tendency was toward a social movement practice of subaltern participation – the pacifying incorporation of popular sectors into the gears of the capitalist state – rather than an autonomous and antagonistic participation, in which the capacity to disrupt and to lay the groundwork for emancipatory and prefigurative inspiration is maintained. The necessary struggle against, within, and beyond the state became instead a muted and moderated struggle captured by the state.[5]

Revolutionary socialism is rooted in the analysis of living forces and their relations, both social and productive; it is both an analysis of capitalist relations of production and a theory of the revolutionary transformation of those relations; that is the meaning of dialectical materialism. Of course that is very obvious. But it is driven not only by what is but by what can 'become' – by a vision of a different future shaped by anti-capitalist or non-capitalist values. The mass movements, in their critical expressions and their social practices often created new forms of social organisation, arising apparently spontaneously out of the practice of struggle – the soviets, the Chilean cordones, the Spanish anti-fascist committees, the Paris Commune and Rojava are all manifestations of that possibility. But the appearance of spontaneity invariably conceals a long process of preparation, ideological and organisational, nourished by multiple traditions. That is the source of the creativity of social movements. Autonomism celebrates the diversity of such expressions, but dismisses any attempt to coordinate them and transform them as instruments of social change as interference. Like John Holloway, they refuse to address the issue of social power – as if the state and its mechanisms of repression and control did not exist. But they do, and they are the blockage on the road to socialism. To ignore it is denial – which in the end amounts to the renunciation of the revolutionary project. It is hard to see it differently, when the Zapatista communities, looking inward, are surrounded by the units of the Mexican army.

The volume edited by Roger Burbach and others[6] is perhaps the most systematic presentation of an autonomist analysis of the pink tide. Each chapter details the wide spectrum of grass roots activities that has marked the last decade and a half – and they are remarkable, imaginative and often inspiring. Yet, as we have shown, the state has grown stronger, more authoritarian and more integrated into the neo-liberal project at the same time. Resistance continues, but this time, and increasingly, against the very state that the movements raised to power. Burbach and others blithely affirm that the answer to capitalist globalisation is to be found in 'globalisation from below'. But that is much more than a celebration of difference and a generalised sympathy for and solidarity with the oppressed. Capitalist globalisation is the most recent chapter in the relentless expansion of capital driven by the laws of accumulation. It is not a conspiracy and only partially planned; competition is at least as formative as the pursuit of profit. But it is driven by a common impulse. We might assume that the shared impulse behind globalisation from below is anti-capitalist; yet the dominant political voices in the movement, who yet enjoy the authority of leadership, appear to distinguish between a bad and a good neo-liberalism, just as Castañeda divided the left into right and wrong.

> It is not the intensity of social conflicts, the willingness of the op-pressed to struggle, or the capacity of the oppressors to control that has substantially changed, but the viability of – and confidence in – a socialist model.[7]

The separation is instructive. For right-wing ideologues like Castañeda, but also for social democratic thinkers and commentators, the present is a given and the future inescapable. The good and the bad left differ for Castañeda by their recognition or failure to recognise this inevitability. In this view it is as if the sustained mass resistance (he was writing in 2006) simply did not exist. Yet the subjects of revolution are those engaged in fighting back against neo-liberalism. The construction of an alternative involves more than resistance. The project is nothing less than the 'self emancipation of the labouring classes' – but the emancipatory project must have strategies for taking power. To renounce that political task, as Holloway does, is to leave those who currently possess and administer power in their own interests, in place and untouched. They will neither surrender it nor fall under their own weight. The development of those strategies is the task of political organisation, informed by a vision as well as an understanding of reality. Socialism does not yet exist, so it must be imagined – unless you adhere to a social democratic idea that capitalism will reach a point of exhaustion out of which socialism will spontaneously flower. In a world that contains President Trump it must now be clear to us all that capitalism has no limit to what it will do to defend itself – including the destruction of the planet by one means or another. Marx's warning at the end of the *Communist Manifesto* was not a metaphor.

But the nature of the political organisation that can develop that strategy is not a given either. The criticism levelled at the revolutionary left is that its horizons were narrow, its methods at best paternalistic and at worst authoritarian. The democratic debate so cherished by the social movements was silenced by the unerring conviction of political leaders who spoke for but not from the working classes. This was not a question of social origin, but of the domination of theory over practice. Theory became dogma and orthodoxy, its legitimation the experience of the Soviet Union even where that included severe criticisms of its evolution. The central tenet of the left was the issue of agency; the subject of the revolution was the proletariat, the industrial working class. In general, that subject did not include the working class in its lived reality beyond the workplace, nor did it discuss the oppressed, the marginalised, the excluded. Their condition would, it was repeated ad nauseam, be resolved by the socialist revolution. The rise of the women's movement challenged that assumption frontally, but its challenge was ultimately separated from the revolutionary parties.

The double crisis produced by the collapse of the Soviet Union and the disarming and disintegration of the industrial working class found the left in disarray. And the new anti-capitalist resistance arose outside its purview. By and large the left had no roots in the new social movements, no discourse that would include them nor a strategy that could materially respond to their concerns with a vision of the future. Where there was some advanced thinking, as in the La Comuna group in Bolivia from which García Linera came, its insights were soon adapted to the necessities of maintaining power in the state.

The subjects of socialist revolution are still the propertyless and exploited, those who have nothing to lose but their chains, the discriminated against and the oppressed. Socialism is their self-government. The working class is multiple, diverse;

> If class is understood as a living, relational phenomenon then it is necessarily conceived as also being multiply determined in and through gender, race and sexuality in present-day Latin American societies. From this vantage point, the latter social oppressions are not dismissed as mere epiphenoma of the class structure.[8]

A revolutionary strategy that consigns them to a passive role on the margins will fail, or perhaps transform itself into a version of social democracy that promises revolution in an indefinite future and meanwhile colludes in the oppression of the subject of revolution today 'for reasons of state'.

On Corruption

The right has claimed a moral high ground on the question of the widespread and persistent corruption that occurred in Brazil and Argentina during the respective administrations of the PT under Lula and Dilma, and of Nestor and Cristina Kirchner. The Odebrecht scandal has revealed the enormous scale of corruption – it seems that the Brazilian construction multinational dispensed $1.3 billion in bribes to individuals in order to gain access to public funds in Cuba, Brazil, Argentina, Peru, Mexico, Venezuela and more. So systemic was the practice that the company had a specific department devoted entirely to paying off public officials.

Corruption is not a new phenomenon, of course; in Mexico it is a pervasive systemic culture, so much so that a gesture, a nod or the raising of an arm is now sufficiently communicative to set the process in motion. Criminals, drug barons, the Mafia, Al Capone and all forms of organised crime have found means to buy themselves politicians, public servants, military and police with impunity through the years.

It is a central issue, however, in any discussion of the pink tide. The Lava Jato case and its repercussions illustrate this point. Dilma was impeached and removed from the presidency, Lula is currently in prison, hundreds of officials have also been jailed or dismissed for their participation in the chains of corruption. In the Brazilian case, Pablo Stefanoni argues in an important article,[9] the anti-corruption campaign set in motion by Lava Jato has been used systematically to undermine and remove the PT from power and replace Dilma in the presidency with Michel Temer, an ultraconservative businessman and a sworn enemy of the PT. But it must also be acknowledged that the net has not only closed around PT officials; Eduardo Cunha, the president of the Senate who launched the impeachment proceedings against Dilma is currently in jail too, as are other parliamentarians of the right. Since corruption is endemic in Brazilian parliamentary institutions, it is hard to imagine where the process will end. Of course, the intention of the right has been to use the charges as a pretext to reverse the decisions of government and introduce neo-liberal structural and economic reforms whose first expression are invariably austerity programmes directed at the majority population – the authors of these initiatives are extremely unlikely to use any of the public services they are dismantling.

The left has responded by creating images of Lula and Dilma in their old guise as activists of an original PT which fought for the poor and argued for a revolutionary transformation unencumbered by Stalinism. But Dilma is no longer the guerrilla warrior tortured and jailed by the military regime. Lula long since ceased to be the factory worker carrying the marks of a childhood in poverty. Both became powerful politicians without changing the system, but instead participating enthusiastically in administering it. To state the glaringly obvious, my enemy's enemy is not always my friend. The left, if it is to rebuild a movement that tells the truth both to power and to its own mass base, cannot collude in the concealment of the real experience of the PT in power. Lula continued the neo-liberal strategies of Cardoso and implemented his own neo-liberal reforms. The schemes to provide money for the poor were individual payments which created a dependency on the state but at the same undermined any possibility of building collective action to change the system that created both their poverty and the wealth – the extreme wealth – of a minority. Lula ended by working in harmony with those reactionary forces, making deals and protecting their interests in return for a share of power. Dilma did the same. In fact in 2014 she lied shamelessly about her intentions, and having won the presidency on an undertaking to address the inequality in Brazil and redirect public funds not just to assistance schemes but to a restructuring, she immediately gave concessions and tax breaks to big capital and imposed restrictive measures on the rest of the population. And to add insult to injury she appointed as her minister of agriculture Katia Abreu, the owner of the wealthiest agro-export business in the country. After the impeachment, PT officials and representatives horse-traded with the very organisations that had launched the impeachment with the simple purpose of retaining its share of power.

The left has a duty to defend progressives and socialists against attacks from the right but not to veil or deny their errors or corruption. The battle against corruption, the misuse of public funds or the abuse of power, is not a right-wing instrument – it can and should be a weapon of the left in the creation of a politics of openness, honesty, accountability and a genuine participatory democracy, which is what the pink tide promised. The promise to do this has been a central element of the successful presidential campaign of Andrés Manuel López Obrador (AMLO) in Mexico, whose campaign focussed on ethics and the war against corruption. His unprecedented levels of support demonstrate the level of public anger that corruption has generated. There is no right or left-wing corruption – there is just corruption. It may be *used* by the right to discredit the left, as it is in this case. And it may end up, as Stefanoni notes in his 2018 *Nueva Sociedad* article 'Disparen contra Lula', by allowing the political vacuum to be occupied by cynics and opportunists like Berlusconi or Trump or Collor in Brazil. But that is not a function of the fight against corruption itself but of its organisational and political support by mass democratic organisations.

In Venezuela today, and among the supporters of the original Bolivarian process, the same dilemma presents itself. The group at the centre of government is guilty of theft and embezzlement on an unimaginable scale, but they have been allowed to get away with it by characterising the very exposure as a right-wing manouevre. In this way, the left becomes complicit in the very processes that have discredited socialism. The history of the left offers innumerable examples of the consequences of this complicity.

The question that remains is why corruption happens? The answer is not be found in generalities about human frailty. In looking at the Latin American examples there is a pattern which can at least bring us closer to an explanation. The first element is power, which itself corrupts but which also brings individuals within reach of enormous resources deployed by wealthy and unscrupulous people. The second concerns state spending itself; the public sector spends on a huge scale, and the individuals charged with that spending administer those funds directly, as the Odebrechts of the world know full well. Bribery and greed are the enemies of ethics and integrity. But it seems to me, curiously enough, that the main issue is the lack of democracy, the absence of transparency and accountability as measures of public office. Corruption is less successful under a bright light. At the same time politicians and people in responsible positions in the public sector need a high level of political consciousness to resist the temptations and largesse that neo-liberalism dispenses with such vigour. AMLO is certainly the first Mexican president to place honesty at the heart of his programme. It remains to be seen whether it will be sufficient to break a system based on political horse-trading, power deals, and corruption.

The Forms of People's Power

The pink tide, conceived as the rise of popular movements, provided a glimpse of what people's power may look like – in the grass roots organisations, the *cabildos abiertos*, the popular assemblies, the Zapatista communities, the MST land occupations. These are only some of the many examples. Their central feature was their democratic, open and participatory nature. They were not always fluid or efficiently organised; they may have contained contradictions.[10] They were noisy, messy, often with kids and dogs and reguetón in attendance. But that is how the creative intervention of the mass movement feels. And at times it produced extraordinary imaginative leaps, like the student demonstrations in Chile in 2012. All of these things were expressions of the unrealised potential for original and imaginative transformations. They were much more than lobbies or pressure groups – they were pointers towards the future. But the absence of political coordination and of thinking about the realities of power and how to address them left a vacuum which was filled by existing political strategies.

In his final writings, Hugo Chávez recognised that the Venezuelan state had not been transformed, though parts of it had been occupied by a new layer of Chavistas. Yet its functions remained largely unchanged, though ministries and ministers had had the words 'people's power' added to their titles. The intention was no doubt good, but what did it signify in terms of a changed relationship between the movement from below and the state? It could be argued that many of the new occupants had come from the working class *barrios*, had been community leaders in their own right. This is certainly true in some cases, but were they charged with speaking on behalf of their base organisations or with carrying the decisions from above to the movement? In an unchanged state, the latter was their role; they were co-opted into the existing institutions. These people's representatives became part of a new bureaucracy overseen by the PSUV, in other words by the state apparatus itself. Steve Ellner, whose analyses of Chavismo are sophisticated and thoughtful, acknowledges the absence of internal democracy in the PSUV in a lengthy 2017 article in *Monthly Review*.[11] His starting point, based on Marta Haernecker, is that 'the old state and a new one will coexist for a long time'. But their coexistence will not be harmonious, indeed it cannot be. It will be, as García Linera insistently reminds us, a contradictory and conflictive relationship, with the two sides pulling in opposite directions. Ellner's defence of the existing Chavista state is based on the tactical necessity of coexisting with the bourgeoisie:

> The government's distinction between the hostile traditional bourgeoisie and a 'friendly' emerging one has remained largely unchanged under Maduro.

Friendly or not, it remains a capitalist class committed to the maintenance of a bourgeois order. Ellner quotes the intervention of one such friendly capitalist at the Constituent Assembly, where he argued fiercely for a return to private ownership of state enterprises.

That could be regarded as a sign of a healthy openness in debate, were Steve able to cite more than one Chavista voice (Julio Escalona) criticising the Maduro government's approach to the bourgeoisie. In any event, a political formation claiming revolutionary credentials cannot take a neutral position between the old and the new states. The question is, where is the 'new state' being formed; in what forums is the debate about a future socialist society being conducted?

Madurismo is not a variety of revolutionary thinking but a state pragmatism, holding the balance between two class forces. In the Marxist vocabulary this is described as Bonapartism, and is by definition a transitional and fragile form. So the legitimate question for socialists to ask is what is being done to strengthen and prepare the new state that will at some time emerge from the old. Because that will be a conscious collective act informed by new values and new purposes. Yet Steve refers to people with a critical position on Venezuela (like myself) in a familiar way.

The disillusionment of many former Chávez sympathizers both in Venezuela and abroad likely stems in part from this privileging of grand goals over immediate challenges.[12]

In other words, all critics are ultraleft utopians. But how often in the history of our movement have grand purposes (like twenty-first century socialism, for example) been sacrificed to immediate challenges that have a curious habit of becoming permanent? 'Revolution now!' is a slogan nobody really uses; it is a parody. But the revolution is a process of preparation, of extending and deepening consciousness, of testing new organs of power, of building that democracy from below, which is what socialism means. Dual power, Ellner, says is 'an approach in which the old state is considered enemy territory'. That is a little crude; but the Poulantzian underpinning to his argument suggests that it is not hostile terrain. The proof lies in the elements in the situation that Steve Ellner does not mention. What does the Arco Minero project, and its definitive move back towards neo-liberalism, signify? It was a defining decision – and the full scale militarisation of the region, the suspension there of constitutional protections and the collusion with massive environmental destruction is not consistent with the building of a socialist alternative – but is its opposite.

What is urgent is to deepen the discussion about the pink tide experience among those committed to socialism under whatever label. Steve Ellner is right to speak about disillusionment, but that does not mean abandoning the field to others, to Castañeda's 'good left'. What the left failed to do in the past, in ideas and in practice, is learn from and with the social movements, what democracy can look like. At the level of ideas, Latin America is not without visionaries and thinkers for the future.

It is no accident that the social movements have rediscovered Latin America's great revolutionary Marxist, José Carlos Mariátegui, who died in 1930, in the course of the struggles of the pink tide. Despite his youth, Mariátegui developed a Marxism that embraced indigenous America and a visionary (some call it romantic) socialism. He was demonised and rejected by the Third International for his refusal to bend to Stalinism. Today he is a source for rethinking the future.[13]

On Populism

Commentators on the collapse of the left governments in Latin America deploy the concept of populism frequently, usually in a deprecating way. As a concept, it is prone to ambiguity and confusion. Yet it points to a real phenomenon that is helpful in understanding the pink tide.

In moments of political crisis – whose causes and nature may vary considerably, from the consequences of economic collapse to internal divisions within the hegemonic class or a collapse brought about by the dramatic loss of legitimacy of the political system, as has happened in Brazil with the corruption investigations, the ruling class, or class coalition, loses control of the political system. This was manifestly the case in Venezuela, Bolivia and Ecuador in the early part of the new century, and later in Nicaragua; in Brazil and Mexico in more recent times. This leaves a political vacuum with no collective political actor able to assume leadership. At such moments what Laclau has called 'the empty signifier' which 'signifies a totality which is literally impossible' fills the space amid what may well be a 'catastrophic equilibrium', as Garcia Linera described in the period 2003–5 in Bolivia. I do not share the general conclusions of Laclau, but the concept is useful. As I understand it, describes a moment in time, transitional and unstable, whose outcome is unclear. In that moment a new concept or discourse emerges which is by its nature ambiguous; it may well be eclectic, taking elements of different ideologies and melding them into a new symbolic referent. The ideological space is not, however, as Laclau suggests, empty, but it draws on contradictory elements – and for a period it may engage with different and opposing class interests. But it is also a battleground between social forces seeking to fill the concept with its own meanings. It is also a phenomenon that offers new possibilities or the promise of them, material or symbolic, to a wide enough range of groups in society to maintain control, though not yet hegemony. The populist discourse is not universal; it is forged out of elements of culture tradition, the collective memory and the remnants of other ideologies.

The conjunction of crisis and the emergence of a leader whose social roots and loyalties are sufficiently ambiguous clearly describes Venezuela in 1988, Bolivia in the wake of the Gas War in 2005–6, Ecuador in 2006 after the fall of Lucio Gutiérrez and Argentina in 2001, where the slogan *que se vayan todos* – let's get rid of them all – perfectly exemplified the phenomenon. Brazil and Mexico lived through major crises in 1999 but they were resolved in each case without a breakdown in the system; in Brazil with the intervention of Lula, the Workers Party candidate. The financial crisis of 2008 hit the countries of pink tide differentially in the succeeding years but they weathered the storm at the time politically, though not economically, as we have argued. But they did not escape the longer term effects. By 2018, Mexico and Brazil were once again immersed in a profound political crisis, while the Macri regime elected in Argentina in 2015 has devoted itself to reimposing the core measures of neo-liberalism, dismantling public services and privatising the national economy. The imminent elections in Mexico illustrate the problem to perfection. The hegemonic party, the PRI, entered an effective alliance during the previous presidency with the right-wing Catholic party PAN as its own internal crisis ended its seventy year monopoly of power. In the last two elections its presidential candidates faced Andres Manuel Lopez Obrador, a left critic of the old system who enjoyed wide popular support across the country and in the capital, Mexico City. Obrador claimed that the results on both occasions were fraudulent – and that would not be out of character with the exercise of politics in Mexico. Yet he has also responded to his double defeat by presenting himself in a very different light in 2018 – where his campaign has carried him to the presidency. In the meantime, the PRI-PAN collusion has collapsed, though both parties share an unshaken commitment to neo-liberalism. Over 20 years of neo-liberalism have produced a disaster in Mexico. The spread of violence and criminality, far from being brought under control by the military and the police, have penetrated and criminalised both. The murder of 46 students in the state of Guerrero was not an isolated incident, but it was especially savage and the final straw, with the open complicity of the state police and governor. Violence against workers, a systemic femicide, the murder of over

100 candidates in the current election round, are the tip of the iceberg, together with privatisation, particularly of the oil industry. The ruling bloc has lost control of the situation and the level of popular rage is rising, though it has no unified political expression. Against that background, Obrador has moved to occupy the space vacated by the PRI, not by building a clear left bloc but by absorbing elements from across the political spectrum under the banner of unity. The ambiguities in his current speeches illustrate the point.

For the left, the dilemma that presents itself is all too familiar. Like Lula, Obrador has moved to the right in order to gain power, and made compromises with business sectors and members of the old ruling castes to that end. Nonetheless, his past reputation is sufficient to create expectations among working people and the poor, reinforced by the propaganda war the right is waging against him, and the insistent comparisons with Chávez, which do him very little harm among the majority population. What is certain is that his prior commitments indicate a continuing neo-liberal direction, and some elements of state welfare provision. What we can assume is that he will not offer an alternative strategy for the achievement of a society of equality and social and economic justice. On the other hand, Massimo Modonnesi sees hope in Obrador's moral campaign and his emphasis on honesty in the notoriously corrupt Mexican political system. That is to be encouraged and supported, but its limitations can be anticipated and prepared for.

For all its radical rhetoric the pink tide was a movement whose economic thinking was shaped by developmentalism, or what is sometimes called productivism. It has demonstrated once again its limitations, as it did during the import substitution period. The future will pose the same problems again.

There is imaginative and visionary thinking emerging from Latin America even amidst the crises of the moment. Alberto Acosta in Ecuador, Edgardo Lander and Roland Denis in Venezuela, Marisvella Stampa in Argentina, Pablo Stefanoni in Bolivia, Raul Zibechi from Uruguay offer us important starting points for a new discussion directed at the future. But for us all, the starting point must be a rigorous and honest appraisal of the present. Manuel Sutherland, the young Venezuelan Marxist economist makes the point well:

The left should criticize the 'progressive governments' with the same wisdom and insight that it applies to right-wing anti-working class regimes. There is no reason to ignore the problems that arise in those countries; the left should instead collaborate in an urgent search for meaningful proposals, and this will involve analyzing objectively the 'progressive' governments and criticizing them with the methods of dialectical understanding. If the Titanic sank, there is no justification for denying the wreckage in the name of solidarity and anti-imperialism.

Notes

INTRODUCTION: Neo-liberalism on the Attack

1. No work has begun on the canal whose Chinese financier was bankrupted by the Chinese financial crisis of 2015. The likelihood is that the project has been effectively cancelled.
2. Frances Fukuyama, *The end of history and the last man,* Free Press, New York, 1992.
3. See Tom Hayden (ed) *The Zapatista Reader,* Nation Books, New York, 2002; Subcomandante Marcos *Our word is our weapon,* Serpent's Tail, London, 2001.
4. See M. Gonzalez, 'The Zapatistas: the challenges of revolution in the new millennium', in T. Hayden (2002) pp. 430–51.
5. Marcos developed several voices including an old man and a beetle, Don Durito. He has written children's stories, including the popular *Libro de los Colores,* and a detective story with Paco Ignacio Taibo, *The uncomfortable dead.*
6. See Marcos (2001).
7. See P. O'Brien, I. Roxborough and J. Roddick, *State and revolution in Chile,* Macmillan, London, 1975.
8. Pablo Larrain's 2012 film 'No' deals with the events of 1989.
9. See below, pp. 37-8.
10. See Jeffery Webber, *The last day of oppression and the first day of the same,* Haymarket Books, Chicago, 2017, pp. 32-5.
11. See Dan LeBotz, *What went wrong? The Nicaraguan revolution: a Marxist analysis,* Haymarket Books, Chicago, 2018.
12. See Jenny Pearce, *Under the Eagle: U.S. intervention in Central America and the Caribbean,* Latin America Bureau, London, 1982.
13. John Beverley, *Latin Americanism after 9/11,* Duke University Press, Durham N.C., 2012, p. 101.
14. And most famously by Oliver North representing Reagan.
15. Beverley (2012).
16. Emir Sader, *The new mole: paths of the Latin American left,* Verso, London, 2011, p. 31.

17. See C. Bazdresch and P. C. Elizondo, 'Privatization: The Mexican case', in *The Quarterly Review of Economics and Finance* Vol 33, Supp 1, 1993, pp. 45–66.

18. Gerardo Muñoz 'Beyond Identity and the State: The Crisis of the Latin American Progressive Cycle' in *Alternautas* Vol. 3, no. 1, July 2016, pp. 84–93.

19. Sader 2011, p. 31.

20. See He Li 'China and India' in *NACLA Report* Vol. 45, no.2, 2012. See too 'Latin America's risky China boom' in *NACLA Report 47/3, Fall 2014*.

21. See the comprehensive report on land rights in Brazil by Rita Damasceno, Joana Chiavari and Cristina Leme Lopes 'Evolution of land rights in rural Brazil' for *Climate Policy Initiative*, Rio de Janeiro, 2017 at https://climate policyinitiative.org/ (Accessed Jan 2018).

22. Cargill's global profits exceeded $1 billion a quarter for the first time in 2008. 'The 86% rise was credited to global food shortages and the expanding biofuels industry that, in turn, caused a rise in demand for Cargill's core areas of agricultural commodities and technology,' (Wikipedia).

23. Sader, 2011, p. 37.

24. José Carlos Mariátegui, the Peruvian Marxist, sees the 'ayllu' in some ways as a model of alternative production and a basis for a different social order. See M. Gonzalez, *In the red corner: the Marxism of José Carlos Mariátegui*, Haymarket Books, Chicago, 2018, Chapter 7.

25. Webber (2017) Chapter 3.

26. See G. Ciccariello-Maher, *We created Chávez*, Duke University Press, Durham N.C., 2013.

27. See the writing of Marc Becker, in particular *Pachakutik: Indigenous Movements and Electoral Politics in Ecuador*, Lanham, M.D., Rowman & Littlefield Publishers, Inc., 2011.

28. The "Killer" demonstration, which reproduced Michael Jackson's video for his global hit of that name was one; and when the Minister of Education brought forward the summer holiday in order to close the universities and put a stop to their demonstrations, the students created their own beach outside the presidential palace and occupied it in bathing costumes. See more generally Webber, 2017, Chapter 5 and Patricio Silva, 'Swimming against the tide', in G. Lievesley and Steve Ludlam (eds) *Reclaiming Latin America: experiments in radical social democracy*, Zed books, London, 2009.

29. John Holloway, *Change the world without taking power: the meaning of revolution today*, Pluto Press, London, 2003.

30. Chis Harman, 'Anticapitalism, theory and practice', in *International Socialism Journal* Autumn 2:88, 2000.

31. James Petras and Henry Veldtmeyer, 'Latin America and the paradoxes of anti-imperialism and class struggle', at http://petras.lahaine.org (Accessed April 2018).

32. See Esteban Flores,'Misery in the maquiladoras', in *Harvard International Review* 22 March 2017 at http://hir.harvard.edu/article/?a=14424 (Accessed August 2018).

33. See chapter 6 below, where Mexico is discussed in greater detail.

34. Katz, October 2007 at https://katz.lahaine.org/ (Accessed July 2017).

1: From the Caracazo to Chávez

1. Cicciarello-Maher, 2013.
2. The party of the Venezuelan Revolution, formed by Douglas Bravo after a split in the Communist Party over armed struggle strategy. See Douglas Bravo and Mike Gonzalez, 'The Civic-Military Alliance: Venezuela 1958–1990', in M.Gonzalez and H.Barekat (eds) *Arms and the people*, Pluto Press, London, 2012. See also Cicciarello-Maher, 2013.
3. See Sam Farber, *The politics of Che Guevara*, Haymarket Books, Chicago, 2016. See also my *Che Guevara and the Cuban revolution*, Bookmarks, London, 2004.
4. See Dario Azzelini, 'Veneuela guerrilla movements 1960s to 1980s', in Immanuel Ness et al. (eds) *International Encyclopedia of Revolution and Protest*, Wiley-Blackwell, New York, 2009.
5. Fabricio Ojeda (1929–66) was the leader of the Patriotic Junta that overthrew the Pérez Jiménez dictatorship in 1958. A member of the Democratic Republican Union (URD), he was elected to Congress in 1958 but he and his organisation were marginalised by the Democratic Action and COPEI parties who set up the Puntofijo power-sharing agreement. He joined the launch of the FALN (Armed Forces of National Liberation) from prison in 1962 and escaped a year later to become commander of one of the guerrilla fronts. He was captured in 1966 and appeared dead, murdered, in prison a few days later.
6. See Cicariello-Maher, 2013, pp. 48–52.
7. There was a second coup attempt in November 1992. It was better organised and armed. But the government was prepared, and over a hundred fighters died. Curiously, it is rarely mentioned in the Chavista version of events.
8. See Bravo and Gonzalez, 2012.
9. Luis Miquilena (1919–2016) was briefly a member of the communist party before leaving it in protest against their support for Betancourt. He later joined URD, which he left in 1962 and retired to a life in business. He visited Chávez in prison in 1993 and became a firm ally in Chávez's early career. He chaired the Constituent Assembly of 1999 and was Minister of Justice. The two men fell out over the issue of Cuban influence and thereafter Miquilena became a very vocal and public opponent.
10. Ciccariello-Maher 2013, pp. 168–9.
11. See Paul Foot, *The Vote*, Bookmarks, London, 2012.
12. See the section 'Biología del fascismo' in J. C. Mariátegui, *La escena contemporánea* (Amauta, Lima, 1925). See too M. Gonzalez, *In the red corner*, 2018.
13. Beverley 2012, p. 122.
14. Ciccariello-Maher, 2013, p. 235. Ali Primera was Venezuela's outstanding radical singer-songwriter, who died in suspect circumstances in 1985.
15. 'Vargas el dolor de un pueblo' is a five-part documentary made by Digber Enriquez Dávila which gives some sense of the dimensions of the tragedy. It is available on YouTube.

16. The organisation had, after all, been founded by a Venezuelan, Juan Pablo Pérez Alfonzo.
17. See Bravo and Gonzalez, 2012.
18. 'The revolution will not be televised' (2003), an RTE documentary directed by Kim Bartley and Donnacha O'Briain.
19. Gustavo Cisneros is listed by Forbes magazine as among the world's richest men, with a personal fortune estimated at $1.8 billion. His activities cover holdings in media (Venevisión TV), entertainment (telenovelas, Miss Venezuela, the Leones de Caracas baseball team), consumer goods, as well as the multi-million dollar resort of Tropicalia in the Dominican Republic. Originally close to Chávez, he supported the 2002 coup. It is curious that none of his enterprises have been touched.
20. He was appointed in 2005 to put into practice his ideas on 'co-management'. See https://venezuelanalysis.com/analysis/1431 (Accessed July 2018).
21. D. L. Raby, *Democracy and revolution*, Pluto Press, London, 2006.
22. Raby, 2006, p. 132.
23. Raby, 2006, p. 169.
24. Webber, 2017, p. 276.
25. See Rafael Enciso Patiño, 'Modelo de Gestión Múltiple Socialista y Empresas de Propiedad Social (EPS) en Venezuela – Aciertos, Dificultades, Perspectivas' at http://www.workerscontrol.net, January 2012 (Accessed June 2018).
26. See Steve Ellner, 'Social Programs in Venezuela Under the Chavista Governments' at https://thenextsystem.org/learn/stories/social-programs-venezuela-under-chavista-governments (Accessed May 2018).

2: Bolivia Rises

1. Augusto Céspedes novel, *El Metal del Diablo* (The Devil's Metal) (1946), narrates Patiño's rise to riches. See too June Nash, *We eat the mines and the mines eat us*, Columbia University Press, 1993.
2. Eduardo Galeano, *The open veins of Latin America: five centuries of the pillage of a continent*, MR Press, New York, 1997.
3. Jeffery Webber, *Red October: Left-Indigenous Struggles in Modern Bolivia*, Haymarket Books, Chicago, 2012, p. 53.
4. See Webber, 2012. Also Robert J. Alexander, *The Bolivian National Revolution*, Rutgers University Press, New Brunswick, 1958 and James Dunkerley, *Rebellion in the Veins: Political Struggle in Bolivia, 1952–82*, Verso, London, 1984.
5. Webber, 2012, p. 65.
6. Webber, 2012, pp. 70–71.
7. Alexander, 1958.
8. Che Guevara's arrival in Bolivia in 1966, and his death there a year later, occurred at the height of this repression. Yet the curious thing is how little the revolutionary miners figure in his *Bolivian Diary*; he is exclusively concerned with the creation of a rural guerrilla, whose failure can in part be attributed to ignorance of Barrientos' policies towards the indigenous question and his recent limited land reforms.

9. The Plan Condor was a joint repressive strategy agreed between the Chilean, Argentine and Uruguayan military with U.S. support. Its objectives were to share intelligence and the persecution of political opponents.

10. Forrest Hylton and Sinclair Thomson, *Revolutionary horizons: past and present in Bolivian politics*, Verso, London, 2007, p. 96.

11. Webber ,2012, p. 113.

12. See the World Bank's Bolivia data base at https://data.worldbank.org/country/bolivia (Accessed August 2018).

13. John Crabtree and Ann Chaplin, *Bolivia: processes of change*, Zed Books, London, 2013. See also Crabtree's *Patterns of Protest: Politics and Social Movements in Bolivia*, London, 2005.

14. See M. Gonzalez and M. Yanes, *The last drop; the politics of water*, Pluto Press, London, 2015.

15. The issue is brilliantly addressed in the context of the long history of colonial exploitation in Iciar Bollaín and Gael García Bernal's film *También la lluvia* (Even the rain) (2010).

16. Or to put it in Spanish, the last drop that overflowed the glass (*la última gota que colmó el vaso*).

17. The most thorough account of Cochabamba's Water Wars is O. Olivera and Tom Lewis, *Cochabamba!: Water Rebellion in Bolivia*, South End Press, Chicago, 2004. See too Benjamin Dangle's, *The price of fire*, A.K. Press, Chico Cal, 2007, pp. 57–69.

18. Jim Schultz of the Democracy Center at http://www.democracyctr.org lives in Cochabamba and has reported for many years on Bolivian politics. His site carried a series of eye witness reports during the Water War.

19. Crabtree in Crabtree 2005, pp. 30-31, gives a brief summary of the subsequent developments in the region. The reality is that lack of investment on the one hand, and on the other, extreme inequalities in access to water, had left the situation still unresolved. In subsequent years, the state resumed the administration of water, but it is a complex issue still in process of resolution. While some communities administer their own wells directly, and a joint state enterprise runs water supplies primarily, there are still water tankers selling water at high prices to some households in the region. It is an ongoing battle.

20. 'Water beyond the state: a letter from Cochabamba', in Gonzalez and Yanes 2015, p. 106.

21. Ioan Grillo: *Gangster warlords; drug dollars, killing fields and the new politics of Latin America*, Bloomsbury, London, 2017, Chapter 49.

22. Webber, 2012, p. 171.

23. Hylton and Thomson, 2007, p. 50.

24. As above.

25. R Zibechi, 'El Alto: un mundo nuevo desde la diferencia', 23 August 2005, at http://www.ircamericas.org (Accessed July 2018).

26. See Crabtree, 2007.

27. Dangl, 2007, p. 110.

28. For a detailed account see Hylton and Thomson, 2007, Chapter 10.

29. Reproduced in Olivera and Lewis, 2004.

30. Garcia Linera interviewed by Pablo Stafononi in *International Viewpoint*, 20 December 2005 at http://www.internationalviewpoint.org/spip.php?article938 (Accessed December 2017).
31. Published on http://www.econoticiasbolivia.com, 30 July 2005.

3: Evo Morales in Power

1. Webber, 2012, p. 231.
2. Alvaro Garcia Linera, as vice-president, has been responsible for developing and arguing the ideological case for the policies and politics of Evo Morales and the MAS. He is extremely prolific in his own writings and equally in his readiness to speak and be interviewed by interested people around the world. While we will be referring to some of his specific contibutions there are a very large number of writings and debates online. Two interesting examples are that edited by Roberto Cavooris, 'A Bolivian Marxist seduced' at https://www.viewpointmag.com/2015/02/25/alvaro-garcia-linera-a-bolivian-marxist-seduced/ and a number of articles, including an insightful essay by Alberto Moreiras in the journal *Culture, Theory and Critique* Volume 56, 2015, Issue 3, available at https://www.tandfonline.com/doi/full/10.1080 (Accessed July 2018).
3. Some of his writings have been published in English, i.e. *Plebeian Power: Collective Action and Indigenous, Working-Class and Popular Identities in Bolivia* in *Historical Materialism*, Volume 55, January 2015.
4. See Webber, 'The evolution of a state manager', in Cavooris et al., p. 259.
5. See Peter Baker's essay in *Culture Theory and Critique,* 2015.
6. Forrest Hylton (2005) quote in Webber, 2012, p. 85.
7. Dangl, 2007, p. 201.
8. Dangl, 2007, p. 201, see also Webber, 2012, pp. 252–3.
9. See J. Crabtree, 'Bolivia: playing by the new rules', in G. LIevesley and S Ludlam, 2009.
10. Hylton and Thomson, 2007, p. 141.
11. For another account of these events see Roger Burbach, 'Morales confronts the insurrection', at http://www.counterpunch.org, 15 September 2008 (Accessed July 2018).
12. See Fernando Molina, 'Tendencias socio-electorales en la Bolivia del caudillismo', in *Nueva Sociedad* January/February 2018, p. 7 at www.nuso.org (Accessed July 2018).
13. A. Garcia Linera, *Las tensiones creativas de la revolución: la quinta fase del proceso de cambio,* at www.rebelion.org. See too 'Bolivia's Garcia Linera, "Moving beyond capitalism is a creative task"' at www.links.org.au, 19 February 2012.
14. Webber, 2017, pp. 184-5.
15. Jeffery Webber, 'The revolution against progress: the TIPNIS struggle and class contradictions in Bolivia', in *International Socialism Journal* no. 133, 2012.
16. Webber, as above .
17. Forrest Hylton, 'Old Wine, New Bottles: In Search of Dialectics' in *Dialectical Anthropology* 35, 2011. Quoted in Webber '…the revolution…'.

18. Webber, as above.
19. See note 4 for this chapter, above.
20. Garcia Linera Closing Plenary at the 4th Euopean Left Conference 2013.
21. See Molina, 2018.
22. Pablo Stefanoni, 'Evo for ever?' 2018 in www.rebelion.org (Accessed August 2018).

4: Ecuador and the Battle for Yasuni

1. See Marc Becker, *Pachakutik: Indigenous Movements and Electoral Politics in Ecuador*, Rowman and Littlefield, Lenham M.D., 2012 and for background Carlos de la Torre and Steve Striffler, *The Ecuador Reader: History, Culture, Politics*, Duke University Press, Durham N.C., 2009. See too 'Ecuador's impasse' in Webber, 2018.
2. Pablo Davalos, 'Movimientos ciudadanos, Asamblea Constituyente y neoliberalismo', 16 January 2007, http://www.alainet.com.
3. Jonathan Watts, 'New round of oil drilling goes deeper into Ecuador's Yasuní national park', http://www.guardian.co.uk, 10 January 2018.
4. See Gonzalez/Yanes, 2015, p. 86 and Todd Gordon and J. Webber, *Blood of extraction: Canadian imperialism in Latin America*, Fernwood, Black Point Nova Scotia, 2016.
5. Interview with Luis Macas in Webber, 2018.
6. J. Webber, 'A new indigenous left in Ecuador', in *NACLA Report on the Americas* Volume 44, 2011, published online 31 May 2016 at https://doi.org/10.1080/10714839.2011.11722137.
7. See Webber, 2016.
8. M. Becker, 'Ecuador's buen vivir socialism', in R. Burbach, M. Fox and F. Fuentes (eds) *Latin America's turbulent transitions*, Zedbooks, London, 2013.
9. *ibid.*
10. See Becker in G. Prevost, Carlos Oliva Campos and H. Vanden, *Social movements and leftist governments in Latin America*, Zedbooks, London, 2012, p. 126.
11. See my 'Honduras is not just another banana republic' in *International Socialism Journal*, no. 125, 2009. See also Todd Gordon and Jeffery Webber, 'The overthrow of a moderate and the birth of a radicalizing resistance', in J. Webber and B. Carr, *The new Latin American left: cracks in the empire*, Rowman and Littlefield, Lenham M.D., 2013.
12. Cf. his compelling contribution to the 2014 Alice Colloqium at www.youtube.com/watch?v=SXMWMqooVpU (Accessed August 2018).
13. Becker in Burbach, 2013.
14. The preceding figures come largely from John Cajas Guijarro's article 'Hacia donde va el Ecuador de Moreno' in *Nueva Sociedad* June 2018.
15. Webber, 2017, p. 72.
16. This paragraph is based on an article by Sunniva Labarthe and Marc Saint Upéry 'Leninismo versus Correismo', in *Nueva Sociedad,* November/December

2017 published at http://nuso.org/articulo/leninismo-versus-correismo
-la-tercera-vuelta-en-ecuador/.

17. They include the equivalent of the Treasury Minister Carlos Pólit (hiding in
Miami), the ex-Oil Minister Carlos Pareja Yanuzzelli (in jail) and Ramiro
González, ex-president of Ecuador's Social Security Institute.

18. J. Cajas Guijardo, 'Hacia dónde va el Ecuador de Lanin Moreno', in *Nueva
Sociedad* June 2018.

19. A. Acosta and John Cajas Guijarro, 'Correa un neo-liberal' in *Rebelion*
7 February 2017 at www.rebelion.org.

5: Venezuela: Decline and Fall

1. The figures come from the latest report from the economist Manuel Sutherland, 'La ruina de Venezuela no se debe al, 'socialismo', ni a la 'revolución'
(The ruin of Venezuela has has nothing to do with socialism or revolution)
in *Nueva Sociedad March/April 2018* also at www.nuso.org. His regular and
well researched reports help to fill the vacuum left by the absence of any
official analysis of the Venezuelan economy.

2. Steve Ellner has lived in Venezuela for many years and written about it for as
long. He is a consistent defender of the current regime though he has critical
positions on a number of issues. His blog is a consistent anthology of his
arguments. http://steveellnersblog.blogspot.com/.

3. See Rolando Astarita, 'La tragedia social de Venezuela' at www.rolandoastarita.
wordpress.com.

4. Cf. Sutherland, 2018.

5. L. Vera, 'Como explicar la catástrofe', in *Nueva Sociedad* March/April 2018.

6. Steve Ellner, 'The Implications of Marxist State Theory and How They Play
Out in Venezuela' at https://venezuelanalysis.com/analysis/13386 (Accessed
May 2018).

7. Military spending hit a peak of $1036.1 million in 2008, and $895 million in
2013, falling significantly in 2017/18. See https://tradingeconomics.com/
venezuela/military-expenditure.

8. Raby, 2006, p. 169.

9. This is discussed at some length in H. Barekat and M. Gonzalez, *Arms and
the people*, Pluto Press, London, 2012.

10. As published by 'Dólar Today'.

11. Sutherland, 2018.

12. See the interview with Lander conducted by Gabiel Mêndez, 'Venezuela
must face its civilizational crisis' at https://venezuelanalysis.com/.

13. Ciccariello-Maher, 2013.

14. Sutherland, 2018.

15. http://blog.chavez.org.ve/programa-patria-venezuela-2013-2019/#.W3ApIV
59i80 (Accessed August 2018).

16. It is worth noting that Fidel Castro made it very clear that there were to be no
statues or monuments to him after his death, let alone attempts to deify him.

17. The figure comes from the observatory of Venezuelan violence, OVV, at https://observatoriodeviolencia.org.ve/ (Accessed August 2018).

18. Rafael Ramirez addressing the National Assembly, 27 May 2005 at https://www.aporrea.org/energia/a14338.html (Accessed August 2018).

19. Sutherland, 2018.

20. See '¿Cómo es la cosa? Exministro Eduardo Samán: Tenemos que volver a la medicina de uso artesanal y natural', 24 March 2017 at https://maduradas.com/tag/eduardo-saman/ (Accessed August 2018).

21. Although since the Lava Jato investigations in Brazil, it may well be Odebrecht's own future that is in question.

22. Lander, 'The civilizational crisis', see above.

23. Lander, as above.

24. Sutherland, 2018.

25. Julia Buxton, 'Venezuela after Chávez', in New Left Review 99, May–June 2016, p. 6.

26. James Petras, 'The great land giveaway', 12 January 2008 at https://petras.lahaine.org/ (Accessed August 2018).

27. Fabrice Adnereani, 'Las vias enmarañadas del autoritarismo bolivariano', in NS Mar/April 2018. In June 2018 a UN Report denounced the close to 1000 deaths their operations had caused.

28. Roland Denis in aporrea.org.

6: On the Margins of the Pink Tide: Mexico, Brazil, Argentina

1. See R. Roman and Edur Velasco Arregui, 'Neoliberal authoritarianism, the "Democratic Transition" and the Mexican Left', in Webber and Carr, 2012.

2. This was made more plausible by the exposure of Salinas's corruption and plots to rid himself of opponents. He subsequently became an exile in Ireland.

3. Diego Enrique Osorno, Oaxaca: la primera insurrección del siglo XXI, Ed Grijalbo, Mexico, 2007. See also R. Zibechi, Territories in Resistance, AK Press, Chico Cal, 2012.

4. See Grillo, 2017.

5. http://www.atlanticcouncil.org/blogs/new-atlanticist/mexico-s-energy-reforms-the-prospects-under-an-amlo-administration (Accessed 3rd July 2018).

6. Ramon I. Centeno, 'Lopez Obrador con los ricos o con los pobres?', in www.rebelion.org, 6th June 2018 (Accessed 15 June 2018).

7. M. Modonesi, 'Sobre el alcance histórico de la elección de AMLO', in Nueva Sociedad, July 2018 also at www.nuso.org (Accessed 18 July 2018).

8. M. Modonesi, in www.rebelion.org, 3 July 2018.

9. See S. Branford and Jan Rocha, Cutting the wire: the story of the landless movement in Brazil, Latin America Bureau, London, 2002.

10. Sue Branford, 'Brazil: has the dream ended?', in Lievesley and Ludlam, 2009.

11. H. Vanden in Prevost, 2012, p. 43.

12. Silva, a well-known environmentalist campaigner, left the PT in 2009 and stood as presidential candidate for the Green Party in 2010. She was an

Evangelical Christian whose opposition to abortion alienated her from the Brazilian left.

13. Webber, 2017, p. 56.
14. See Benjamon Fogel, in 'Lessons Earned: a conversation', in *Jacobin* 29, 19 May 2017.
15. Webber, 2017.
16. Fabian Bielinsky's film 'Nine Queens' (2000) represents the situation to great comic effect.
17. Katz at www.katz.lahaine.org, 30 December 2001.
18. See also the account by Marina Sitrin in Stahler-Stolk et al., 2014, pp. 209–32.
19. Katz, www.katz.lahaine.org, March 2002.
20. P. Audivert quoted in Katz, 5 March 2002.
21. I visited a rope making factory in the Echeverria suburb, a poor, working class industrial area, which had been taken over by its small workforce when its manager tried to remove the machinery. The riot police arrived to remove them but the entire district had mobilised to defend the workers and eventually they continued production on their antiquated machines and began to sell their products directly. It was just one example.
22. See Webber and Carr, 2012, pp. 237–40.
23. See Conclusion.
24. See Karl Marx, *The civil war in France* writing about the Paris Commune. 'Public functions ceased to be the private property of the tools of the Central Government. Not only municipal administration, but the whole initiative hitherto exercised by the state was laid into the hands of the Commune.'
25. Webber and Carr, 2012, pp. 240–41.
26. As above.
27. Katz, www.katz.lahaine.org, 16th August 2004.
28. Webber and Carr, 2012, p. 248.
29. Despite the enormous level of support for the legislation, the abortion proposal was rejected by the Argentine Senate in August 2018. This was the direct result of the active intervention of the Catholic Church and the ostensibly progressive Argentine Pope. It was a defeat for the vibrant +NiUna-Menos movement as well as the abortion campaign and the wider struggle for womens rights.
30. Caudio Katz, 'Who will pay for the crisis, them or us?', at www.katz.lahaine.org (Accessed 3 July 2018).

CONCLUSION

1. Ref 'Latin America's left turn', in *Foreign Affairs* May/June 2006 and *Utopia Unarmed*, Vintage Books, New York, 1994.
2. See Patrick Iber, 'The two lefts of Jorge Castañeda' in *Dissent*, Winter 2016.
3. See Burbach et al., 2013, Chapter 2, 'The pink tide and the challenge to U.S. hegemony'.
4. Zibechi, 2012, p. 79.

5. Webber and Carr, 2012, p. 40.
6. Burbach et al., 2013.
7. Webber and Carr, 2012, p. 40.
8. Webber, 2017, p. 291.
9. 'Disparen contra Lula', in *Nueva Sociedad*, April 2018. See also at www. nuso.org.
10. I can't resist quoting Walt Whitman here. 'Do I contradict myself? I contain multitudes.'
11. Steve Ellner, 'Venezuela's fragile revolution', in *Monthly Review*, 1 October 2017.
12. As above.
13. See Webber, 2017 and M. Gonzalez, *In the red corner; the Marxism of Jose Carlos Mariategui*, Haymarket, Chicago, 2018.

Index